Discovery Travel Adventures™

AUSTRALIAN OUTBACK

Scott Forbes
Editor

John Gattuso
Series Editor

Discovery Communications, Inc.

Discovery Communications, Inc.
John S. Hendricks, *Founder, Chairman, and Chief Executive Officer*
Judith A. McHale, *President and Chief Operating Officer*
Judy L. Harris, *Senior Vice President and General Manager, Consumer Products*

Discovery Publishing
Rita Thievon Mullin, *Editorial Director*
Michael Hentges, *Design Director*
Mary Kalamaras, *Senior Editor*
Rick Ludwick, *Managing Editor*
Jill Gordon, *Marketing Specialist*

Discovery Channel Retail
Tracy Fortini, *Product Development*
Steve Manning, *Naturalist*

Insight Guides
Jeremy Westwood, *Managing Director*
Brian Bell, *Editorial Director*
John Gattuso, *Series Editor*
Siu-Li Low, *General Manager, Books*

Distribution
United States
Langenscheidt Publishers, Inc.
46–35 54th Road, Maspeth, NY 11378
Fax: 718-784-0640

Worldwide
APA Publications GmbH & Co.
Verlag KG Singapore Branch, Singapore
38 Joo Koon Road, Singapore 628990
Tel: 65-865-1600. Fax: 65-861-6438

Discovery Communications produces high-quality nonfiction television programming, interactive media, books, films, and consumer products. Discovery Networks, a division of Discovery Communications, Inc., operates and manages the Discovery Channel, TLC, Animal Planet, Travel Channel, and Discovery Health Channel. Visit Discovery Channel Online at www.discovery.com.

Although every effort is made to provide accurate information in this publication, we would appreciate readers calling our attention to any errors or outdated information by writing us at: Insight Guides, PO Box 7910, London SE1 1WE, England; fax: 44-20-7403-0290; e-mail: insight@apaguide.demon.co.uk

Printed by Insight Print Services (Pte) Ltd, 38 Joo Koon Road, Singapore 628990.

Library of Congress Cataloging-in-Publication Data
Australian outback / Scott Forbes, editor.
        p. cm. – (Discovery travel adventures)
    Includes bibliographical references and index.
    ISBN 1-56331-932-2 (pbk.)
      1. Australia – Guidebooks. I. Forbes, Scott, 1963– II. Series.

DU95 .A83 2000
919.404'7 – dc21

00-043160

*A*ustralian Outback combines the interests and enthusiasm of two of the world's best-known information providers: **Insight Guides**, whose titles have set the standard for visual travel guides since 1970, and **Discovery Communications**, the world's premier source of nonfiction entertainment. The editors of Insight Guides provide both practical advice and general understanding about a destination's history, culture, institutions, and people. Discovery Channel and its website, www.discovery.com, help millions of viewers explore their world from the comfort of their home and encourage them to explore it firsthand.

About This Book

This book reflects the contributions of dedicated editors and writers familiar with Australia's wild places. Series editor **John Gattuso**, of Stone Creek Publications in New Jersey, worked with Insight Guides and Discovery Channel to conceive and direct the series. Gattuso looked to **Scott Forbes**, a Sydney-based editor and writer who has worked on numerous travel guides and nonfiction books, to serve as project editor. Having spent most of his life in somewhat more temperate and densely populated Scotland, Forbes is particularly intrigued by the enormity of Australia's desert landscapes. "It's that air of mystery, the sense that there are places out there where perhaps no one has set foot."

All the contributors share this fascination with Australia's wide-open spaces and its extraordinary native species. As the author of an exhaustive guide to the Kimberley, award-winning writer **Daniel Scott** was a natural choice to write about one of Australia's last great frontiers, while his long diving experience ensured the right perspective on the Great Barrier Reef. A recent tour of the southwest provided him with his first taste of the rugged Stirling Range, and return visits helped him craft the chapter on its botanical bounty. One of Australia's most widely published travel writers, **Marc Llewellyn** has firsthand knowledge of a broad range of the continent's environments. Among his many publications are guides to Tasmania and the Victorian High Country as well as a plethora of articles on Kangaroo Island, which he describes as "a giant wildlife park where the sea lions call the shots." He has penned chapters on all three areas for this book.

Amanda Burdon, who covers the remote, dusty Pilbara and the lush Wet Tropics, grew up in New South Wales and credits her parents for her passion for the outdoors. Formerly an associate editor with *Australian Geographic*, Amanda now works as a freelance writer and editor, specializing in environmental, travel, and social topics. "Escaping to the bush every now and then is what sustains me; I guess I'm still a country girl at heart," she says. **Margaret McPhee** has written extensively on Australia's wilderness areas. Here she confines herself to two favorites: Fraser Island and New South Wales' Corner Country. She first visited the Corner in 1978. "I was struck by its timelessness: hard-baked hearths remain as they were left by Aboriginal families a century or more ago, the land is much as it was when the first European explorers battled through it."

After several years as a senior writer with *Australian Geographic*, travel and nature writer **Pip Moran** is now based in Taiwan. She rates her top wildlife encounter to date as diving with giant Australian cuttlefish, but it's the remote terrestrial realms of her homeland – particularly Uluru-Kata Tjuta and Kakadu National Parks, which she describes here – that have captured her heart. "Uluru has an awesome, unforgettable presence," she says. "No one should visit Australia without making a pilgrimage to see it." **Peter Prineas**, author of chapters on the MacDonnell Ranges and Lamington National Park, has been fascinated by Australia's wild places for as long as he can remember. "Traveling with my parents between country towns as a child, I would see some distant blue hills and plead to go there – it was instinctive." He later spent nearly a decade exploring the potential of many of New South Wales's "distant blue hills" as pre-serves, on behalf of the National Parks Association of New South Wales. Since then he has contributed to a wide range of books on wilderness areas and conservation.

During a journalistic career that spans nearly 30 years, **Peter Meredith** has canoed among hippos on the Zambezi, bushwalked among elephants in Zimbabwe, and soared alongside Australian wedge-tailed eagles in a hang glider. Based in Sydney since 1980, he has traveled widely both on assign-ment and for simple enjoyment. His love of the bush and knowledge of the history of its transformation and preservation inform his chapters on wilderness conservation and the Blue Mountains. **Bruce Elder** is a senior travel writer with the *Sydney Morning Herald* and the director of its Web-based guide to Australia, a role that has taken him to more than 1,000 Australian towns. He rates Shark Bay, which he writes about here, as one of the most beautiful areas he has visited. His chapter on Aboriginal history reflects a long interest in this subject, which saw its fullest expres-sion in his book *Blood on the Wattle: The Massacres and Maltreatment of Australian Aborigines since 1788*, recently nominated as one of the 10 most influential Australian works of nonfiction in the 20th century.

Reg Morrison has been photographing and writing about Australia's plants, animals, geology, and people for almost four decades. As reflected in his chapter "In Splendid Isolation," he is passionate about the evolu-tionary and environmental issues implicit in this extraordinary conti-nent. Originally a newspaperman, he switched to books in 1972 and has since written three natural-history titles, supplied the photos for more than a dozen others, and become an Associate of the Australian Museum. **Matthew Cawood** worked as a cowboy on the black-soil plains of New South Wales and Queensland before turning to writing about travel, agriculture, and the environment. Although he had driven between Sydney and Perth nine times during a footloose youth, he took time to get to know the Flinders Ranges, which he covers here, only on his last transcontinental journey – which also happened to be his honeymoon. "Maybe it was the circumstances, but the atmosphere and the hues of the ranges really gripped me," he says. "I've been back six times in five years." Our guide to the practicalities of observing Australian wildlife, **Terence Lindsey**, has studied, written about, and taught natural history for most of his life. He was born in England and raised and educated in Canada but has been based in Australia for many years. An Associate of the Australian Museum and a former tutor at the University of Sydney, he has published widely on the wildlife of North America, Australia, New Zealand, and Southeast Asia.

Thanks to Michael Adams, who helped compile the travel tips, to the many park rangers and tourist associations who reviewed the text, and to the members of Stone Creek's editorial team: Judith Dunham, Edward A. Jardim, Enid Stubin, Sallie Graziano, and Nicole Buchenholz.

Outback dwellers, as epito-mized by the hardy stockman (above), have learned to cope with isolation, limited services, and climatic extremes.

Water lilies (opposite) cover Yellow Water billabong during the wet season in Kakadu National Park, Northern Territory.

Laughing kookaburras (below), named for their cackling calls, are found throughout eastern and southwestern Australia.

Preceding pages: Traditions still play a central role in the lifestyles of Australia's indigenous peoples.

Following pages: Climbers ascend the walls of Bungonia Gorge in New South Wales.

Table of Contents

MAPS

t's fair to say that after centuries of conjecture, mapping, and exploration, the realities of the Great South Land came as something of a disappointment to the 17th-century Dutch and English sailors who were the first travelers from the Northern Hemisphere to reach its shores. The continent appeared to be neither *provincia aurifera* ("gold-producing land") nor *scatans aromatibus* ("overflowing with spices"), as contemporary map legends indicated. Nor was there any sign of the densely populated and materially wealthy civilizations reported by some travelers. The first British settlers echoed the sailors' dismay, finding the landscapes of Terra Australis "barren and forbidding," the wildlife unnervingly odd.   ◆   But northern eyes have grown accustomed to this land where "nature is reversed," and priorities have changed. From the perspective of today's travelers, living **Visitors to Australia are regularly** in a world of expanding human popula- **astounded by its unspoiled** tions, large-scale urbanization, and **wilderness, diverse landscapes,** ever-increasing globalization, it is precisely **and thrillingly exotic wildlife.** those facets of the continent that so dismayed earlier, more materialistic visitors – the emptiness, the ancient and specialized nature of its indigenous culture, the strangeness of its wildlife – that lure them southward. For these modern-day treasure seekers, Australia is a land of immeasurable wealth.   ◆   Cartographically speaking, the country remains peripheral. Consult a world map and you'll probably find it tucked in a bottom corner. Projections tend to curl and contort the landmass, disguising its true scale: the only nation to encompass a continent, Australia is as large as the lower 48 states. Yet it has a population no larger than that of New York State; what's more, 84 percent of its citizens, who cluster in the cities and conurbations that

Hikers savor the sweeping views from the rim of Kings Canyon in Watarrka National Park, Northern Territory.

Preceding pages: Cathedral Gorge, Bungle Bungle Range, Western Australia; a western pygmy-possum feeding on nectar; Palm Valley in Finke Gorge National Park, Northern Territory.

Space and solitude (left) await the outback traveler, as well as rich and varied wildlife.

Eastern grey kangaroos (right) inhabit much of eastern Australia, while their western grey relatives are confined to arid areas of the south. The two were once thought to be separate species.

cling to the east, southeast, and southwest coasts, occupy just one percent of the country. That means the rest – barely three million people – are scattered across more than 2.9 million square miles. Start doing the math and your mind will begin to race at the prospect of entering a land where you can still drive, hike, or raft for days without encountering another soul.

If travelers have a preconceived image of this wilderness, it almost certainly features shimmering red sands, ancient rock formations, and flawless blue skies. The outback, as the arid zones are known, indeed occupies much of the continent and a prominent place in the national ethos. But if you thought an immensity of desert was all Australia has to offer, think again.

Green tree frogs have adapted readily to the presence of humans, taking up residence in gardens and buildings.

Think swathes of eucalypt woodlands and plains carpeted with wildflowers. Picture glacier-carved ranges enclosing sparkling mountain lakes. Imagine lush tropical forests edged by white-sand beaches, and the largest system of coral reefs on Earth.

Australia's distinctive fauna is now one of the country's prime drawing cards, and visitors flock to parks and reserves seeking a glimpse of a koala, platypus, or kangaroo. But these iconic marsupials merely hint at the astonishing range of endemic wildlife on display: approximately 82 percent of all Australia's mammals, 89 percent of its reptiles, and 85 percent of its vascular plants are found nowhere else on Earth. The diversity is equally staggering: a given area of the seemingly barren outback holds two to three times as many reptile species as its American or African equivalent; the state of Victoria has more orchid species than the whole of North America or Europe; and a small nature reserve near Canberra shelters more ant

species than the British Isles.

The early settlers' misreading of the continent's indigenous civilization had tragic and lasting effects. The apparent simplicity of Aboriginal culture belied the fact that it was the result of 40,000 years of attunement to the rhythms and harsh realities of a generally arid land. Aboriginal peoples now generously share their deep knowledge of the environment with those eager to understand the continent's marvels – scientists keen to learn about the estimated 200,000 plant and animal species that have yet to be classified, archaeologists hunting for clues to the continent's original colonization, and, of course, travelers seeking precious insights into its timeless landscapes.

The treasures of this island continent can't be measured, weighed, or sold, won't boost your bank account or even pay your passage home. But they will surprise and astonish you, expand your knowledge of the myriad ways and forms of nature, redefine your place in the world. They *will* enrich you. So read on and let your mind sail forth. The hunt starts here.

Wild
Australia

*Your journey into wild Australia will be all the
more fulfilling if you take time to learn about
the diversity and status of its environments,
the distribution of its wildlife, and the history
and culture of its indigenous inhabitants.*

In Splendid Isolation

CHAPTER 1

There is a line of rocky hills near the western edge of Australia where you may unroll your sleeping bag under a blaze of southern stars and know that you will be cradled to sleep aboard what is possibly the oldest raft of land crust anywhere on Earth. The sedimentary rocks that formed these hills, known as the Narryer Range, originated under northern skies at least 3.65 billion years ago and have since drifted right around the globe not once, but twice. ◆ Four hundred and fifty miles (750 km) northeast of the Narryer Range, in a region so remote and inhospitable that it was whimsically nicknamed the North Pole by prospectors, lies another tangle of hills of similar antiquity. Pick your way upward through the prickly tussock grasses to a particular ridge line, and you can run a finger over one of the oldest signatures of life on Earth – a tiny column of layered sediments that originated as a pile of bacterial waste in a muddy tidal bay some 3½ billion years ago. ◆ To see a modern version of this signature, you need **Long separated from other landmasses, this ancient continent has given rise to distinctive and diverse flora and fauna.** only head southwest to the turquoise waters of Shark Bay. Wade into the warm waters of one of its shallowest arms, and you will find yourself surrounded by waist-high mounds. Known as stromatolites, these bacterial deposits – many of which have been growing for thousands of years – are the living descendants of the North Pole fossils. Here, our wildest *Jurassic Park* fantasies are utterly dwarfed. ◆ The entire Australian continent constitutes an incomparable diary of planetary evolution, written both in stone and in the genetic codes of its modern life-forms. On the one hand, its remarkable geological record spans 90 percent of the Earth's existence

The white bark of a snappy gum glows in fading light. Gum trees, or eucalypts, are among the most distinctive Australian plants.

Preceding pages: Termite mounds rise like islands amid a sea of wildflowers in the Pilbara. These extraordinary constructions can rise more than 20 feet in height.

Subtropical rain forest (right) grows even in moist pockets of temperate zones such as southwestern Victoria.

and outlines the entire crustal history of this small, fertile planet. On the other, its plants and animals represent a branch of southern life that has for the past 40 million years evolved in splendid isolation.

With the exception of Antarctica, Australia is the flattest, driest, and most sparsely inhabited continent. Its small population shares the country's arid, impoverished soils with one of the strangest assemblies of plants and animals to be found anywhere in the world – one that possesses a degree of distinction that prompted even the great naturalist Charles Darwin to ponder yet again the origin of species and the mechanics of evolution. He could not have come to a more fitting place for such musing.

Diary in Stone

The 3.65-billion-year-old rocks of Narryer are not the oldest rocks in the world – even more ancient outcrops have been found in Canada and Greenland – but they form part of a huge shard of primordial crust that underlies much of Australia's western shoulder. No other land crust fragment of this size and age remains on Earth. Furthermore, the Narryer rocks have yielded minute grains of zircon that began to crystallize almost 4¼ billion years ago. These crystals are the oldest fragments of earthly material ever found.

Just as astounding is the fact that Australia's geological record begins not in the Southern Hemisphere but in the north; so the continent

Weathered rock formations in Watarrka National Park attest to the antiquity of central Australia's desert landscapes.

Billabongs (right) brim with life following the monsoonal rains that drench northern Australia each summer.

also provides us with an account of its crustal wanderings, a journey that appears to have taken it to both poles twice. During that epic journey, other pieces of land crust welded themselves to this primordial fragment, enlarging it to form a block that now makes up more than two-thirds of the continent. Meanwhile, it was by turns squeezed and stretched, inundated by seas, and ravaged by sheets of ice.

During the last billion years, plate collisions and volcanic eruptions plastered other fragments of crust to the eastern side of the landmass, enlarging it to its present size, while prolonged erosion and glaciation ground the continent flat. Draped in a shroud of sediments, its old bones now barely break the surface, reappearing extensively only in Western Australia's Pilbara and Kimberley regions, and in the far north, as the Arnhem Land plateau.

For several hundred million years, Australia and its crustal twin, Antarctica, formed the core of a vast agglomeration of southern landmasses known as Gondwana, which also included South America, Africa, India, Tibet, parts of Southeast Asia, and part of China. Much of this supercontinent was cool and wet, and cloaked in dense rain forests. About 100 million years ago, a new pattern of heat flow in Earth's mantle

The Wet

It might be a monsoon to the meteorologist, but to most who live in northern Australia it is simply the Wet. It arrives in early January behind a three-month crescendo of electrical storms. As the thunderous fanfare subsides, the monsoon unfurls its grey curtains of rain, launching itself in smoking torrents from the ancient battlements of Arnhem Land and thundering down the volcanic escarpments of the Atherton Tableland. Within days, the region's vast networks of lowland water holes and wetlands have begun to overflow, spreading sheets of water across the plains.

It is a time of abundance, and the earth erupts with new growth. Millions of waterbirds that recently fought for room in shrinking mud holes swiftly disperse across a green and glittering land to search out old nest sites. On flooded plains, beneath clouds of insects, fish grow fat. In the deep pools, the giant lotus rolls out platforms of leaves where male jacanas build their nests; in their shade, aquatic file snakes populate the reed beds with wriggling young. Water spiders lie in wait among floating flowers, and crocodile mothers ferry squawking hatchlings from their mud-bank nests.

For creatures that neither swim nor fly, this is a time of crisis. Many animals that live underground are forced to seek temporary refuge above water level and often find themselves sharing that refuge with their deadliest enemies. By April, however, most of the survivors are back in their burrows and the rhythms of life return to normal.

began to tear Gondwana apart. A large fragment including Australia and Antarctica drifted northward. Some 80 million years ago, rifting on the eastern side of this fragment thrust a sliver of land eastward, forming the islands of New Zealand and New Caledonia. A by-product of this rifting was the Great Dividing Range, Australia's only major upland formation, which now runs the full length of its eastern side.

By 40 million years ago, Australia's continental raft had separated from Antarctica

and begun a journey that would take it more than 1,300 miles (2,100 km) north, into the tropics. This relocation occurred as an ice age began to tighten its grip on the planet, and the combination of continental drift and climate change was to rewrite the rules for all life in Australia. Sealed into their continental test tube by a moat of open seas, Australia's plants and animals became guinea pigs in a laboratory of evolution. As the climate became more arid and unreliable, they were forced to adapt or perish. It

species take refuge from the region's searing heat in tunnels and burrows, with many emerging only at night. The termite is the predominant herbivore of these regions, but among the predators, skinks and lizards rule by day, while small marsupial carnivores, snakes, and geckoes dominate the night shift – ably assisted by scorpions, spiders, and centipedes.

Seasons count for little here: rainfall is unpredictable and opportunism rules. Plants and animals bide their time, awaiting the next downpour. When it finally appears, the response is little short of miraculous. Almost before the last storm cloud has passed, a silent explosion begins as billions of seeds burst their casings and seedlings race to establish a genetic foothold on the future. After surviving for months – perhaps even a year – inside mucous cocoons, water-holding frogs emerge lusting and blinking into the glistening world above. Ephemeral pools fill with shield shrimps, the air thrums with the beating wings of midges, and barren sandplains submerge beneath a tide of flowers – poached-egg daisies, billy buttons, purple mulla mullas, and golden everlastings. Such bursts of desert abundance are brief, however. In a matter of weeks, the pools evaporate and life disappears

was their remarkable genetic solutions that so intrigued Darwin – and still command our curiosity today.

Land Without Seasons

The most significant product of that momentous voyage was an enormous arid heartland – the outback. Not only is 70 percent of this environment inhospitable to humans, but its prickly hummock-grass

plains seem at first glance to support little more than a handful of reptiles, the odd bird, and a few billion termites. Nothing could be farther from the truth. The maze of tiny footprints delicately etched into the desert's floor each morning gives the game away: Australia's biological resources are still in place; they have merely gone underground. Innumerable

from view, leaving the wind to distribute the genetic harvest – billions of new seeds and microscopic eggs.

This inherent environmental instability is due in part to irregular climatic disturbances known as El Niño events. The result of unusual heating of the lower atmosphere, they are heralded by an eastward flow of warm surface water in the Pacific Ocean. In response, tropical trade winds subside, the monsoon fails in Southeast Asia, and drought grips many regions, notably in Australia and Africa. Typically, each El Niño drought is followed by widespread flooding, as normal weather patterns reestablish themselves.

Coastal Patterns

Only along Australia's coastal fringes does this climatic instability diminish and rainfall become seasonal. Along northern coastlines, the northeast monsoon – the Wet, as it is known locally – brings massive electrical storms, torrential rain, and widespread flooding just after Christmas, the height of the Southern Hemisphere's summer. Winters here are by contrast mild, clear,

Bushfires (top) destroy but also regenerate: many native plant species rely on fire to trigger germination.

Colonies of termites construct their giant chambers (right) using chewed vegetation, soil, and droppings.

and dry. Such predictability guarantees distinct and identifiable responses from native plants and animals. Indeed, so predictable is the monsoon that the Aboriginal inhabitants of Arnhem Land were able to subdivide their year into six discrete seasons and to vary their lives accordingly.

In the far north, or Top End as it is known locally, this climate creates vast seasonal wetlands that attract immense flocks of wetland birds and are home to turtles, frogs, and most of Australia's crocodiles. In the northeast – the wettest part of the continent – it preserves remnants of tropical rain forests that harbor primitive flowering plants, arboreal marsupials including two species of tree-climbing kangaroo, and the cassowary, a cousin of the emu.

Between the climatic extremes of the arid heartland and the monsoonal north lies a belt of tropical savanna, characterized by heavy summer rainfall and tall-growing annual grasses. This environment is highly prone to bushfires, which are often triggered by lightning. Similarly, in the south, where central aridity gives way to occasional winter rains, the prickly hummock grasses known as spinifex blend into true grassland and grassy woodland. It was the growth of these two transitional belts that allowed the ancestors of modern kangaroos and wallabies to prosper and diversify as aridity increased during the past 10 million years. The kangaroos' success hinged not only on their ability to utilize poor fodder and travel with unrivaled economy of effort, but on their peculiar ability to regulate their fertility and transport their young. The transitional grasslands are also home to reptiles and small burrowing mammals,

as well as the ubiquitous emu and Australia's only coursing predator, the dingo.

The southern coastal fringe of the continent is often described as Mediterranean, receiving most of its rain during the cool, mid-year winter months and sweltering in the dry Christmas heat. But the seasons are ill defined here and subject to the vagaries of the high- and low-pressure weather systems that drift from west to east. Consequently, the plants and animals of these regions are adapted not only to poor soils and uncertain winter rains but to frequent summer bushfires. The dominant trees and shrubs – eucalypts, banksias, and acacias – are slow-breathing, fire-resistant energy misers. Forests of this tough-leaved vegetation, known as sclerophyll, are

Wizards of Oz

The increasing environmental stress experienced by Australian plants and animals during the past 40 million years of continental drift and climate change has produced a land of specialists. These descendants of Gondwanan species have honed their survival mechanisms into some of the most complex and bizarre strategies ever to appear on this planet.

Kangaroos, for example, can provide three different forms of nutrient to three different generations of offspring at any one time, carry their young in pouches, delay gestation during times of hardship, and travel rapidly over great distances using only two of their toes. The platypus has a poison-loaded claw, carries a form of sonar equipment in its ducklike beak, lays eggs, and yet suckles its young. Many plants have not only fireproofed themselves – they even employ fire to midwife their reproduction process. The grotesque bull banksia of southwestern Australia, for example, depends entirely on fire to release and germinate its big, woody seeds.

Then there are possums known as gliders that plane from tree to tree on winglike flaps of skin, dexterous bolas spiders that "angle" for moths with baited lines, and the drought-proof salamander fish, which can bury itself in a dry riverbed and survive many waterless weeks by breathing air and living on body fats. There was even a frog that swallowed its fertilized eggs, turned its stomach into a kind of uterus, and gave birth through its mouth, but that was back in 1985. The gastric-brooding frog has since disappeared, and its fate remains a mystery.

Lush oases rimmed by ancient palm species (top) are concealed in many of the gorges of northern central Australia.

The marsupial mole (left) is blind, lives almost entirely underground, and feeds mainly on invertebrates.

Gastric-brooding frogs (below) were last seen in eastern Queensland but may now be extinct.

largely confined to the northeastern, southeastern, and southwestern corners and the Great Dividing Range. Perhaps the most famous inhabitant of this forest environment is the koala. Its modern range is limited to the southeast, however, and shrinking fast.

On the highest peaks of the Great Dividing Range, which straddle the Victoria–New South Wales border, alpine conditions create winter snowfields as large as those of Switzerland. This is the realm of hardy specialists such as snow gums and corroboree frogs. To the north, on the range's well-watered eastern slopes, pockets of subtropical rain forest provide glimpses of the continent's Gondwanan past.

Island Stronghold

The major stronghold of Gondwanan species in Australia, however, is the island of Tasmania. Its cool-temperate rain forests and alpine heathlands altered little during Australia's voyage north, as did their inhabitants. The mossy *Nothofagus* forests of the southwest look much as they did when dinosaurs walked the Earth, and high above those forests in icy pools lives a small crustacean, the Tasmanian mountain shrimp, whose segmented body and external gills precisely mirror those of a primitive ancestor that dwelled there

some 250 million years ago. And while most large marsupial carnivores became extinct on the mainland tens of thousands of years ago, three – the Tasmanian devil and two quoll species – still prowl the island's forests.

Evolutionary relics such as these open a window in the fabric of time. For the traveler who takes the trouble to

learn something of Australia's astonishing past and seek out the right vantage points, the view from here is unrivaled.

The Australian Alps (right), in the southeast of the country, are blanketed with snow for most of the winter.

Eric Naylor, a tribal elder with the Yuin people, an Aboriginal group living near Wallaga Lake on the south coast of New South Wales, tells the Dreaming story of Gulaga as he mixes a paste of white ocher in a small tin bowl. ◆ "This mountain is Gulaga, the mother," he says to visitors standing near the top of a peak known to white Australia as Mount Dromedary. "In the Dreaming, she had two sons." Naylor explains how her sons ran toward the sea, though Gulaga pleaded with them to stay. The younger son, Najanuga, who was slower and more cautious, became a rocky headland, later named Point Dromedary by Europeans. The elder son, Barunguba, swam out to sea, where today he stands as the windswept outcrop known to settlers as Montague Island. ◆ Naylor dips his index finger in the bowl and carefully paints a single line down a visitor's fore-head. "This is your third eye. It will let you experience the spirits who live

Aboriginal guides offer insight into the culture of Australia's indigenous people and a new perspective on its landscapes.

here. And this" – he dabs the ocher on the left cheek – "is to allow you to open your mind." A simple mark on the right cheek "will help you to listen," and a touch of ocher on the chin "will help you to be quiet." As he paints, Naylor relates how for thousands of years the Yuin people have made the arduous five-hour trek up the mountain to this spot to learn from elders "how to look after and respect the land and all its creatures." ◆ Their faces suitably daubed, the visitors enter the sacred site. Behind thick scrub, hidden from the hikers who trek the local trails, lie huge, round, moss- and lichen-encrusted granite monoliths, ancient rocks worn smooth and sensual. The spiritual aura of the site is immediately obvious, and Naylor's timeless

Aboriginal peoples throughout Australia are willing to explain their traditions and rich cultural heritage to overseas visitors as well as their nonindigenous compatriots.

stories ensure that no visitor can fail to sense it.

The spirituality and stories have always been there. For Aboriginal people, they date back to the beginning of time, a period known as the Dreaming, or Dreamtime. During the Dreaming, supernatural ancestors emerged from the spirit world to roam the then-featureless land. Their activities shaped the landscape, and many of the spirits eventually assumed the form of landmarks, people, and animals. Each Aboriginal group has its own Dreaming stories that explain the creation of its lands and all natural phenomena. These narratives also contain the laws and moral codes on which all social customs and religious practices are based. For each group, certain sites represent key episodes in the stories and therefore have particular spiritual significance. Many remain off-limits to travelers, but at some, including Gulaga, the local people are willing to explain their beliefs and the significance of the site to outsiders.

Traditional Culture

Archaeologists explain the presence of Aborigines in Australia in terms of the great human migratory movements. Most argue that the first migrants reached the coast of northern Australia about 60,000 years ago, crossing from Indonesia via a land bridge that formed when the sea level was more than 400 feet lower than it is today.

By about 40,000 years ago, most parts of the continent had been settled. Archaeological artifacts trace the spread and development of Aboriginal societies. Stone tools unearthed in the Northern Territory date to 60,000 years ago; others retrieved at Swan River near Perth are around 39,500 years old. Rock art found in the Kimberley and dated to 40,000 years ago represents some of the earliest evidence of human artistic endeavor. By comparison, the famous cave paintings at Lascaux in France – the first utterance of European artistic expression – date from 15,000 to 17,000 years ago. Remains recovered at Lake Mungo in western New South Wales indicate that by 25,000 years ago Aboriginal people were practicing cremation. This is the earliest evidence of complex death rites found anywhere in the world.

Traditional Aboriginal society was based on small

groups of nomadic hunter-gatherers, but lifestyles varied according to the environment. Peoples living in fertile regions tended to be more sedentary, whereas groups living in arid areas moved frequently to take advantage of seasonal supplies of food and water. By doing so, they ensured that the local ecology was allowed to regenerate.

Common to all groups was a deep belief in equality: there is no evidence of the formation of political hierarchies, although social distinctions were made on the basis of age and gender. Kinship was defined by a complex series of rules and bonds, and the combination of kinship and Dreaming affiliation often dictated marital eligibility and religious duties including the stewardship of sacred sites. Social connections with other groups were established through trade and at regular ceremonial gatherings. On meeting, groups would exchange and compare not only goods such as ocher and flint but also Dreaming stories, frequently in the form of songs. Connections would be established, with one group's Dreaming ancestor appearing in the song of a neighboring people or the story of one ancestor being continued in another group's narrative. In such a way, the Dreaming stories linked widely separate peoples

Aboriginal art (right) has enjoyed great commercial success in recent years, helping to revitalize many communities.

Rock art (opposite) dating to 2,000 BC is preserved in the "Art Gallery" in Carnarvon National Park, Queensland.

Indigenous communities (right) normally welcome visitors but may request that they register upon arrival or obtain a travel permit.

and formed an intricate, continent-wide web of oral culture, sometimes called "the songlines."

Frontier Strife

By the time Europeans arrived in the late 18th century, Australia was inhabited by more than 300,000 people speaking approximately 250 languages. Captain James Cook saw many Aborigines as he sailed up the eastern coast of Australia, yet, on August 22, 1770, on Possession

Island off the Cape York Peninsula, he claimed most of the continent for King George III. The implication of this, that the land was undeveloped and therefore uninhabited, became the basis of the infamous legal fiction known as *terra nullius* – a Latin term meaning "no one's land" – that was used by settlers to justify the seizure of Aboriginal

Indigenous Experiences

Revenue from tourism has become the economic mainstay of many indigenous communities. One of the most successful indigenous developments is the **Tjapukai Aboriginal Cultural Park**, near Cairns in northern Queensland. Nearly a decade ago, the Tjapukai Dance Theatre was established, led by Djabugay didgeridoo virtuoso David Hudson, with artistic assistance from two New York theater impresarios. In 1997, the theater became a cultural park – the country's largest private-enterprise employer of Aboriginal people.

At the park, visitors can see displays of Djabugay artifacts and a beautifully made documentary charting the history of the Djabugay. In the Creation Theatre, the native belief system is presented in the Djabugay tongue, which is translated for the audience into seven languages. There are also demonstrations of didgeridoos and bush foods and medicines, and lessons in spear- and boomerang-throwing.

Near Tenterfield in northern New South Wales, Woollool Aboriginal Cultural Tours takes visitors to **Bald Rock**, the largest exposed granite monolith in Australia and a sacred site for the Bundjalung people. At **Camp Coorong** near Meningie in South Australia, visitors can stay with the Ngarrindjeri people and learn about their lifestyle and customs from tribal elders. And at the **Umbarra Aboriginal Cultural Centre** at Wallaga Lake, Eric Naylor's half-day and day tours of **Gulaga** include a guided tour of the mountain and a range of cultural activities at the center. Not surprisingly, the Northern Territory has the widest range of Aboriginal-operated activities.

Travelers visiting indigenous communities should be sensitive to cultural differences. Always ask before you photograph or film people, and don't be offended if the subjects refuse. You should also heed any requests that you refrain from photographing sacred sites. Never bargain for artifacts, as this is not usual practice. And if you're planning to drive across Aboriginal lands, find out from the local Land Council whether a permit is required.

Tour guide Karina Lester (above) explains the cultural and religious significance of Uluru to a group of visitors.

land until as late as 1992.

The arrival of the First Fleet in January 1788 saw the beginning of nearly 200 years of antagonism between Europeans and Aborigines. As settlers spread out, the rules of engagement remained remarkably consistent. By clearing forests and introducing livestock, the newcomers damaged the delicate ecological balance maintained by indigenous people and depleted their supplies of food and water. In response, Aborigines, who perceived all animals – even sheep and cattle – as natural resources, began to hunt livestock.

Settlers responded violently to what they saw as theft, and massacres of Aborigines occurred all along the frontier. Only occasionally were the perpetrators brought to justice. At Myall Creek in northern New South Wales in 1838, a posse of laborers and convicts murdered 28 unarmed Aborigines. Seven of the men were subsequently caught, tried, and hanged in Sydney. But such justice was rare: the massacres in the Gippsland area of East Victoria in the 1840s, for example, were so poorly reported that the chief perpetrator, a landowner named Angus McMillan, was eventually appointed, without a hint of irony, the state's Protector of Aborigines.

By 1901, the Aboriginal population had dropped to less than a third of its 1788 level. Many of the survivors were forced into or took refuge in mission stations, where they became highly institutionalized. Around this time, in a misguided attempt to integrate Aborigines into white culture, the states began to remove Aboriginal children from their families and place them in white foster families or children's homes. This practice, which continued until the 1960s, resulted in the so-called stolen generation, an entire generation of Aborigines who were cut off from their traditional culture, their land, and its spirituality.

After falling to a historic low of around 74,000 in 1933, today's indigenous population, while still only two percent of the Australian total, exceeds 352,000. The largest concentrations – in excess of 70,000 people – live in New South Wales and Queensland, although Aborigines make up 23 percent of the Northern Territory's small population.

Reclaiming the Land

In the 1960s, taking their lead from the racial integration movements of North America, Aborigines started to demand equality and attempt to reclaim some of their homelands. The land rights movement reached a high point in 1992, when, as a result of a claim brought by Koiki (Eddie) Mabo and the Meriam people of Murray Island in the Torres Strait, the Australian High Court declared that indigenous people held native title to traditional lands. Thus, the legal fiction of *terra nullius* was finally overturned.

Despite this, state governments, pastoralists, and mining companies continue to block native title claims. Furthermore, two centuries of maltreatment and oppression have left many Aborigines disheartened. Some still have little access to adequate social services and live in squalid conditions more commonly found in developing countries.

However, the process of reconciliation and healing continues. Many government agencies, particularly at a local and state level, have apologized to the indigenous community for past wrongs. Furthermore, there is a growing awareness that Aboriginal history, rarely taught in schools in the past, is an integral and vital part of the fabric of Australian history and society. And in an act of remarkable assertiveness, many Aboriginal communities have begun to educate white Australians and overseas visitors in the country's first – and most ancient – culture.

Boomerangs (right) were once used for hunting, but today their role is more likely to be decorative rather than functional.

Ceremonial gatherings (below) provide a focus for widely scattered indigenous groups.

Preserving Wilderness

n 1838, Sir James Martin, an Irish-born politician and judge, attempted to sum up the feelings of unease he had experienced in his new homeland of New South Wales: "Trees retained their leaves and shed their bark instead, the more frequent the trees, the more sterile the soil, the birds did not sing, the swans were black, the eagles white, the bees were stingless, some mammals had pockets, others laid eggs, it was warmest on the hills and coolest in the valleys, even the blackberries were red ... such is *Terra Australis*." ◆ Martin's bewilderment was shared by many of the convicts and settlers who arrived in Australia following the founding of the British penal colony at Sydney in 1788. Beyond the confines of the settlement spread a seemingly endless woodland filled with bizarre plants and outlandish creatures. It was a scene of such menacing strangeness that to many of the settlers, the harsh but famil-iar realities of jail in the colony seemed preferable to life in what one military official called the "absolute, howling wilderness." ◆ To the new colony's

Growing environmental awareness has radically altered Australian attitudes to wilderness and given rise to an extensive system of protected areas.

first governor, Arthur Phillip, the "endless continuance of perplexity" on all sides was begging for the imposition of "order and useful arrangement." Consequently, the colonists set out to create order out of apparent chaos. Following on the heels of pioneering explorers who began venturing away from Sydney in the early 1800s, land-hungry emancipated convicts and retired officers assaulted the vegetation with vindictive zeal, clearing trees and planting crops. Within 50 years they had taken over all the viable land in the southeast, and by the end of the 19th century they had occupied

A ranger prepares an orphaned wedge-tailed eagle for its return to the wild. Public and private reserves play a critical role in preserving wildlife and wilderness.

most of the inhabitable parts of the continent.

Although forests were cleared mainly to permit farming, the continent's trees had value in themselves and were exploited early. Red cedar, which yields a highly versatile timber, was one of the first species to fall to the axe. Growing from southern New South Wales to northern Queensland, it was so ferociously harvested that today very few specimens remain.

The combination of settlement and logging decimated the continent's forests. By 1996, 40 percent had been cut down and much of the rest had been logged and thinned. Only about a quarter of Australia's original forest remains untouched.

Species under Assault

Convinced of the absolute rightness of the European approach, 19th-century settlers not only imposed their brand of farming on their new home but also introduced their own animals. For the first time, Australia's ancient and fragile soil, which had hitherto felt only the soft footpads of native animals, endured the hard hooves of sheep and cattle. A mere 100 years after settlement, the continent carried eight million cattle and 100 million sheep.

Overgrazed, broken up, and trampled to dust, large areas of topsoil were washed or blown away. Livestock numbers continued to increase, and today 70 percent of Australia is devoted to grazing, with some outback farm properties as large as small European countries.

Native plants dwindled before this onslaught. So too did the smaller native animals – the bettongs, potoroos, and bandicoots – that depended on the vegetation for cover and food. Initially, some of the larger species, such as kangaroos and wallabies, benefited from the change from woodland to grassland and extended their ranges over large areas of the country. But they soon came to be seen as pests that competed for fodder with introduced stock, and farmers began to cull them by the million. This practice continues as roo numbers are still much higher than before colonization.

Sheep and cattle were followed by wave after wave of other introduced creatures, including rabbits, foxes, cats, horses, goats, donkeys, water buffaloes, and pigs. The most destructive were rabbits, which had attained plague numbers in the east by 1890. Spreading across the continent at the rate of 68 miles a year and creating deserts wherever they hopped, they reached

Cattle (left) have had a devastating effect on the Australian landscape, consuming vast areas of vegetation and wreaking havoc on fragile soils with their hard hooves.

Habitat destruction, erosion, pollution, and introduced species continue to take a heavy toll on wildlife. Endangered or vulnerable natives include (from left to right) the dusky hopping mouse, the little bent-wing bat, and the burrowing bettong.

the west coast in 1907. Foxes, introduced for sport in the mid-1800s, followed the rabbits, preying on them as well as on small Australian animals. Concerned settlers released cats into the bush in an effort to control the rabbit plague, but these predators merely increased the threat to native wildlife, particularly small mammals and ground-nesting birds. In the 1950s, the introduction of the disease myxomatosis almost brought the rabbit population under control, but survivors soon became immune to the virus and numbers swelled again to reach 300 million by 1995. The introduction of a new rabbit-culling disease, calcivirus, has met with varying success. Where a decline in rabbit numbers has been highest, however, native vegetation and animals have bounced back.

The combined effects of habitat destruction, hunting, erosion, and introduced species have taken a heavy toll on Australia's wildlife. Since settlement, 19 of the continent's 268 ground-dwelling animals have become extinct – Australia has the world's worst record for mammalian extinctions – as have 20 of its 777 bird species and 76 of its 20,000 flowering plants.

Campaigning for Conservation

Even behind the clamor for national development and progress in the mid-19th century, small voices had raised concerns about the environmental cost. They grew louder in the late 1800s. Deeply worried by the disappearance of animal and plant species, scientists and nature lovers formed learned societies that began campaigning for the protection of native animals and wilderness.

Ferdinand von Mueller, government botanist of the state of Victoria, was among the most vociferous of the early scientists. "I regard the forest as a heritage given to us by nature, not for spoil or to devastate, but to be wisely used, reverently honoured, and carefully maintained," he said in 1871. Eight years later, Australia declared the world's first national park, near Sydney. In the early 1900s, the Australian public, inspired by the accounts of explorers and adventurers and by a patriotic pride in what made their newly independent country distinctive, took to outdoor recreation with enthusiasm. Bush walkers became zealous supporters of von Mueller's view, and as their numbers swelled, so did their influence. By 1916, there was a national park in every state.

After World War II, however, the emphasis on postwar

Conservation groups (left) have succeeded in attracting widespread support, and their protest marches regularly draw large numbers of people from all walks of life.

reconstruction gave Australia's resource industries a renewed respectability and influence. Wild places came under attack from mining, forestry, and urbanization. These greater threats demanded a more vigorous approach. No longer were polite letters and respectable deputations to Parliament enough; to preserve the wilderness, conservationists would have to mobilize the Australian people.

With the highly politicized anti-Vietnam War movement pointing the way, the scene was set for the great confrontations that shaped today's Australian conservation movement. The most significant was a campaign to prevent a company from mining 50 million tons of limestone for cement in the southern Blue Mountains in

the late 1960s and early 1970s. The operation, near a cave system known as the Colong Caves, threatened to scar pristine wilderness irreparably and obstruct and pollute a wild river. The Colong campaign became a blueprint for future battles against obdurate resource-hunters. Campaigners aroused the public's indignation through a media blitz, commissioned scientific investigations, staged street rallies, stood for Parliament, and – for the first time in Australia – used shareholder rights to take the fight into the mining organization's boardroom. Outwitted, the company gave up.

This increasingly professional approach was refined during the 1970s. Environmentalists successfully prevented sand mining on Fraser Island, thwarted the building of a dam on the Franklin River in Tasmania's wild southwest, lobbied stubbornly for the protection of the teeming wetlands and escarpments of Kakadu in the Northern Territory, opposed uranium mining in Kakadu and at Roxby Downs in South Australia, protested against the logging of ancient forests, and fought for the preservation of wilderness areas. Their campaigns helped increase the amount of land under

Lady Musgrave Island (top) is part of Great Barrier Reef Marine Park, one of 13 World Heritage Areas in Australia.

Ranger One (right), a uranium mine located inside Kakadu National Park, has long been a focus of environmental protests.

government protection. Today, Australia's national parks and other reserves cover almost 150,000 sq. miles (390,000 sq. km) – 5 percent of the country. There are more than 500 national parks (administered by state bodies rather than the federal government), as well as numerous other kinds of preserves including conservation reserves, coastal parks, scenic reserves, and state forests.

Additional protection has come through international recognition of Australia's ecological treasures. To date, 13 areas have been awarded World Heritage listing by UNESCO. Properties on the World Heritage List are considered to be of outstanding universal value, and as a signatory to the World Heritage Convention, Australia is obliged to protect and conserve these areas. This has helped conservationists raise international support for campaigns such as the one against the proposed expansion of uranium mining in Kakadu.

Looking Ahead

The past 200 years have seen a dramatic change in attitudes to the land among nonindigenous Australians. From being repelled by it, they have grown to understand and love it. Today, they're positively proud of its strangeness and, alongside their indigenous compatriots, delight in showing it off to visitors from other

Winifred Falls is just one of many scenic splendors that draw visitors to Royal National Park.

countries. This enthusiasm, combined with a sense that Australia's potential for nature tourism has been only partially tapped, has given rise to numerous ecotourism ventures, and recent years have seen a substantial increase in the number of overseas travelers visiting national parks and participating in nature-based activities.

There is a danger, of course, that overdevelopment may result in the degradation of the very qualities these travelers appreciate. Yet, if a balance can be maintained between access and conservation, nature tourism will undoubtedly play a crucial role in preserving the continent's extraordinary natural heritage for countless generations of Australians and overseas visitors to come.

The World's First National Park

On Friday, March 21, 1879, John Lucas stood up in the New South Wales Parliament and suggested to his fellow MPs that "to ensure a healthy and consequently vigorous and intelligent community … all cities, towns, and villages should possess places of public recreation." A majority

in the house agreed with him, and on April 26, the New South Wales government formally dedicated 18,000 acres of bushland on Sydney's southern outskirts as The National Park.

This was the first reserve in the world to bear this name. Although it is widely believed that Yellowstone merits this honor, the American park was dedicated a "public park" in 1872 and did not officially acquire the title "national park" until 1883. Yellowstone has often been cited as the inspiration for The National Park, but more likely models were the large reserves created on the outskirts of London in the mid-1800s, such as Hampstead Heath, which became a park in 1872.

In 1880, The National Park was expanded to 35,000 acres (14,000 hectares), a size that catered to the growing numbers of visitors. When England's Queen Elizabeth II passed by the park in 1954, she agreed to grant it royal status, and the following year it was renamed the Royal National Park.

During the 20th century, the park's function has tilted away from recreation toward protection of native plants and animals. Its complex array of habitats includes heaths, swamps, woodlands, and rain forests, which harbor a wide range of species, from the red-necked wallaby and New Holland mouse to the satin bowerbird and the superb lyrebird. One of several reserves that now form an almost unbroken ring of green around Australia's major city, the Royal is a historic gem.

t might be an epic three-week trek in a convoy of radio-equipped four-wheel drives across the mammoth, sunbaked dunes and spinifex-spiked scrub of the remote Simpson Desert. Or perhaps an extended hike through the glacier-carved highlands of Tasmania, with days spent observing curious pademelons and rare relict plants, and evenings swapping tales around the stove of a snug mountain hut. Or simply a few days diving on the outer rim of the Great Barrier Reef amid the kaleidoscopic colors of coral and fish, followed by a weekend of indulgence at an exclusive rain-forest retreat. Whatever your mental image of your Australian eco-odyssey, turning the daydream into reality depends on careful planning and an acquaintance with the quirks and commonplaces that constitute this particular land of Oz. ◆ Australia's cities will look reassuringly familiar to visitors from other Western countries, especially the United States, and most state capitals offer a sophisticated range

The journey may be long and the roads a little dusty, but the natural wonders are abundant compensation.

of services and attractions that is likely to waylay even seasoned travelers. But the contrast between urban and rural Australia remains pronounced. Drive a few hours inland from any of the major centers – go bush, as the locals would have it – and things start to change. Soon you're hitting dirt roads, the towns are rapidly shrinking in size, the choice of hotels and eateries is dwindling, and it's three hours to the next gas station. ◆ So before you vault the oceans in a jumbo, hop into a rental car at the airport and make straight for Uluru – better still, before you even book your trip – consider your options carefully. Australia's wildness may be its major attraction, but it's not without its challenges and perils.

Outback travel often involves long drives through inhospitable country. Travelers must be wary of the dangers of driver fatigue, and carry spares and emergency provisions.

Seasons in Reverse

Down under, Christmas is celebrated in searing summer heat, wildflowers begin to bloom in August, and skiers plummet down pistes from June to September. Australia's unfamiliar Southern Hemisphere seasons and widely variable climate mean that you have to time your visit carefully. Scorching heat in the outback and torrential rains that engulf the Top End during the monsoon should dissuade you from visiting these regions between November and April. If that's not enough, consider this: during those months it's almost impossible to cool off in the ocean anywhere north of the Tropic of Capricorn due to the presence of deadly box jellyfish.

On the other hand, winters are perfect for traveling in the outback and tropics: the days are bright, warm, and clear, the nights cool and dry; the floods that fill canyons and cover plains have dwindled to bubbling creeks and muddy billabongs frequented by abundant wildlife – and the seas are free of box jellyfish.

Summer is ideal for touring and hiking in cooler regions such as Tasmania and the Victorian High Country, which may be blanketed in snow in winter (though December through January is also peak holiday season and many wilderness areas may be busy). Spring and fall are best for warmer southern destinations such as the Blue Mountains in New South Wales. To some extent, however, your departure date should be determined by your interests. For example, botanists should be sure to arrive in Western Australia in time to catch the state's extraordinary wildflowers in bloom – a wave of color that ripples down the western side of the continent between August and November.

Natural Hazards

Few antipodean animals pose a threat to travelers, but it pays to tread carefully. Australia has more venomous snakes than any other country, and several of the most deadly. Boots and long trousers will offer some protection, but you can also comfort yourself with the knowledge that almost all snakes beat a hasty retreat as soon as they sense your approach and that Australia's annual tally of fatalities per million inhabitants is a minuscule 0.13. To treat a bite, bind the wound tightly, then get the injured person to a doctor at once. Antivenins are widely available.

Several species of spider can inflict a painful and sometimes life-threatening bite, so treat all arachnids with caution. The most deadly spider is the Sydney funnelweb; fortunately, this species is restricted to the Sydney region and an antivenin is seldom far away.

Toxins carried by bush ticks can paralyze and even kill. After hiking in eastern grasslands or forests, check your body thoroughly. If you find a tick, soak it in methylated spirits and then draw it out carefully using tweezers. Try not to squeeze the tick's body, as this will force more toxin into the system.

The only large, aggressive land animal is the saltwater crocodile, which inhabits the rivers and swamps of the far north. Fatalities occur regularly, so keep away from the water's edge in croc country.

Offshore, steer clear of stonefish, pufferfish, porcupine fish, and stingrays. Despite their reputation, sharks seldom attack humans, but make sure you heed shark alerts. Of more concern is the box jellyfish, which is common in tropical waters between October and May. Its long tentacles can inflict agonizing stings that cause occasionally fatal burns and respiratory problems. Emergency treatment involves dousing the wounds with vinegar, supplies of which are positioned on many northern beaches, but prompt medical attention is essential.

Redback spiders (above, left) are notorious for their painful and highly toxic bite, which can be fatal.

Warning signs (left) placed on tropical beaches in summer alert swimmers to the dangers of box jellyfish.

Flies (above) can drive travelers to distraction. Veils, available in many outback areas, provide some relief.

Diving (right) on Australia's reefs is never a solitary experience. This underwater explorer is accompanied by schooling fish, including double-header and moon wrasse.

Travel Options

Driving long distances in remote country may not daunt the average North American traveler, but it's one thing to cover 500 miles (800 km) in a day when the highways are six lanes wide and there are frequent hotels, diners, and service stations; it's quite another to cover the same distance on a narrow, rutted, two-lane road in 110°F (43°C) heat when the only thing between you and your destination is a fuel station that may or may not be open. Most roads in and around Australia's cities, along the east and southwest coasts, and in Tasmania are good, though there's little that resembles an American freeway. But outside of these areas, many of the highways are poorly maintained. So

think twice before you opt to drive from one end of the country to another.

Trains and buses offer only limited alternatives for long-distance travel, particularly to outback and wilderness destinations. True, Australia still offers some of the world's last great rail journeys including the epic cross-continent *Indian-Pacific* route, which passes through desert country and covers the longest straight stretch of railway in the world (297 miles). But outside the southeastern corner of the

country, services are limited; in addition, fares are relatively expensive and the going is slow. The bus network is more economical, extensive, and popular, and remains the choice of budget travelers with time to spare.

By far the most efficient way to reach far-flung parts of the country is to fly. Air services are regular, safe, and frequent, and Australia's domestic airlines offer a range of air passes that permit you to fly to several destinations. International carriers regularly offer deals that include internal

flights along with the long-haul ticket to Australia. Check the latest deals with your travel agent. Be warned, however, that flights from the east coast to some isolated centers – Broome, for example – may be heavily booked.

One way to save time and energy is to join an organized tour. A reliable ecotravel operator will get you to the places and creatures you want to see with a minimum of fuss and a good deal of informed commentary. Specialized tours range from month-long air cruises of the entire continent to birding tours of the eastern rain forests and escorted hikes along major trails such as the Overland Track in Tasmania. Choose your outfitter carefully: use reputable companies that have been endorsed by conservation or ecotravel organizations. The Ecotourism Association of Australia can provide a list of approved operators.

On the (Dirt) Road

Having reached a regional center, travelers of a more independent disposition will pick up a rental vehicle. Find out in advance whether a conventional car will get you where you want to go. Once you leave the highways, it's likely that you'll have to cope with unpaved roads, ranging from smooth gravel to soft sand, and endless corrugations that will keep your teeth chattering and bones rattling long after you've come to a halt. Bear in mind that standard insurance may not cover a conventional rental car when it's on a dirt track.

In the outback in particular, a four-wheel-drive vehicle will be preferable, if not essential. It will be more expensive and guzzle more of Australia's costly gas, but it offers a higher level of security

Hang gliding (left) offers thrilling sport and a bird's-eye view of the bush. Opportunities for outdoor adventures like this abound in Australia.

Overland travel (left) is the only way to appreciate the enormous scale of Australia's outback landscapes.

as well as greater scope for adventure. No extensive four-wheel-drive trip should be undertaken lightly, and don't even contemplate any of the country's famously treacherous long-distance tracks unless you are experienced and well prepared. On the other hand, if your journeys will be short and follow well-traveled routes, don't let the fact that you haven't driven a four-wheel drive put you off. Most rental companies will provide instruction, and it won't be long before you're negotiating sandy tracks and fording shallow creeks.

Whatever kind of vehicle you set off in, remember that Australians drive on the left and give way to traffic coming from the right, seat belts are compulsory front and back, and you should keep to 30–35 mph (50–55 km/ph) in urban areas and no more than 70 mph (110 km/ph) on highways (although exact limits vary from state to state). In rural areas, inquire about road

conditions before you set off. If you're heading down a particularly remote track, report your departure to the police and then confirm your arrival at the other end. It's a good idea to carry some spares – say, two additional tires, a replacement fan belt, and extra fuses – and it's essential to equip yourself with a plentiful supply of fresh water (nine pints per person per day) and emergency foodstuffs in case you should break down. If that occurs on an outback road, whatever you do, stay with your vehicle. In recent years, several people have perished from heat exhaustion because they attempted to walk to find help. Even on an isolated road, another vehicle is likely to appear sooner or later, and you're more likely to be spotted from the air if a search is organized.

As you cruise the red roads of the outback, you may wonder why so many vehicles have oversized bumpers. If you're rash enough to drive at night, you'll soon find out. Come dusk, cattle and kangaroos and other nocturnal mammals are prone to wander – often into the path of oncoming traffic. Having a kangaroo come through your windshield is *not* the best

Multiday hikes (right) can be demanding. Walkers should make sure they are in good physical condition and carry appropriate equipment.

way to get your first close-up view of Australia's national icon, so avoid road travel in outback areas between dusk and dawn.

Always slow down as you pass other vehicles on narrow gravel roads, as flying grit can shatter windscreens. And if you see one of Australia's giant road trains – articulated trucks that tow up to four huge semitrailers – heading toward you on a narrow highway, don't just slow down – pull off the road and stop. Road trains take about as long to come to a halt as a 747, and if their drivers have to choose between endangering their valuable loads and nudging you off the road, guess which way they are going to jump?

Despite these hazards, driving the wide open roads of Australia can be a great way to appreciate the vastness

Cool waters (right) restore and refresh, but care must be taken not to pollute waterways with soaps or detergents.

River rafting trips (below) can be organized in many areas and often provide access to remote wilderness.

and wildness of the continent. But try to resist the temptation to cram too much into a driving tour. After all, spending half of your vacation inside a vehicle hardly qualifies as a wilderness experience.

Bush Lodging

When is a hotel not a hotel? When it's an Australian pub. At one time, all pubs in Australia were required to offer accommodation to passing travelers. Now that those laws have lapsed, many watering holes in city and rural areas are hotels in name only. Some rural establishments continue to offer lodging, but it may consist of a spartan room above the bar or a bunk in a dorm. Fortunately, a much wider range of bush accommodation is now available. Travelers heading for coastal areas such as the Wet Tropics will be spoiled for choice, and the growth of nature tourism has seen numerous ecoresorts spring up in many wilderness areas.

To fully explore the wildest parts of the country, however, your best option – possibly the only one in some areas – is to camp. Before you shudder and shake your head, remember that camping doesn't have to be an uncomfortable experience. Many specialist outfitters run catered camping tours that provide a level of luxury to match top resorts. In addition, Australia's generally predictable, warm, dry weather creates ideal conditions for sleeping outdoors, and, with one or two notable exceptions, the continent's

Covering Your Tracks

Choose your campsite carefully (right). Seek shade and shelter from prevailing winds, and avoid low ground that may be prone to flash floods.

Australia's impoverished soils and limited rainfall mean that the country is particularly susceptible to bushfire, erosion, and other forms of environmental damage. You can minimize your impact on fragile habitats by adhering to the following guidelines:

● Collect all your trash in plastic bags and take it with you when you leave. Do not bury it, as erosion or animals may unearth it.

● Keep to existing trails and avoid cutting across switchbacks.

● Always use existing campgrounds. If no campground is available, select flat, hard ground where you won't damage vegetation.

● Use a fuel stove. If you have to make a fire, build it in an existing fireplace. Do not cut vegetation for firewood; use only wood provided or, as a last resort, deadwood.

● Observe all fire bans: these are regularly in operation in summer months in national parks and state forests, with the current alert displayed at the park entrance.

● To avoid polluting water, wash well away from watercourses. Never use detergents in or near any natural water source.

● Bury human waste at least 6 inches (15 cm) deep[and 250 feet (75 meters) away from watercourses.

● When driving through private land, leave gates as you find them, even if they are open.

● Never remove any objects, such as rocks, plants, or shells, from wilderness areas. Take only photographs.

● Use your influence as an ecotraveler: select only environmentally friendly accommodations, and ask your tour operators what guidelines they follow and how they contribute to preserving the environments they visit.

plants and animals are unlikely to spoil your fun.

Those going it alone can rent camping gear from outdoor equipment shops and car rental companies. If you do so, take a tip: check all your equipment before you set off. Driving for five hours to a remote bush campsite before discovering that you don't know how to set up the tent or that the stove doesn't work could leave you facing a miserable night. What's more, backtracking to the rental office could totally disrupt your carefully planned itinerary.

One of the joys of camping is the number of fellow travelers you encounter, and you'll soon find yourself swapping bush tales around the camp barbecue with people from all walks of life. But the greatest delight is the proximity to nature. It's watching wallabies graze mere feet away from where you rest or seeing dingoes slink through the shadows at the edge of camp. It's waking to the cacophonous laughter of the kookaburra – the "bushman's alarm clock" – or the catalogue of sounds created by the pied butcherbird, whose impressive repertoire may have you ready to tick off another five species on your life list before you flip back the tent flap and find yourself confronted by a lone black-and-white junior

magpie whooping it up on its perch like some avian jazz legend. And on balmy nights, it's gazing at great flocks of flying foxes as they flap silently past a mist-veiled moon, or casting aside the canvas in favor of the vast, astonishing canopy that is the southern night sky.

Whether you camp or opt for a luxury resort, whether you fly, drive, or backpack, traveling through wilderness areas is about accumulating experiences such as these, experiences that will sustain you for many moons to come – or at the very least, until you next go bush.

Hemmed in by giant trees, a dozen travelers shuffle along a narrow trail through the utter darkness of a tropical highland rain forest. Up ahead, their guide is using a powerful portable spotlight to sweep the foliage high above, but behind her the group is straggling in the feeble glimmer of a dozen flashlights, skeptical of seeing anything in the vast and stygian gloom. ◆ Presently, the guide halts. Gathering around to peer along the beam of light, the walkers at first can make out only the red glow of a pair of eyes. But slowly, like the Cheshire Cat, an image builds around the glow to reveal a green ringtail possum peering down at its enthralled audience. The guide has found a "hot spot" of activity, and within an hour she has shown her group at least four species of possums, as well as a rufous owl, some flying foxes, and a blossom bat – **You'll see more creatures,** not to mention various frogs and **from kangaroos to tropical birds,** other small fry. ◆ Suddenly, there's **when you know what to** an almighty crash as a tree-kangaroo **look for and where to search.** leaps a full 15 feet (4.6 meters) from a branch, then bounds away into the blackness. The guide knows a good exit line when she hears one, and directs the party homeward. There's no topping this beast: a kangaroo that climbs trees – now that's worth a stiff neck, a damp collar, and a struggle with a bit of jet lag. ◆ The Australian continent is crammed with extraordinary plants and animals of every kind, many of them found nowhere else on Earth. This combination of diversity and uniqueness presents significant challenges, even to experienced wildlife watchers. As a result, your trip is likely to be far more rewarding if you take some time to learn about the animals that interest you and the environments they inhabit – preferably before you leave home.

Bilbies were once widespread in arid areas, but populations have declined dramatically in recent years as a result of predation by foxes and competition with cattle for food supplies.

Knowing where to look is an important part of successful wildlife-watching (right). Opting for a specialist tour can save valuable time.

Australia Online

Compared with North America and Europe, Australian national parks are undeveloped. A few of the most important have visitor centers, resident naturalists, and marked trails, but many others are simply big chunks of wilderness where you can wander as you please, soaking up the extraordinary wildlife.

The downside of this is that detailed information on animals and plants can be hard to obtain locally. Fortunately, in these days of the World Wide Web, preliminary research, even from the other side of the world, is a no-brainer. Just connect to the Internet, log on to your favorite search engine, and type in "butterflies Australia" or whatever else you'd like to know more about, and then take your pick.

Rainbow lorikeets, which are common along northern and eastern coasts, live up to their name with stunning, multihued plumage.

If you don't get quite what you want, look up the scientific names of any creatures that interest you and type them in (inside quotes). If all else fails, e-mail a polite query to the information officer at any Australian museum – all states have at least one.

Regional Strategies

Zoologists divide Australia into three regions: the arid interior (or outback), the tropical north, and the mainly temperate eucalypt forests and woodlands of the southeast and far southwest. The wildlife of each region is distinct, although there are exceptions. One of the echidna's more extraordinary features, among a host of oddities, is that it is the only one of the continent's 220 or so mammal species that you'll find almost everywhere. If you'd like more oddities: it's also the sole Australian

mammal that hibernates, and it can beat any cat hands-down in laboratory intelligence tests.

The outback, or Eyrian region, as it is known to zoologists, encompasses all of Australia's deserts and almost none of its people or infrastructure. For an overseas visitor interested in wildlife, it's undeniably the most daunting of the three regions and also perhaps the most quintessentially Australian. In this vast aridity, the basic techniques of finding animals – those that really apply anywhere – assume special importance. For example, it's essential to start early in the morning. The birds are most active then, and the local lizards and other reptiles sit conspicuously on rocks, soaking up the early sun, just as they do in Arizona or Texas.

During the heat of the day, check patches of vegetation

for shade-seekers of any kind – goannas, small birds, and kangaroos. If you're traveling by car, don't drive too fast – many reptiles including snakes, frilled lizards, and shinglebacks are most likely to be seen crossing roads. And if you see only one tree between you and the horizon, then there's a fair chance an ol' man red kangaroo will be taking his ease in the shade beneath it. Thoroughly survey any water holes you come across – finches and small honeyeaters in particular visit such places all day long.

Treasures of the Tropics

Almost everywhere you travel in Australia, you will be struck by the abundance of birds. True, there are mammals, frogs, and reptiles aplenty, but they are undeniably less obvious and harder to find: most Australian mammals, for example, are active only at night. But birds are obvious everywhere.

The ubiquity of birds is just as true in tropical Australia – the Torresian region – as elsewhere. Kakadu's wetlands, for example, shelter vast numbers of magpie geese and other wildfowl, and even the remote badlands of the Kimberley are noted for their endemic birds. But the bewildering diversity of tropical bird life – and wildlife generally – reaches its peak in the highland rain forests of northeastern Queensland. The Atherton Tableland near Cairns alone has nine species of endemic birds and seven mammals, plus numerous frogs, skinks, geckoes, freshwater fish, and insects found nowhere else.

Painted dragons (below) are among the most colorful of the Ctenophorus dragons of arid Australia.

The honey possum (bottom) of southwestern Australia is about the size of a small mouse and survives entirely on nectar and pollen.

Rain-forest birds present special problems for nature watchers. To begin with, a small bird can be fiendishly difficult to spot amid the riot of a billion leaves, and the rain-forest light is always deceptive – a kaleidoscope of torrid glare and inky shadows, or else it's raining and everything is reduced to shades of misty grey. Worse, many of the most interesting birds are 200 feet away, directly above your head, leading to stiff necks and aching backs.

The vast majority of tropical mammals is nocturnal, but daytime wonders include the black-and-yellow Cairns birdwing butterfly – with a wingspan the size of your hand, it is one of the largest of all butterflies and a sight to take your breath away. It's a good idea to carry a small flashlight in rain forests and use it to peer under bark or into cavities. You never know what small frog, gecko, or beetle might peer blearily back at you, disturbed from its midday slumber.

Two techniques are most effective for dealing with such challenges. If you're alone, walk until you find a fruiting tree, then stop. Most of whatever is around is almost sure to visit the tree during the next hour or two. If you're in a group, carry at least one tripod-mounted spotting scope (20x to 30x is ideal) and wander slowly along a broad track. The most skilled practitioner can then be nominated to spot the creature and line it up in the scope, and everyone else can briskly line up behind for a quick peek. If you can find a track following a high ridge or along a steep hillside allowing you to view the canopy from above, so much the better.

Freshwater crocodiles (top) inhabit the waterways of northern central Australia.

Blue angelfish (right) are one of 30 species of angelfish found in Australian waters, principally on coral reefs.

Humpback whales (below) spend summer feeding in Antarctic waters before migrating to their breeding grounds in the tropics.

Coastal Creatures

Kangaroos and other Australian landlubbers tend to top the wish lists of most visitors, but the country's marine life is so diverse it demands your attention.

All around the coastline, opportunities abound for getting close to sea creatures of every kind. In winter, you can view wandering albatrosses off Wollongong in New South Wales; in spring, you can follow the migration of humpback whales at several points along the east and west coasts. Summer travelers can watch southern right whale mothers nurse their calves from cliff-tops almost anywhere along the Great Australian Bight and witness the evening parades of fairy penguins returning to their nests on Philip Island in Victoria or Kangaroo Island in South Australia.

And all this without even a mention of the mecca of dive enthusiasts from around the globe, the Great Barrier Reef. By far the largest organic object on earth, it sprawls for 1,430 miles along the coast of Queensland. Almost anyone who can swim can don snorkel and flippers and explore the reefs that fringe numerous islands, and in places you can simply wade along a reef at low tide (but wear thongs – coral is sharp).

The best way to experience this underwater wonderland is to join a dive trip to the outer reef. You can get a close-up view of hundreds of species of multi-hued coral while having your fingers nibbled by a kaleidoscope of small fishes so varied in color and pattern that sometimes it seems no two are alike.

Koalas (right) are choosy about the kinds of eucalypt trees they inhabit: only 35 out of 600 species provide the kind of leaves they prefer.

Patrolling the Boundaries

About nine-tenths of the Australian human population lives in the temperate, or Bassian, region, but that still leaves ample room for some of the country's most intriguing wildlife. This region tends to be dominated by trees, especially eucalypts, but the woodlands may be open and scattered, or so tall and dense they may be mistaken for rain forest.

The diversity of bird life is particularly striking here, mainly because of the abundance of parrots and cockatoos, charismatic birds that can hardly be described as shy, unobtrusive, or retiring. Crimson rosellas, for example, come to be hand-fed at many a forest picnic spot (as do some wallabies and pademelons).

In temperate zones, it's especially important to understand the significance of ecotones, a term referring to the interface between two habitats, such as the boundary between grassland and forest. Usually, this is where the action is. The best birding, for example, can be had by wandering along a seldom-used forestry track or country road, particularly one with fields on one side and forest on the other. Especially around May, when many birds are shuffling between their summer and winter

homes, seeing 100 species in a mile is not unusual, and if there are plenty of flowering eucalypts – about one-quarter of all Australia's land birds are strongly associated with flowering eucalypts – then it's possible to see 20 species of honeyeater in a single tree.

With mammals, serendipity is everything, though you're almost sure to see kangaroos or wallabies during such rambles, and perhaps a wombat or an echidna into the bargain. Koalas are extremely patchy in distribution, and you really need local help to find one. But if you just happen to hear the most extraordinary roaring and bellowing sounds you've ever encountered, investigate promptly – you've probably just made contact with a male koala on the hunt for a mate.

◆

Australian Destinations

◆

From the breathtaking rockscapes of the Red Centre to the teeming turquoise waters of the Great Barrier Reef and the verdant high plains of the Victorian Alps, Australia offers some of the world's most awe-inspiring yet accessible wilderness areas.

Uluru–Kata Tjuta National Park
Northern Territory

CHAPTER **6**

A string of camels threads its way through red dunes, the riders rocking in rhythm to their animals' steady gait. The eastern sky glows fiery red, brightening gradually to reveal the landscape in a muted light. Here and there in this open and vast country, old, shaggy desert oaks clad in thick, black bark and weeping grey-green foliage stand tall at the base of the dunes. Smaller mulga trees cluster in the hollows, and assorted shrubs and circular clumps of prickly spinifex grass speckle the dunes. ◆ Birds begin to awaken and stir. A brown falcon perches on the gnarled limb of a dead desert oak, silent and watchful, while a small flock of green budgerigars flies by, low and swift. Delicate lines, swirls, and indentations decorate the sand – evidence of the nocturnal activities of small marsupials. ◆ The camel riders reach the crest of a high dune and stop, watching in silent wonder as the sun bursts over the horizon, igniting the monumental rock whose rounded bulk

Australia's most distinctive landmark is both a sacred site for indigenous people and a sanctuary for wildlife.

dominates the skyline. Another day has dawned at **Uluru–Kata Tjuta National Park**. ◆ Possibly Australia's greatest tourist drawing card, **Uluru** (Ayers Rock) is a national icon with an enduring mystique that attracts hundreds of thousands of visitors each year. Those who make the pilgrimage to see "the Rock," and its lesser known but equally spectacular counterpart **Kata Tjuta** (the Olgas), enter a starkly beautiful world of ancient landforms, brilliant blue skies, blood-red sands, diverse wildlife, and 30,000 years of Aboriginal culture. ◆ The World Heritage-listed park encompasses 511 sq. miles (1,320 sq. km) of the continent's bone-dry heart and is managed jointly by its traditional owners – the Anangu Aboriginal people – and Environment

Uluru is a place of pilgrimage for travelers, many of whom are learning to appreciate the immense religious significance of the rock to the Anangu people.

Preceding pages: The Pinnacles in Nambung National Park, Western Australia, are limestone columns exposed by erosion.

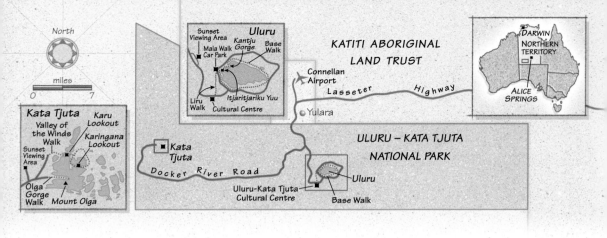

North

miles

0   7

Sunset Viewing Area · Uluru
Mala Walk · Kantju Gorge · Base Walk
Car Park
Liru Walk · Itjaritjariku Yuu · Cultural Centre

KATITI ABORIGINAL LAND TRUST

Connellan Airport

Lasseter   Highway

DARWIN
NORTHERN TERRITORY

ALICE SPRINGS

Yulara

Kata Tjuta
Valley of the Winds Walk
Sunset Viewing Area
Olga Gorge Walk · Mount Olga

Karu Lookout
Karingana Lookout

Kata Tjuta

Docker River Road

ULURU – KATA TJUTA NATIONAL PARK

Uluru-Kata Tjuta Cultural Centre

Uluru

Base Walk

Australia. This is a region of extremes where rainfall is erratic, droughts can last for several years, and temperatures fluctuate between several degrees below freezing on winter nights and more than 104°F (40°C) on many summer days. Evolution has borne these vagaries well: diversity abounds, together with examples of remarkable adaptation. The park is home to some 566 species of plants, 178 birds, 72 reptiles, 24 native mammals, and six introduced species, including the camel – the "ship of the desert" that opened up so much of inland Australia.

Around the Rock

Rising 1,141 feet above the shimmering plain and with a circumference of 5.8 miles (9.3 km) is the ancient weather-scarred bulk of Uluru. Like Kata Tjuta, this enormous monolith is the visible tip of a huge slab of rock that extends far beneath the ground – possibly as far as 3.7 miles (6 km). There

Tawny frogmouths (above) are named for their wide gapes and for their muted plumage.

An Aboriginal guide (right) demonstrates how to obtain nectar from honey grevillea flowers.

are two explanations for the creation of these awesome formations. Geologically speaking, both Uluru and Kata Tjuta are remnants of the debris washed down from the giant Petermann Ranges, which stretched through central Australia some 600 million years ago.

The other explanation, that of the Anangu, stems from the Tjukurpa, the creation period during which ancestral beings traveled across the land, their movements and activities forming every living thing and every feature of the landscape. Tjukurpa also refers to the collection of history, knowledge, religion, morality, and law that governs the way in which the Anangu look after each other and the country.

To learn more about Tjukurpa and the Anangu people, make your first stop the **Cultural Centre**, about half a mile (0.8 km) from Uluru. Here, dynamic displays describe the park's history and wildlife as well as aspects of Anangu life. An appreciation of Anangu culture encourages visitors to reassess that long-prized Uluru experience, "the Climb." For both spiritual and safety reasons, the Anangu would prefer that visitors didn't scale the rock. The marked trail to the top follows a sacred route taken by ancestral Mala men during the Tjukurpa. It is also steep and strenuous, and a number of people have died attempting it.

A more profitable and respectful way to investigate Uluru is to explore the many trails around its base. Several of the walks are self-guided, or you can join any number of tours conducted on foot and by vehicle. Anangu-led walks can be an unforgettable experience. Guides unlock many of the mysteries of the bush, demonstrating the collection and preparation of foods and medicines, the making of tools and implements, and aspects of the Tjukurpa.

The complete circuit, known as the **Base Walk**, is an easy amble, taking at least three hours. The Mala Walk parking lot is a good place to start. As you wander along the track, the features that lend so much character to the rock's surface – the caves, overhangs, crevices, hollows, and blackened lines of water-courses – are revealed in a new light. One Tjukurpa story tells how the small cave near the start of the walk, **Itjaritjariku Yuu**, was built as a shelter by Itjaritjari, the marsupial mole, and that the wedge-shaped stone lying on its side at the entrance is the *yuu*, or windbreak. Itjaritjari's modern-day incarnation is a distinctive creature: the marsupial mole is completely blind and has short powerful limbs that it uses to "swim" through the sand. Living

almost entirely underground, it is rarely seen, though you may spot its tracks – wavy lines in the sand that end at a small mound.

The main trail continues past thickets of plumbush, sticky hopbush, and stands of bloodwood where birds such as crested pigeons, black-faced cuckoo-shrikes, and little wood swallows flit through the treetops. Sharp-eyed observers may see a nocturnal tawny frogmouth roosting on a limb, its

Rainwater carves deep grooves in the sides of Uluru (right) and sustains pockets of vegetation such as these bloodwood trees.

Shield shrimps (left) appear in numbers in puddles and pools around Uluru and Kata Tjuta following rains.

mottled plumage blending perfectly with the rough, flaky eucalypt bark. At **Kantju Gorge**, one of the few reliable water holes around Uluru, look for the large tadpoles of the water-holding frog, which survives long dry spells by entombing itself in a watertight cocoon made from its own shed skin. Keep an eye out, too, for black-headed goannas sunning themselves on the rock's surface. Along the northern, drier side of Uluru, the vegetation is sparser and the caves more abundant. Those just above ground level are frequented by euros, or hill kangaroos. Overhead, majestic wedge-tailed eagles soar on thermals, searching for prey.

Come late afternoon, there is only one place to be: a sunset viewing area. Though you're likely to share the spectacle of Uluru's famous color changes – from pink through mauve to fiery red and deep orange – with crowds of other camera-toting tourists, it is nevertheless an obligatory experience. Note, however, that the quality of the performance can vary depending on atmospheric conditions. The color changes result from the reflection of the sun's dying light, mainly from the red part of the spectrum, on the rock and sand.

Among the Domes

When explorer Ernest Giles reached Kata Tjuta in 1873, he described the formation's 36 conglomerate domes, which rise up to 1,791 feet, as "extraordinary freaks or convulsions of nature." Somewhat more prosaically, he observed that the formation was "composed of untold masses of round stones of all kinds and size, mixed as plums in a pudding and set in vast and rounded shapes upon the ground."

Though accurate from a geological point of view, his descriptions gave no hint of the immense spiritual significance of the formation to the local people. Much of Kata

Watarrka National Park

It has been called Australia's Grand Canyon – and **Kings Canyon**, **Watarrka National Park**'s star feature, is a majestic affair. Its ancient sandstone walls soar 330–490 feet (100–150 meters) to a plateau of beehive-shaped domes whose austere beauty contrasts with the **Garden of Eden**, a cool, moist valley at the bottom of the gorge.

Encompassing the western end of the rugged George Gill Range, 186 miles (300 km) northeast of Uluru, the park is one of Central Australia's most important botanical areas. More than 600 plant species have been recorded here, 60 of them rare or relict. The park is rich in wildlife, too, protecting 20 mammal species, 71 reptiles, and 140 birds.

Reasonably fit visitors should take the 3.7-mile (6-km) walk around the canyon rim, which includes a detour to "the Garden." Though strenuous and steep in places, it provides spectacular views of the park's rugged landscape as well as distant desert sand plains, and offers plentiful opportunities for encounters with wildlife, including euros, falcons, red-tailed black cockatoos, and ring-tailed dragons. There are also a few shorter walks and guided tours departing from **Lilla**, an Aboriginal homeland within the park.

Kings Canyon (above) formed when layers of sandstone were uplifted and fractured around 300 million years ago.

A thorny devil (opposite, bottom) is certainly not camera shy. The devil relies on its spines to deter predators.

Tjuta is associated with sacred stories and rituals that are the exclusive knowledge of initiated men. Consequently, no Tjukurpa stories can be passed on to the general public. However, Kata Tjuta's natural wonders are on open display and best viewed on the two walks that depart from the parking lot.

The 3.2-mile (5.1-km) **Olga Gorge Walk** provides fine views of the open country to the west before leading into the imposing gorge. Longer but more rewarding is the **Valley of the Winds Walk**. The track winds for 4.6 miles (7.4 km) around and between several domes; apart from a short, steep section leading to the breathtaking **Karingana Lookout**, it's a comfortable walk, taking about three hours. During the warmer months, discerning observers may spot superbly camouflaged earless dragons and perenties – at up to 6½ feet (2 meters) long, Australia's largest lizards – on the stony slopes. Bird life is prolific: seed-eaters such as zebra finches, crested pigeons, and budgerigars flit in and out of the forested valleys; magpies, grey shrike-thrushes, and pied butcherbirds burst into sporadic song, their caroling voices echoing in the canyons; singing and grey-headed honeyeaters forage for insects among the foliage; and kestrels nest in rocky hollows high up on the domes.

After rain, look for shield shrimps in the rock pools lining the ephemeral creek that runs alongside the track below the **Karu Lookout**, the first viewpoint. These tiny crustaceans live as long as there is water, laying thousands of eggs that survive until the next downpour fills the pools. Spring rains also trigger displays of wildflowers such as early Nancy lilies, whose delicate pink blooms decorate the creek edges.

If you start the walk in mid-afternoon, you can arrive at the nearby sunset viewing area in time to watch Kata Tjuta's color changes – a spectacle to equal that of Uluru but usually enjoyed by fewer spectators.

In Uluru-Kata Tjuta National Park, nature has stripped away the fat of the land to reveal the bare and beautiful bones of one of her most spectacular desert environments. Time spent here, no matter how brief, instills a sense of wonder – for the limitless plains, the massive, sometimes surreal formations, the remarkable plants and wildlife, and the rich indigenous culture that binds them all together.

TRAVEL TIPS

DETAILS

When to Go

April to September is the most comfortable period to visit, with average maximum temperatures ranging from about 68°F (20°C) in June and July to about 86°F (30°C) in April and September. Winter nights, however, can drop to below freezing. December, January, and February are the hottest months, with daytime temperatures often topping 104°F (40°C). Rain can fall in any month but is less likely from April to August.

How to Get There

There are regular direct flights from major cities and Alice Springs to Connellan Airport, which is 4.3 miles (7 km) from Ayers Rock Resort and Yulara, the park's service village. Car rentals are available at both Connellan and Alice Springs airports; the drive from Alice Springs to Uluru is 289 miles (465 km). Greyhound Pioneer, tel: 07-3258 1701, and McCafferty's, tel: 07-4690 9888, both have daily bus services from Alice Springs to Uluru. The ride takes about 5½ hours.

Watarrka National Park is about 190 miles (300 km) northeast of Uluru and 200 miles (330 km) southwest of Alice Springs. For an off-the-beaten track adventure, travel via the gravel Mereenie Loop Road. Check road conditions with the Alice Springs Visitor Information Centre, tel: 08-8952 5800, before setting out. For those without their own vehicle, there are a host of tour options for both parks.

Special Planning

The desert sun is very strong, even in the cooler months, so come prepared. If undertaking any walks, wear a broad-brimmed hat, sturdy shoes, long sleeves, and plenty of sunscreen. In the hotter months, carry and drink a quart of water per hour and conduct all strenuous activities during the cooler early morning hours.

Permits and Entry Fees

Entry tickets providing unlimited access to Uluru–Kata Tjuta National Park for up to five days can be purchased from the visitor and information centers at Yulara or the park entrance station. Entrance to Watarrka National Park is free.

Visitors traveling to Watarrka National Park from Alice Springs via the Mereenie Loop Road, which traverses Aboriginal land, will need to purchase a permit from the Central Australian Tourism Industry Association office in Alice Springs, tel: 08-8952 5800.

INFORMATION

Central Australian Tourism Industry Association

60 Gregory Terrace, Alice Springs, NT 0871; tel: 08-8952 5800.

Tour and Information Centre

Ayers Rock Resort, Yulara, NT 0872; tel: 08-8956 2240.

Uluru-Kata Tjuta National Park Cultural Centre

P.O. Box 119, Yulara, NT 0872; tel: 08-8956 3138; web: www.biodiversity.environment. gov.au/protecte/intro.htm

Visitors Centre

Ayers Rock Resort, Yulara, NT 0872; tel: 08-8957 7377.

Watarrka National Park

Parks and Wildlife Commission of the Northern Territory, P.O. Box 1046, Alice Springs, NT 0871; tel: 08-8951 8211; web: www.nt.gov.au/paw

CAMPING

No camping is permitted in Uluru–Kata Tjuta National Park.

Ayers Rock Campground

Ayers Rock Resort, Yulara, NT 0872; tel: 08-8956 2055.

This commercial campground has tent and powered sites, plus 14 air-conditioned, six-bed cabins. Facilities include showers and toilets, a swimming pool, and free gas barbecues. $–$$

LODGING

> **PRICE GUIDE** – double occupancy
>
> $ = up to $49 $$ = $50–$99
> $$$ = $100–$149 $$$$ = $150+

Kings Canyon Resort

Luritja Road, Watarrka National Park, NT 0872; tel: 02-9360 9099; e-mail: rockres@ayersrock.aust.com

Just 4 miles (7 km) from Kings Canyon, this 132-room resort set in stunning wilderness offers Watarrka's sole accommodation. Options include standard and deluxe hotel rooms, budget lodge rooms, trailer parks, known as caravans, and campsites. Recreational facilities include two swimming pools and a tennis court. $–$$$$

Outback Pioneer Hotel and Lodge

Ayers Rock Resort, Yulara, NT 0872; tel: 02-9360 9099; e-mail: rockres@ayersrock.aust.com

Traditional Aussie hospitality is the order of the day at this relaxed, country-style hotel and lodge at Ayers Rock Resort, 12½ miles (20 km) from Uluru and 33 miles (53 km) from Kata Tjuta. The Outback has 125 hotel rooms with private bathrooms, 12 cabins, and several air-conditioned dormitories. Amenities include a swimming pool, a barbecue, and a restaurant. $–$$$$

Sails in the Desert Hotel

Ayers Rock Resort, Yulara, NT 0872; tel: 02-9360 9099; e-mail: rockres@ayersrock. aust.com

Featuring an award-winning native garden, Ayers Rock Resort's premier hotel offers 228 rooms, including six with spas and two suites. Facilities include a swimming pool, tennis court, putting green, three restaurants, a clothing and gift shop, and an art gallery. $$$$

TOURS & OUTFITTERS

Anangu Tours

P.O. Box 435, Yulara, NT 0872; tel: 08-8956 2123; web: www.users.bigpond.com/LBANA NGU/ or e-mail: lbanangu@ bigpond.com

Aborigine-led tours offer visitors an opportunity to learn about Anangu culture.

Frontier Camel Tours

P.O. Box 275, Yulara, NT 0872; tel: 08-8956 2444; web: www.ozemail.com.au/~camelfro or e-mail: camelroc@ozemail.com.au

Peaceful sunrise and sunset camel rides travel among red dunes to view Uluru.

Lilla Aboriginal Tours

Lilla Community, P.M.B. 136, Kings Canyon via Alice Springs, NT 0872; tel: 08-8956 7417.

Short, easy, guided walking tours are available at this Aboriginal out-station within Watarrka National Park.

Uluru Experience

P.O. Box 25, Yulara, NT 0872; tel: 08-8956 2563.

Local experts lead personalized walking and vehicle-based tours around Uluru and Kata Tjuta. Some of the four-wheel-drive tours visit a nearby working cattle station.

Excursions

Chambers Pillar Historical Reserve

Parks and Wildlife Commission of the Northern Territory, Tom Hare Building, South Stuart Highway, Alice Springs, NT 0870; tel: 08-8951 8211; web: www.nt.gov.au/paw

Towering 164 feet above the surrounding red plain, this sandstone pillar is a sight to behold, especially at sunset when it glows like a burning ember in the sun's dying light. Named by John McDouall Stuart – the first European to see it – in 1860, the pillar served as a navigational landmark for explorers, and visitors can see the names of many of these pioneers carved into the soft sandstone. The reserve lies 100 miles (160 km) south of Alice Springs, with the final section of the journey requiring a four-wheel-drive vehicle.

Henbury Meteorites Conservation Reserve

Parks and Wildlife Commission of the Northern Territory, Tom Hare Building, South Stuart Highway, Alice Springs, NT 0870; tel: 08-8951 8211; web: www.nt.gov.au/paw

Twelve meteorite craters, formed 4,700 years ago when a meteorite disintegrated just before impact, are protected in this reserve 90 miles (145 km) southwest of Alice Springs. A self-guided walking track allows visitors to view the craters at close range. The largest crater is 590 feet wide and 49 feet deep with a 20-foot-high rim.

Rainbow Valley Conservation Reserve

Parks and Wildlife Commission of the Northern Territory, Tom Hare Building, South Stuart Highway, Alice Springs, NT 0870; tel: 08-8951 8211; web: www.nt.gov.au/paw

Locals regard Rainbow Valley as one of the Red Centre's best-kept secrets. The 6,133-acre (2,480-hectare) reserve's has

dramatic sandstone bluffs and cliffs whose iron red and leached white bands of color light up in the rays of the setting sun. Accessible only by four-wheel-drive, the park is 60 miles (100 km) southwest of Alice Springs. There is a campsite but bring your own water, food, and firewood.

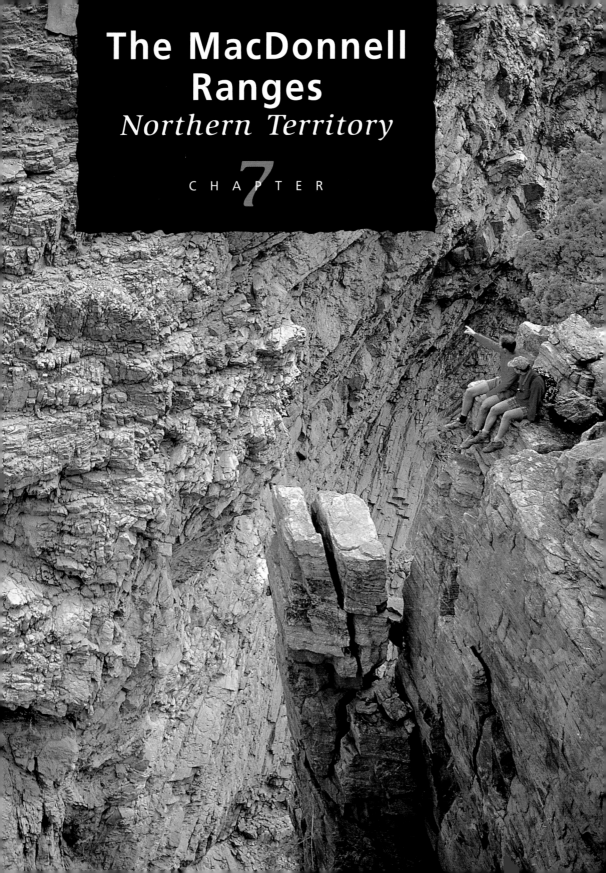

The MacDonnell Ranges
Northern Territory

Viewed from the quartzite ridge at **Counts Point**, the **MacDonnell Ranges** extend from the eastern horizon to the west, their great folds and ridges falling and rising, seemingly without end. A series of parallel ranges rather than a single chain, the mountains stretch out across Australia's arid heart like great stone lizards basking in the sun. ◆ The slopes are sparsely covered with cypress pine, spinifex grass, and mulga bush, and their rocky outlines and warm shades of red, gold, and brown stand out boldly in the clear desert air. To the northwest, the tallest peak in the MacDonnells, **Mount Zeil**, is clearly visible; even more impressive is its neighbor, **Mount Sonder**, with its mauve coloring and majestic lines. ◆ Between the ranges, dark-green mulga bushes dot broad valleys of red earth, and the white-sand beds of watercourses, fringed by red gum trees, wend their way across the flats. These rivers have not seen a permanent flow of water for thousands of years, but over eons they have cut deep

The hidden pools of these ancient ranges have long been a lifeline for Central Australia's plants, animals, and human inhabitants.

gorges through the iron-stained ranges. In their cool shadows grow ferns and mosses, and palmlike cycads that are relics of a past age when the rain forests of Central Australia spread down to the shores of an ancient sea. ◆ Known to the local Arrernte people as Altjira, the MacDonnell Ranges extend 90 miles (145 km) on either side of **Alice Springs**. The mountains consist mainly of quartzite rock derived from sand laid down 850 million years ago on the bed of an ancient sea. Some 350 million years ago, tectonic forces thrust the ranges to a height of 15,000 feet, but erosion has since worn them down so that only a few peaks approach 5,000 feet.

Perched precariously above Serpentine Gorge, walkers study the surrounding rocks. Far below, the gorge's waters sustain lush pockets of ancient plant species.

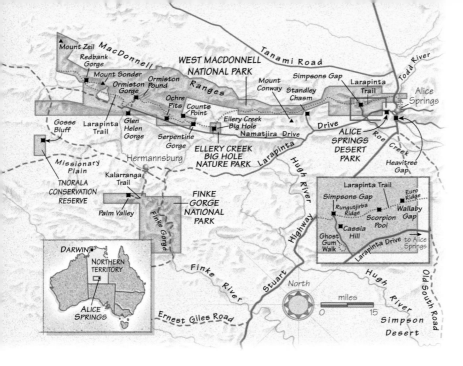

The MacDonnells mark the northern edge of Australia's greatest internal drainage basin, centered on the vast salt pan of **Lake Eyre**, 300 miles (480 km) to the southeast. During infrequent floods, the usually dry Finke, Hugh, Todd, and Hale rivers flow from the ranges toward the lake, their waters gradually evaporating in the heat of the **Simpson Desert**.

Tropical and temperate climates mingle over the MacDonnells, producing wide variations in rainfall. Combined with the diverse landforms, this gives the mountains a much greater range of environments than the surrounding desert plains. More than 600 species of native plants grow here, many of them ignoring the seasons and responding only to rain, so that during a wet spell the slopes may be brightened by masses of white everlasting and yellowtop daisies. The valleys support modest woodlands of eucalypts such as red gums, ghost gums, and bloodwoods, and hardy cypress pines grow sparsely on the ridges. In the gorges, ancient oases sustain relict

Zebra finches (right) are among the most widespread finches. Highly social, they often gather in large flocks.

plant species, such as the palmlike Australian cycad and the guinea flower, which first took root millions of years ago when the region's climate was much wetter than it is today.

About 148 species of birds inhabit the ranges. At water holes, you're likely to spot seedeaters such as the spinifex pigeon, with its prominent plume and white "necklace," and the tiny zebra finch, with its black-and-white striped tail. Watch for little variegated wrens on the dry ridges and wedge-tailed eagles soaring overhead.

Native mammal numbers have declined since the arrival of European settlers and introduced predators such as foxes and cats, and the 56 species that once lived in central Australia have been gradually reduced to 43. Happily, however, some species thought to be extinct, such as the central rock-rat and a mouse-sized marsupial known as the long-tailed dunnart, have recently been rediscovered. Perhaps the most surprising feature of these arid ranges is the wealth of aquatic life found in the seemingly modest water holes: the pools support as many as 10 species of native fish.

The Alice

The first European to enter the MacDonnells was the determined Scotsman John McDouall Stuart, who trekked north from Adelaide in the 1860s and crossed the ranges repeatedly before finding an overland route to Australia's northern coastline. In the 1870s, the Overland Telegraph Line from Adelaide was strung through the ranges at **Heavitree Gap**. A telegraph station was established at a nearby pool and named Alice Springs for Alice Todd, the wife of the Postmaster-General of South Australia, Charles Todd. The town that sprang up later and is often referred to as "the Alice" is now the administrative and commercial hub of Central Australia.

Most of the mountains to the west of Alice Springs are contained within the 1,125,000-acre **West MacDonnell National Park**; much smaller parks and reserves protect places of interest to the east. The national park encompasses many of the ranges' most spectacular and accessible gorges as well as their highest peaks. Well-maintained roads allow conventional vehicles to reach the main sights, although a four-wheel-drive vehicle permits wider exploration. Trails wind through and around most of the gorges, and eager walkers can experience the full grandeur of these ancient desert mountains by hiking the **Larapinta Trail**. Most of the trail's 13 sections are open, and when fully completed, it will wend for 137 miles (220 km) along the backbone of the western MacDonnells from the

The long-tailed dunnart (left) uses its impressive tail to help it balance on rocky ground.

The Larapinta Trail (below) offers a comprehensive experience and stunning views of the MacDonnells.

old telegraph station near Alice Springs, ending just beyond Mount Razorback. Each section starts and ends at a roadhead, so the trail can be enjoyed in stages and provides even novice walkers with access to some of the wildest parts of the ranges.

Visitors can walk, drive, or even cycle from Alice Springs to the park's most popular destination, **Simpsons Gap**. The bicycle track starts from the grave of the Reverend John Flynn, founder of Australia's Royal Flying Doctor Service, 4 miles (7 km) out of town on Larapinta Drive, and keeps to a comfortable grade as it meanders through rolling

bushland. Situated 14 miles (22 km) west of Alice Springs, Simpsons Gap is an arresting cleft in the red quartzite rock of **Rungutjirba Ridge**, eroded by the floodwaters that pour infrequently down Roe Creek. A colony of rare black-footed rock-wallabies lives among the great boulders on the eastern bank. The 15-minute **Ghost Gum Walk** provides an excellent introduction to the region's flora, and the one-mile trail leading to the top of **Cassia Hill** offers fine views of the ranges.

Most walkers take two days to cover the distance to Simpsons Gap along the first section of the Larapinta Trail, staying overnight

at the **Wallaby Gap** campground. The trail provides good views of Alice Springs from boulder outcrops overlooking the town, and at **Euro Ridge** visitors can see a striking panorama of the western ranges as far as Mounts Conway and Laughlen. Parts of the trail pass through shrub lands of many-stemmed witchetty bushes, prized by Aborigines for the fat moth larvae, called witchetty grubs, that live in their surface roots. Euros, or hill kangaroos, inhabit the ridges, and there is another colony of black-footed rock-wallabies at Wallaby Gap. At **Scorpion Pool**, you may come across the pied butcherbird, with its melodious, organlike calls.

Most visitors arrive at **Standley Chasm**, an Aboriginal-owned reserve outside the park on **Larapinta Drive**, around midday. That is the only time when the rays of the sun reach down directly into the gorge and illuminate its sheer red walls. Beyond Standley Chasm the road forks, with Larapinta Drive continuing southwest while **Namatjira Drive** heads west, hugging the ranges.

Follow Namatjira Drive to **Ellery Creek Big Hole**, a deep pool flanked by gum trees and shaded by steep red rock faces, and **Serpentine Gorge**, where the high cliffs and

Ellery Creek Big Hole (left) is a popular swimming spot.

Arid plains (right) around the range give little hint of the abundant wildlife concealed in its valleys.

Camel safaris (opposite, below) are available locally. Australia has the world's only wild camel population, numbering around 100,000.

permanent water provide a refuge for cycads and other relict species. The gorge was also kept as a sanctuary under traditional Arrernte law, which held that certain water holes should remain free from hunting and gathering to ensure the regeneration of the local ecology. Ancestral spirits in the form of a water serpent and a wedge-tailed eagle were said to guard the southern entrance to the gorge and punish anyone who violated the law. From Serpentine Gorge, it is a three-and-a-half-hour walk up the Larapinta Trail to **Counts Point**, with its magnificent views, and another five and a half hours to **Ochre Pits**, where Aboriginal people quarried the yellow clay for ceremonial and other uses.

Farther along Namatjira Drive, a side road leads to **Ormiston Gorge**, which opens out into **Ormiston Pound**, a broad drainage basin surrounded by mountains. With its wide, tree-lined riverbed and deep, near-permanent water hole, the gorge is one of the most spectacular places in the Western MacDonnells. In summer, the water offers welcome relief from the heat; in the cooler months, the 4.4-mile (7-km) loop trail through the pound is one of the region's best walks. At nearby **Glen Helen Gorge**, the main channel of the Finke River flows through a narrow gap in the sandstone walls of the ranges and spills onto Missionary Plain.

Central Rock-Rat

In 1996, a team of volunteers building a section of the Larapinta Trail trapped some small, unusual-looking mammals. Photographs were taken and sent to biologists at the Northern Territory Parks and Wildlife Commission, and the animals were soon identified as central rock-rats. This came as a great surprise, for the species had not been seen for 36 years and was thought to be extinct. Subsequently, more rock-rats were found, including a population at Ormiston Gorge.

The central rock-rat is brownish grey and smaller than a common rat: you could hold a large adult male in the palm of your hand. Its short, fat tail is shaped like a carrot, with the thickest part close to the body. Remarkably, the tail drops off when the animal is disturbed – simply handling the rock-rat is enough to dislodge it – and it does not grow back. This adaptation seems to be a strategy for escaping predators. Rock-rats found in the wild sometimes lack tails but can apparently survive without them, for they consist of thickened skin and bone and do not serve to store fat.

The central rock-rat is being bred at **Alice Springs Desert Park** where scientists are attempting to study the animals closely – while keeping them attached to their tails.

Fossilized remains indicate that the central rock-rat (below) was once abundant in the mountain ranges of central Australia.

Desert Survival

Through Dreaming stories, the Arrernte people are spiritually linked to their country. These stories not only operate as a system of law, they also incorporate valuable knowledge of the land and its ecological cycles. This knowledge has helped the Arrernte to maintain a balanced relationship with their surroundings and survive in a harsh desert environment for thousands of years.

Traditional Arrernte life was centered on numerous groups or clans. Each clan had a territory over which its people hunted kangaroo and wallaby; gathered lizards, witchetty grubs, bush tomato, and native orange fruits; collected grasses and other materials for making fibers; searched out stone, bone, and mulga wood for implements; and obtained substances such as the sap of the bloodwood tree for medicinal use.

In the desert, however, nothing is more important than water, and it was the availability of this essential resource that had the strongest influence on the Arrernte's patterns of movement. During droughts, several clans would retreat to a deep water hole in the ranges. When the rains came, the Arrernte would leave the ranges and spread out to forage in parts of their territory that were normally barren. They would not return to their refuge until the next dry spell, thus ensuring that its resources were conserved.

Even when far from the nearest water hole, the Arrernte had ways of quenching their thirst. As a last resort, they knew where to dig for the water-holding frog and squeeze out the water stored in its bloated body.

Arrernte guides (left) explain their culture and traditions to visitors in Alice Springs.

The folded layers of the ranges (bottom) convey a powerful sense of the immense geological forces that created them.

Land of Colors

Beyond Glen Helen the road is unpaved. Travelers equipped with a four-wheel-drive vehicle can continue west beyond **Redbank Gorge** and then south past Tnorala (Gosse Bluff Meteor Crater) to **Hermannsburg**, 77 miles (124 km) southwest of Alice Springs. Those traveling in conventional vehicles should backtrack and drive to Hermannsburg along Larapinta Drive.

The MacDonnell Ranges are extraordinarily rich in color. Depending on the geology, light, and perspective, you may see the rock faces glowing gold, suffused with mauve, or blazing red, and there is little to equal the white trunk of a ghost gum against the intense blue of the Central Australian sky. Aboriginal artist Albert Namatjira was born into this land of colors at the Hermannsburg Aboriginal Mission in 1902. In 1934, he met the artist Rex Batterbee and soon became an accomplished painter of watercolor landscapes. By the 1950s, Namatjira was famous, and prints of his scenes of the MacDonnell Ranges hung on the walls of thousands of Australian homes. The artist died in 1959, but his distinctive style of painting is continued today by Arrernte artists of the Namatjira school, and a number of his paintings are displayed at Hermannsburg.

Located on the Missionary Plain where the Finke River wends its way toward the Simpson Desert, Hermannsburg was started as a religious mission in 1877 by German Lutheran missionaries who established a church and school and set about baptizing

and educating Arrernte children. In the process, they learned much about Arrernte culture and recorded it in great detail. These records provided an invaluable source of information for later generations of Arrernte people seeking to reclaim their traditional customs and knowledge. Today, Hermannsburg is a cattle station and community settlement owned by the Arrernte, but the Lutherans' whitewashed, German farmhouse-style buildings remain and have been carefully restored. The old missionary house is now a tea room, and there is also a museum and art gallery.

The road that leaves Larapinta Drive near Hermannsburg and heads south to **Finke Gorge National Park** should be attempted only in a four-wheel-drive vehicle. For the last 10 miles it runs along the sandy bed of the Finke River and is impassable after heavy rain. The drive into the park is spectacular, with the road passing beneath the high, red cliffs of **Finke Gorge**. At **Palm Valley**, several trails allow you to explore the dramatic escarpments and hidden gorges, including the **Kalarranga Trail**, which follows in the footsteps of an

Aboriginal Dreaming ancestor. Palm Valley is noted and named for its red cabbage palms, an ancient species found only here; its closest relative grows on the coast of New South Wales, 1,400 miles (2,250 km) away. After a day spent exploring, you can camp at an oasis amid the palms, and as you drift into sleep, you might easily imagine the sound of waves breaking on the shore of the Central Australian sea, so long ago.

Red cabbage palms (right) have grown in Palm Valley for at least 10,000 years and are found nowhere else on Earth.

TRAVEL TIPS

DETAILS

When to Go

The most comfortable time to visit is from mid-April to mid-September, when the maximum average daily temperatures are 65°–80°F (18–27°C). At night, however, the temperature drops dramatically, with an average minimum in July of just 39°F (4°C). Between late September and early April, the temperature soars, with an average maximum in January of 96°F (36°C).

How to Get There

Alice Springs Airport is 7½ miles (12 km) north of the ranges. Car rentals are available. The major sights of West MacDonnell National Park can be seen in a day trip by following Larapinta and Namatjira Drives from Alice Springs. The Eastern MacDonnell Ranges stretch 60 miles (100 km) east of Alice Springs, and most of their attractions can be reached from the Ross Highway. The Mereenie Loop Road links the MacDonnell Ranges with Watarrka (Kings Canyon) National Park as well as Uluru–Kata Tjuta National Park.

Special Planning

Many roads in the Northern Territory are unfenced, so drivers should be wary of kangaroos and wandering livestock, particularly around dusk and dawn. Unpaved roads are common; check road conditions in advance of traveling and keep your speed down. Visitors should carry sufficient fuel, food, and water, a jack, a tow rope, and basic spare parts and tools. If hiking, wear a hat, loose protective clothing, sunscreen, and sturdy shoes, and carry a water bottle.

Permits and Entry Fees

Standley Chasm is on Aboriginal land and an entry fee applies. A day permit is necessary to travel the Mereenie Loop Road and visit Tnorala Conservation Reserve (Gosse Bluff). These are available from the Central Australian Tourism Industry Association office in Alice Springs, tel: 08-8952 5800.

INFORMATION

Central Australian Tourism Industry Association

60 Gregory Terrace, Alice Springs, NT 0871; tel: 08-8952 5800.

Parks and Wildlife Commission of the Northern Territory

P.O. Box 1046, Alice Springs, NT 0871; tel: 08-8951 8211; web: www.nt.gov.au/paw

CAMPING

In the Western MacDonnell Ranges, bush camping is allowed at Ellery Creek Big Hole, Ormiston Gorge, and Redbank Gorge. In the Eastern MacDonnell Ranges, camping is permitted at Trephina Gorge, N'Dhala Gorge, and Ruby Gap National Park. Camping fees are payable at park ranger stations. If ranger stations are unattended, visitors should put the appropriate fee into the "honesty box" provided.

LODGING

PRICE GUIDE – double occupancy	
$ = up to $49	$$ = $50–$99
$$$ = $100–$149	$$$$ = $150+

Arltunga Bush Hotel

P.O. Box 8194, Alice Springs, NT 0870; tel: 08-8956 9797.

Located in the Eastern MacDonnell Ranges, this hotel has four simple, pleasant rooms and a basic campground. At night, the hotel's generator is turned off, providing visitors with spectacular views of the star-studded sky. The hotel is adjacent to the Arltunga Historical Reserve, and facilities include a barbecue area and a restaurant that is open for meals all day. Travelers should book well in advance. $

Ross River Homestead

P.O. Box 3271, Alice Springs, NT 0871; tel: 1800 241 711 in Australia, or 08-8956 9711; web: www.ozemail.com.au/~rrhca or e-mail: rrhca@ozemail.com.au

The homestead offers 30 rustic-style cabins with private bathrooms, a campground, and 48 beds for backpackers. Facilities include a swimming pool and restaurant; staff members provide bush-walking, camel-riding, and horseback-riding tours. $–$$

Wallace Rock Hole Community

Via Alice Springs, NT 0871; tel: 08-8956 7993.

This Arrernte Aboriginal community is 72 miles (117 km) west of Alice Springs off Larapinta Drive. Accommodations include campgrounds, two on-site trailers, and two self-contained cabins. The staff leads cultural tours, bush-tucker (food-gathering) courses (minimum of four people), and rock-art tours (minimum of three people). $–$$

TOURS & OUTFITTERS

AAT King's Australian Tours

74 Todd Street, Alice Springs, NT 0870; tel: 08-8952 1700; web: www.aatkings.com.au

This bus company offers a one-day tour of the Western MacDonnell Ranges departing from Alice Springs. Destinations include John Flynn's Grave, Ormiston Gorge, Simpsons Gap, and Standley Chasm.

CentreView Tours

P.O. Box 8702, Alice Springs, NT 0871; tel: 08-8952 4301; web: www.centreviewtours.com.au or e-mail: booking@centreview tours.com.au

Two four-wheel-drive tours view

the MacDonnell Ranges. A half-day tour explores the Eastern MacDonnell Ranges, stopping at Emily and Jessie Gaps, Corroboree Rock, and Trephina Gorge; it includes the opportunity to ride a camel, throw a boomerang, or crack a whip. A full-day tour visits the Western MacDonnell Ranges, taking in Flynn's Grave, Simpsons Gap, Ellery Creek, and Ormiston Gorge. A minimum of two people per tour is required.

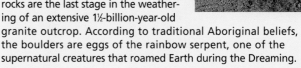

Murray Cosson's Australian Outback Flights

30 Giles Street, Alice Springs, NT 0871; tel: 08-8952 4625 or 041 9 804 386; web: www. australianoutbackflights.com.au or e-mail: mcosson@dove.net.au

Kings Canyon and Uluru scenic flights fly along the Western MacDonnell Ranges, offering views of gorges, canyons, and the giant meteorite crater in Tnorala Conservation Reserve (Gosse Bluff). A minimum of two people per tour is required. The price includes lunch and bus tours at Kings Canyon and Uluru.

Roving Outback Tours

P.O. Box 237, Warooka, SA 5577; tel: 08-8855 3451; web: www.ozemail.com.au/~alicwand /outbacktours/ or e-mail: alicwand@ozemail.com.au

Three- to nine-day four-wheel-drive tours and safaris from Alice Springs explore the Eastern and Western MacDonnell Ranges. Destinations include Flynn's Grave, Simpsons Gap, Redbank and Ormiston Gorges, Ross River, and Arltunga Historical Reserve.

Excursions

Arltunga Historical Reserve

Parks and Wildlife Commission of the Northern Territory, P.O. Box 1046, Alice Springs, NT 0871; tel: 08-8951 8211; web: www.nt.gov.au/paw

Arltunga is an abandoned gold-mining town in the Eastern MacDonnell Ranges, 68 miles (110 km) east of Alice Springs. From 1887 onward, hundreds of people searched for gold here and for a time formed the largest community in Central Australia. As well as old mine workings and cemeteries, you can visit the restored police station and jail; there is also a visitor center containing a historical display.

Devils Marbles Conservation Reserve

Parks and Wildlife Commission of the Northern Territory, P.O. Box 1046, Alice Springs, NT 0871; tel: 08-8951 8211; web: www.nt.gov.au/paw

South of Tennant Creek, the Stuart Highway passes through a field of precariously balanced, rounded granite boulders, many of them bigger than a house. The boulder field is a spectacular sight at sunset, when the rocks take on a reddish glow. The rocks are the last stage in the weathering of an extensive 1½-billion-year-old granite outcrop. According to traditional Aboriginal beliefs, the boulders are eggs of the rainbow serpent, one of the supernatural creatures that roamed Earth during the Dreaming.

Ruby Gap Nature Park

Parks and Wildlife Commission of the Northern Territory, P.O. Box 1046, Alice Springs, NT 0871; tel: 08-8951 8211; web: www.nt.gov.au/paw

Ruby Gap is a rugged gorge in the Eastern MacDonnell Ranges, 87 miles (140 km) east of Alice Springs. The area saw a modest mining rush after 1886 when "rubies" were discovered in the Hale River. The gems proved to be garnets and the rush quickly ended, but gold discoveries continued to attract fortune hunters. Ruby Gap has an air of remoteness and solitude, and a four-wheel-drive vehicle is needed to negotiate the road from Arltunga.

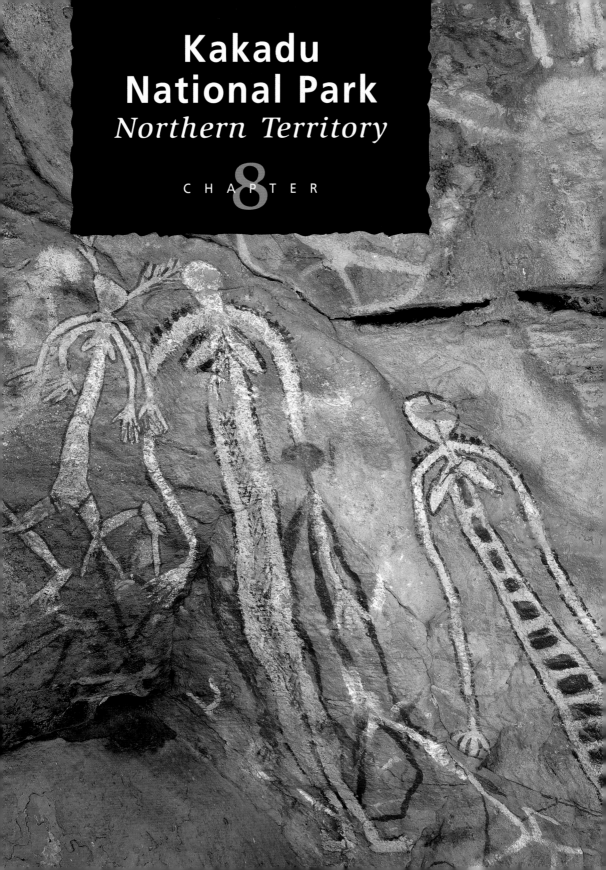

Kakadu
National Park
Northern Territory

CHAPTER 8

The savanna woodlands of **Kakadu National Park** are baking in the fierce midday sun. A casual glance reveals few signs of life: the dominant trees, Darwin woollybutts, raise their smooth white limbs to a sky empty of birds. The red-tailed black cockatoos, blue kingfishers, lorikeets, honeyeaters, and friarbirds that will enliven the treetops at sunset perch out of sight for now. Tucked away in hollows, burrows, and nests, the woodland wildlife awaits the cool of night. Only a few reptiles remain active, and patient observers may, if they sit quietly, spot a sand or yellow-spotted monitor digging deep in the soil for insects and their larvae. ◆ Occupying center stage in this silent landscape is a cluster of giant earthen structures with ornate pillars and fluted buttresses. The architects and builders of these monoliths, some of which exceed 20 feet in height, are the aptly named cathedral termites – one of more than 55 species of termite in the park. ◆ Termites are the lifeblood of ecosystems here in the far north of the Northern Territory, or Top End, as it is known locally. They are busy day and night harvesting, storing, and eating grasses, leaf litter, wood, and soil. As nutrient recyclers, they reign supreme, the insect equivalents of the vast herds of mammals that graze the grasslands of Africa. Their wind-proof, waterproof, and fireproof mounds, particularly evident in Kakadu's southern woodlands, are but one entry in the catalogue of natural wonders that awaits visitors to Australia's largest national park. ◆ World Heritage-listed for its outstanding natural and cultural values, Kakadu National Park, 125 miles (200 km) east of Darwin, encompasses an area of almost

Tropical rivers and woodlands teeming with wildlife – plus astonishing rock art – make this a preserve of international significance.

Nanguluwur Gallery at Nourlangie is one of many rock art sites in Kakadu that constitute a record of more than 20,000 years of Aboriginal occupation.

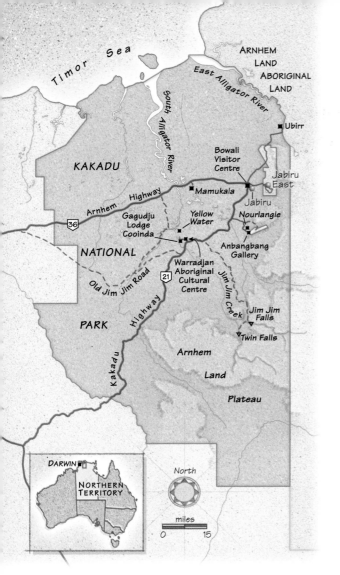

mainly eucalypts and tall grasses such as spear grass. The remainder includes pockets of monsoon forest, rugged stone country, rivers and billabongs, floodplains, paperbark swamps, tidal flats, and coastline.

From this mosaic of habitats stems an astonishing variety and abundance of plants and animals, including one-third of all Australia's known bird species, about one-quarter of its freshwater fishes, more than 60 mammals, nearly 100 reptiles, 10,000 insects, and 1,900 plants. In the kingdom of Kakadu, all subjects – from the native bee to the ubiquitous kapok bush – have had to adapt to a monsoonal climate that swings from the parched heat of the dry season to the flooding rains of the Wet. Through long association with the land, the park's Aboriginal traditional owners, the Bininj, have learned to recognize not two but six distinct seasons, each characterized by a climatic feature and its effect on plant and animal life. Newcomers can tune in to the park's subtle rhythms at the **Bowali Visitor Centre**, near **Jabiru**, which provides an excellent introduction to Kakadu's habitats through displays, videos, and ranger talks.

Creatures of the Water

Kakadu is a bird-watcher's paradise and a croc-spotter's heaven. Its wetlands provide important refuges and feeding grounds for many Australian waterbirds and are significant for at least 30 migratory species. They are also prime territory for saltwater crocodiles, and freshwater crocs can be found in the upper reaches of the rivers. Opportunities to explore the wetlands abound, but without doubt the renowned boat cruise at **Yellow Water** provides one of the richest experiences, particularly during the Dry when the creeks and floodplains recede and wildlife crowds the permanent billabongs.

Stately brolgas, jabirus, and egrets patrol the shallows, ever-watchful of the crocodiles that bask on the shore with mouths opened wide to prevent their brains from overheating. Wheeling flocks of wandering whistling ducks fill the air with shrill cries, while comb-crested jacanas walk across

7,700 square miles and includes the traditional lands of a number of Aboriginal groups. Within its boundaries lie some of the world's finest examples of rock art as well as spectacular scenery, ranging from the rugged sandstone escarpment of the **Arnhem Land Plateau**, which extends 310 miles along the eastern edge of the plains, to the vast wetlands that teem with bird life. It also embraces an entire tropical river system, the **South Alligator**, and examples of most of Australia's Top-End habitats. Nearly 80 percent of the preserve comprises savanna woodlands –

Northern dwarf tree frogs (opposite) inhabit swampy wood-lands, often forming colonies numbering in the thousands.

Water erosion (right) has created these unusual formations in the creekbed of Koolpin Gorge.

Elaborate mounds (below) constructed by cathedral termites form a forest within a forest in the lowland woodlands of Kakadu.

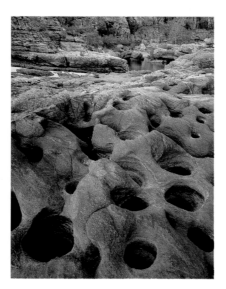

rafts of water lilies with unsinkable aplomb, a feat they perform with the help of an exceptionally long hindtoe measuring about three inches.

Sharp-eyed observers may see Macleay's water snakes swimming gracefully through the billabong, but only a lucky few will glimpse the Arafura file snake, an abundant but rarely seen reptile with a boxlike head

and sagging skin, which spends its days hiding from predators among the roots of water pan-danus. As the boat glides across the still waters of the billabong's paper-bark swamps, look for the nests of birds such as the white-bellied sea eagle, the whistling kite, and the green pygmy goose. Here, too, you're likely to see the darting forms of the blue-winged kookaburra, the forest kingfisher, and the rainbow bee-eater. When in flower, the paperbarks provide food for nectar-feeding birds such as honeyeaters and lorikeets. Late in the day, agile wallabies come to drink and graze at the water's edge.

Commercial boat cruises of the **East Alligator River**, which forms part of the

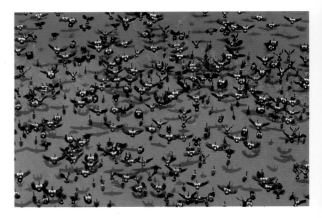

border between Kakadu and Arnhem Land, bring further encounters with wetland wildlife and also focus on Aboriginal culture. Birders in search of yet more things feathered can head for **Mamukala**, wetlands east of the South Alligator River on the Arnhem Highway. At its most dramatic in the late dry season when thousands of magpie geese congregate to feed, Mamukala offers two easy walks, a covered observation platform with a mural illustrating seasonal changes and common waterbirds, and a bird blind. Hearing the thunderous flapping of wings as a huge flock of magpie geese takes to the sky is an unforgettable experience.

Know Your Crocs

The world's largest living reptile, the estuarine (saltwater) crocodile, and its smaller cousin, the freshwater crocodile, are both alive and well in Kakadu, thanks to protective measures introduced in 1971. Prior to that, they were hunted to near extinction.

Despite being members of the same family, the two species display distinctive characteristics, not least of which is the saltie's deserved reputation for aggressiveness. But don't be beguiled by freshwater crocodiles: they, too, can become hostile if provoked. The blanket rule is look to your heart's content, but don't approach either species.

Freshies, which live only in Australia and grow to a maximum size of about 9.8 feet (3 meters), are easily identified by their narrow snout and a single row of large bony lumps called "scutes" situated immediately behind the head. Salties, also found in India, Southeast Asia, and Papua New Guinea, lack scutes and have broader snouts. They are also much bigger, growing to 23 feet (7 meters) in length and weighing almost 3,300 lbs (1,500 kg). Salties generally live longer (more than 70 years), though freshies can attain a ripe old age of at least 50 years.

Though their name suggests otherwise, salties are equally at home in fresh water and estuarine areas; freshwater crocs keep to their namesake habitat and are rarely found in tidal rivers. Both feed on fish, frogs, lizards, snakes, rats, bats, and birds, but salties may also take large land animals – including humans. Hence the need for extreme caution around the park's waterways.

Records in Rock

Kakadu's Aboriginal people rarely paint on rock now, but the sandstone galleries of their forebears constitute one of the world's oldest and best preserved records of human prehistory. Around 5,000 art sites, concentrated along the escarpment, in gorges, and on rock outliers, have been recorded in the park, and an additional 10,000 are thought to exist. Dating back as far as 20,000 years, the paintings are much more than creative expression: they are a visual record depicting the physical, social, and cultural environment of a people who had no written language.

The major sites of **Ubirr** and **Nourlangie** allow visitors to appreciate the beauty of the art and, through this,

Magpie geese (top) feed on aquatic plants and throng the wetlands in the thousands.

Freshwater crocodiles (above, left) can be distinguished from their saltwater relatives by their narrow snouts.

Saltwater crocodiles (left) are Australia's biggest reptiles and the largest crocodiles in the world.

The Arnhem Land Plateau (right) rises above Kakadu's eastern plains. Most of it belongs to Aboriginal people.

the close links between Aboriginal people, the land, and their spiritual heritage. These links can also be explored at the **Warradjan Aboriginal Cultural Centre**, near **Yellow Water**, where Kakadu's Bininj owners have created an outstanding display of cultural materials.

At Ubirr, near the northeastern edge of the park, a 0.6-mile (1-kg) loop trail leads to the main sites. The artistic styles range from simple red ocher paintings like that of the extinct thylacine, or Tasmanian tiger, to more recent (less than 1,500-year-old) "X-ray" images showing the internal structures of animals. You'll also see interesting examples of contact art, which records the arrival and activities of people from other cultures, mostly seafaring Macassans and European explorers and settlers. One "whitefella" is depicted with a pipe in his mouth and his hands on his hips, "bossing us Aboriginal people around," as one Bininj put it. This figure and another clad in trousers, boots, and a shirt are thought to be buffalo hunters, painted around the 1880s.

In the **Main Gallery**, you can view pictures of food items including fish, wallabies, goannas, and possums, which were regularly painted on the back wall, one on top of the other. The artists were not concerned about preserving the images for posterity but simply wanted to pay respect to a particular animal, ensure future hunting success, or illustrate a noteworthy catch.

Just beyond the Main Gallery, a short, moderately steep climb leads to a lookout with a superb 360-degree panorama of the Arnhem Land stone country, the Nardab floodplain, the woodlands, and dark ribbons of rain forest. The view is especially beautiful at sunset when the last light of day gilds the landscape.

Walkers can undertake a similar climb at **Nourlangie**, south of Jabiru – this time to a lookout providing fine views of the Arnhem Land escarpment. But the main interest here is the **Anbangbang** rock shelter and gallery, reached via a 0.9-mile (1.4-km) loop trail.

Water lilies (left) flower in profusion on the park's rivers and billabongs during the wet season.

Gagudju Lodge (below), in the center of the park, provides convenient access to Yellow Water.

An archaeological dig conducted in the 1980s revealed that Aboriginal people had been using the rock shelter for at least 20,000 years. Evidence of their activities is clearly visible: the rear wall is decorated with paintings of wallabies and other food animals, and the large flat rock on the floor is pocked with grinding hollows used for preparing food and crushing ochers.

In the main gallery, the rock art focuses on a story about Namarrgon, the Lightning Man, who is responsible for the violent wet-season storms. The images here are sharper than many others in the park: in 1964 a number of the gallery's figures were renewed by Nayombolmi, a respected artist also known as "Barramundi Charlie," who simply painted over older, similar figures. Repainting is part of the rock-art tradition, although only "authorized" artists are allowed to do it.

Having studied the rock art, look around Nourlangie for endemic chestnut-quilled rock-pigeons, black wallaroos, euros, black-palmed monitors, and Oenpelli pythons – all are sighted from time to time around the galleries.

Gorges and Waterfalls

Only birds and tourists in light aircraft are privy to one of Kakadu's most spectacular wet-season displays: torrents of rainwater thundering down the Arnhem Land escarpment. Scoured by water and wind, this ancient sea cliff ranging in height from a hundred to a thousand feet is slowly retreating at an estimated three feet every thousand years. Kakadu's highest waterfall, **Jim Jim**, in the southeast of the park, cascades for 656 feet into a deep plunge pool; nearby **Twin Falls** is about half that height but just as

Nitmiluk National Park

One of the territory's top attractions – a series of 13 spectacular sandstone gorges, in places almost 200 feet high – can be found in **Nitmiluk (Katherine Gorge) National Park**, just over 200 miles (322 km) south of Darwin. Carved over millions of years by the **Katherine River**, the gorge system cuts deeply into the southern Arnhem Land Plateau, providing habitat for a remarkable range of wildlife including 20 frog species, 75 reptiles, 38 mammals, and 176 birds.

Katherine Gorge (above) is actually a system of 13 gorges, best viewed from a boat.

Little red flying foxes (right) feed on blossoms and will travel long distances to locate adequate supplies.

There are numerous options for exploring the 1,127-square-mile park's wild beauty. A boat trip through the gorges, either as part of a commercial cruise or in a hired canoe, is obligatory, providing superb views of the towering rock walls, basking freshwater crocodiles (there are no saltwater crocs in Nitmiluk), and Merten's lizards. You're also likely to see herons, egrets, and cormorants, though you need venture no farther than the small wharf to see large colonies of black and little red flying foxes roosting in the paperbark trees on the riverbank. Gould's goannas, which grow to an impressive five feet in length, commonly patrol the picnic tables near the boat launch, looking for scraps.

For a stunning bird's-eye view of the park, take to the sky in a helicopter – flights depart regularly from the helipad near the gorge system's entrance. Walkers are well covered, too, with an extensive system of trails ranging from leisurely strolls along the riverbanks to overnight treks. The latter include the challenging four-hour (one way) Smitt Rock Walk, which is well worth the effort: the view of the large rock outcrop rising from the waters of the fifth gorge is one of the most impressive sights in the entire system.

magnificent. The monsoonal rains that inundate Kakadu's creeks and rivers and overflow onto the floodplains also limit road access to these celebrated sites, which is why those wishing to view the falls in their wetseason glory must take a scenic flight from either Jabiru East or Cooinda airstrips.

Come the dry season, you can reach Jim Jim via a bone-rattling 37-mile (60-km) drive over unpaved road followed by a 0.3-mile rock hop through a shady anbinik forest and a tumble of boulders. Along the way you'll pass pools filled with aquatic animals such as the primitive archerfish, which shoots a jet of water up to five feet in the air to knock down its insect prey, and elusive freshwater crocodiles. Merten's water monitors bask on the rocks while firetail skinks dart between patches of shade and iridescent dragonflies flit over the water. In the forest, look for rainbow pittas – colorful, stumpy-tailed birds – foraging in the leaf litter.

Getting to Twin Falls from Jim Jim involves a rough six-mile drive followed by a short walk and a 0.6-mile swim – made easier by an air mattress – through a narrow

gorge. Unlike Jim Jim, Twin Falls is spring-fed and flows year-round, though at a greatly reduced rate during the Dry. The swim through the cool, clear water is the refreshing prelude to one of the park's most beautiful sights – that of the falls cascading into a large pool fringed by a wide, sandy beach and monsoon forest trees.

Kakadu is a place for all seasons. Whether you climb the stone country, cruise the waterways, swim in the numerous plunge pools, amble through the shady monsoon forests, or take time to get acquainted with the unexpected wealth of woodland wildlife, you will be enriched by time spent exploring its habitats. You could spend a lifetime here and never run out of discoveries: if there is an earthly Eden, this is it.

TRAVEL TIPS

DETAILS

When to Go

The dry season (April to September) is the most comfortable and popular time of year to visit. Humidity is relatively low, temperatures range between 70°F and 91°F (21°–33°C), and rain is unusual. During the "buildup" (October and November), temperatures and humidity increase, and thunderstorms are frequent. The peak of the wet season (December to March) is a particularly dynamic time, but humidity is high, rainfall frequent, and many roads are closed.

How to Get There

Darwin International Airport is about 130 miles (210 km) west of the park. Car rentals are available there, and the drive to Jabiru takes about 2½ hours. Greyhound Pioneer, tel: 08-8981 8700, offers a daily bus service from Darwin to the park. Commercial tours of the park are available from Darwin and Jabiru. Nitmiluk National Park is slightly more than 200 miles (320 km) south of Darwin, which will take four hours by car.

Special Planning

Kakadu's tropical climate and biting insects can make life uncomfortable. A long-sleeved shirt, trousers, and a hat will offer protection against sunburn and insect bites. Be sure to pack sunscreen and insect repellent (mosquitoes can carry Ross River virus). Avoid dehydration by drinking plenty of water.

Distances between fuel stops are often long: fill up whenever possible. During the dry season, the main roads can be negotiated in a conventional vehicle, but some tracks, including the one to Jim Jim and Twin Falls, require four-wheel drive. For up-to-date information on road conditions, contact Bowali Visitor Centre.

Permits and Entry Fees

Park-use fees apply and can be paid at the entrance stations or the Bowali Visitor Centre. Tickets are valid for 14 days. Entrance to Nitmiluk National Park is free.

INFORMATION

Bowali Visitor Centre

P.O. Box 71, Jabiru, NT 0886; tel: 08-8938 1120.

Nitmiluk Visitor Centre

P.O. Box 344, Katherine, NT 0851; tel: 08-8972 1886; web: www.nt.gov.au/paw

Parks Australia North

P.O. Box 71, Jabiru, NT 0886; tel: 08-8938 1100; web: www.anca.gov.au

CAMPING

In Kakadu National Park, the major camping areas are at Merl, Muirella Park, Mardugal, and Gunlom. All have solar-heated showers, toilets, and laundry sinks. Fees are payable on site or at Bowali Visitor Centre. Free bush-camping areas, some offering basic toilet and washing facilities, are located throughout the park.

In Nitmiluk National Park, commercially run campgrounds at the gorge and Edith Falls offer car parking and tent and trailer sites. Bush-camping areas have been established for overnight walkers and canoeists, who must obtain a permit at Nitmiluk Centre. A small fee is charged.

LODGING

PRICE GUIDE – double occupancy

$ = up to $49 $$ = $50–$99

$$$ = $100–$149 $$$$ = $150+

Frontier Kakadu Village

Arnhem Highway, Kakadu National Park, NT 0886; tel: 08-8979 0166; web: www. allseasons.com.au or e-mail: ntsales@bigpond.com

Situated near the South Alligator River, this complex provides a variety of accommodations, from 138 air-conditioned motel rooms to powered and unpowered trailer sites, and a camping area. Facilities include a swimming pool, a bar and restaurant, tennis courts, nature walks, and a store. $–$$$

Gagudju Crocodile Hotel

Flinders Street, Jabiru, NT 0886; tel: 08-8979 2800; e-mail: execu tivesec@crocodile.sphc.com.au

This crocodile-shaped hotel offers 110 air-conditioned rooms overlooking an attractive central courtyard with a billabong and shaded pool. Facilities include a restaurant, a coffee lounge, a gift shop, and several bars. $$–$$$

Gagudju Lodge Cooinda

Kakadu Highway, Cooinda, NT 0886; tel: 08-8979 0145.

Well-positioned near Yellow Water Billabong and Warradjan Aboriginal Cultural Centre, this 48-room lodge offers a range of accommodations, from comfortable air-conditioned units and budget rooms to tent sites and trailer sites with power. Amenities include a swimming pool, bistro, restaurant, and store. $–$$

For those visiting Nitmiluk National Park, the nearby town of Katherine offers a wide variety of lodging. Contact the tourist information center, 08-8972 2650.

TOURS & OUTFITTERS

Guluyambi East Alligator River Cruises

P.O. Box 95, Jabiru, NT 0886; tel: 08-8979 2411; web: www.kakair.com.au or e-mail: kakair@kakair.com.au

Daily 1½-hour cruises on the East Alligator River focus on Aboriginal culture.

Kakadu Air Services

P.O. Box 95, Jabiru, NT 0886; tel: 08-8979 2411; web: www.kakair.com.au or e-mail: kakair@kakair.com.au

Half-hour and one-hour scenic flights offer a bird's-eye view of Kakadu and provide the only means of seeing the spectacular Jim Jim and Twin Falls during the Wet.

Nitmiluk Tours

Travel North, 6 Katherine Terrace, Katherine, NT 0850; tel: 08-8972 1044; web: www.travelnorth.com.au or e-mail: info@travelnorth.com.au

Half-, full-, or multiday canoe rentals and guided tours are available, as well as gorge cruises lasting two to eight hours.

North Australian Helicopters

Travel North, 6 Katherine Terrace, Katherine, NT 0850; tel: 08-8972 3150; web: www.travelnorth.com.au or e-mail: info@travelnorth.com.au

Daily 12- and 24-minute helicopter flights provide excellent views of the gorge system, the Arnhem Land Plateau, and wildlife.

Odyssey Safaris

G.P.O. Box 3012, Darwin, NT 0801; tel: 08-8948 0091; web: www.odysaf.com.au or e-mail: info@odysaf.com.au

Experienced naturalists lead small-group interpretive four-wheel-drive tours of Kakadu, Litchfield, and Nitmiluk National Parks. Options include two- to 10-day deluxe camping safaris, fully accommodated tours, or a combination of both.

Yellow Water Cruises

Gagudju Lodge Cooinda, Kakadu Highway, Cooinda, NT 0886; tel: 08-8979 0145.

Daily 1½- to 2-hour boat cruises of the Yellow Water wetlands provide a marvelous opportunity to see abundant bird life and crocodiles.

Excursions

Arnhem Land

Tourist Information Centre, G.P.O. Box 4392, Darwin, NT 0801; tel: 08-8981 4300; e-mail: drtainfo@ozemail.com.au

A wild, ancient landscape occupying the entire north-eastern half of the Top End, Arnhem Land is undoubtedly one of Australia's last frontiers. The region is Aboriginal land, and visitors must obtain permits before entering. It encompasses floodplains, escarpments, and rain forest, and supports a huge range of wildlife, including at least 1,000 plant species, more than 275 birds, 50 mammals, 75 reptiles, 25 frogs, and 55 fish.

Cobourg Peninsula

Parks and Wildlife Commission of the Northern Territory, P.O. Box 496, Palmerston, NT 0831; tel: 08-8999 5511; web: www.nt.gov.au/paw

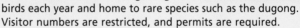

A wilderness of pristine beaches, eucalypt woodlands, paperbark swamps, and coastal grasslands, this peninsula and its waters are entirely protected within Gurig National Park and Cobourg Marine Park. Rich in Aboriginal culture and containing the ruins of early attempts at European settlement, the peninsula is the first landfall for thousands of migrating birds each year and home to rare species such as the dugong. Visitor numbers are restricted, and permits are required.

Litchfield National Park

Parks and Wildlife Commission of the Northern Territory, P.O. Box 496, Palmerston, NT 0831; tel: 08-8999 5511; web: www.nt.gov.au/paw

Spectacular waterfalls tumbling down sandstone cliffs into rain-forest-shrouded pools are the chief attraction of this park, just 80 miles (130 km) south of Darwin. Its 55 square miles protect an array of wonders, including the pillarlike rock formations of the Lost City and termite mounds that dot the plains like headstones in a cemetery, as well as Blyth Homestead, the historic remains of a property built by European settlers.

The Kimberley
Western Australia

CHAPTER **9**

F ive A.M. at **Windjana Gorge National Park** in the western Kimberley, and it's eerily quiet and still. As the deep blue of night recedes, a photographer stands on the sand at the center of the gorge, waiting for sunrise. Submerged in semidarkness, with the 320-foot walls of Windjana looming over her, she can imagine the chasm as it was 350 million years ago: part of a huge reef washed over by a sea that now lies more than 60 miles (100 km) away. ◆ Soon, the sun begins to light up the top of the towering walls, turning the rock cool orange, then fiery red. The forms of fig trees and river red gums emerge at the edge of the river. Yet, nothing moves; still there is no sound. ◆ Then, like the cry of a fractious human baby, amplified by the walls of the gorge, comes the first squawk of a corella. Then another. In minutes, the gorge resounds with their calls as a 20-strong posse of these large white parrots flits from treetop to treetop. Unperturbed by these boisterous antics, a regal-looking grey heron poses motionless on

Verdant waterways and gorges create a startling contrast to the arid plains and fire-red rockscapes that dominate this wild plateau.

a rock, peering into a pool. The water ripples, revealing a Johnston crocodile; nearby, an ungainly freshwater turtle noses into view. ◆ The sights and sounds of the gorge are so entrancing that by the time other travelers arrive an hour or so later, the photographer realizes that she has taken not a single picture. But the memory of this place, where for a moment she felt like the first person on Earth, will live with her forever. ◆ Although Windjana Gorge has its own particular atmosphere, the rugged **Kimberley** region of northwestern Australia offers endless opportunities for such solitary encounters with nature. Indeed the region is so vast – covering 260,400 square miles,

Zebedee Springs at El Questro Station is one of many cool oases concealed among the valleys and gorges of the otherwise arid Kimberley Plateau.

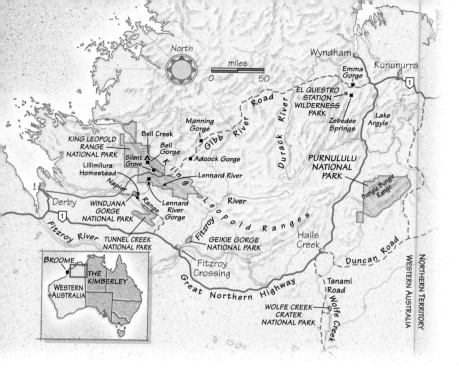

Map labels:
North
miles 0 50
Wyndham
Kununurra
Emma Gorge
EL QUESTRO STATION WILDERNESS PARK
Zebedee Springs
Lake Argyle
Manning Gorge
Gibb River Road
Durack River
Bell Creek
KING LEOPOLD RANGE NATIONAL PARK
Bell Gorge
Silent Grove
Adcock Gorge
Lillimilura Homestead
Lennard River
PURNULULU NATIONAL PARK
Bungle Bungle Range
Derby
WINDJANA GORGE NATIONAL PARK
Napier Range
King Leopold Ranges
Lennard River Gorge
River
Fitzroy River
TUNNEL CREEK NATIONAL PARK
Fitzroy Leopold Ranges
GEIKIE GORGE NATIONAL PARK
Halls Creek
Duncan Road
WESTERN AUSTRALIA
NORTHERN TERRITORY
Fitzroy Crossing
Great Northern Highway
Tanami Road
Wolfe Creek
WOLFE CREEK CRATER NATIONAL PARK

BROOME
THE KIMBERLEY
WESTERN AUSTRALIA

Prehistoric Land

The Kimberley not only remains undeveloped, it offers glimpses of an almost unimaginably distant past. Some of the region's rocks formed as far back as two billion years ago, and much of the terrain has changed little since it was ground by glaciers during two ice ages 700 and 600 million years ago. Parts of the lowlands lay under ocean for most of the Devonian period (360 to 408 million years ago), and many of the gorges of the western Kimberley, with their tall, straight walls, are still recognizable as former reef systems.

The sea has long since retreated from the plateau to create a stunning but treacherous coastline of inlets, channels, and thousands of islands, which, around Derby, is subject to the second-biggest tides in the world. The inland terrain of the Kimberley is no less varied: folded mountains give way to dusty plains; flat-topped plateaus reminiscent of the mesas of the American Southwest rise above vast expanses of savanna grassland; and lush pockets of rain forest thrive beneath lofty escarpments. Although in the dry season, in

it is about half the size of Texas – that finding some space to yourself is seldom a problem, even during the April-to-October tourist season.

Despite its proximity to the populous islands of Indonesia to the north, the Kimberley remains one of the most sparsely inhabited parts of Australia. Aboriginal occupation dates back 40,000 years, and Dutch, English, and French explorers began to investigate the coastline from the 17th century onward, but it was not until the late 1870s that the Kimberley began to be settled by Europeans. This was partly because it was so far from the developing population centers of the southeast coast, such as Sydney and Melbourne, and partly because the rugged terrain posed major obstacles to settlement. Even today, the Kimberley's population is a mere 30,000, most of whom live in the region's few small towns or on vast cattle stations scattered across the plateau.

Dendritic drainage channels (right) appear on the tidal flats of King Sound, near Derby, as the sea retreats.

The red sands of the Kimberley (right) and the turquoise waters of the Indian Ocean create a striking contrast at Roebuck Bay near Broome.

particular, much of the land appears to be semi-desert, every track you follow seems to lead to another miraculous flow of pristine water, another Eden-like oasis surrounded by hot red rock.

Fossil Walls and Bat Caves

Exploring this remote and rugged land requires careful planning. Road access remains limited: the **Great Northern Highway** skirts the southern edge of the plateau, but the main route through the heart of the Kimberley, the **Gibb River Road**, is a dirt track that was once a cattle trail and remains rough going in places.

Practically speaking, the plateau can be divided into western and eastern sections. In the west, the colorful town of **Broome** and the less glamorous but more convenient port of **Derby** serve as good jumping-off points for Windjana and several other national parks and the virtually uninhabited coastline. In the eastern section, the modern town of **Kununurra** provides a base for exploring such wonders as the strange, striped formations of the 360-million-year-old **Bungle Bungle Range**, the giant meteorite crater at **Wolfe Creek**, and huge, artificial **Lake Argyle**, home to thousands of crocodiles.

For those with limited time, a three- to five-day loop tour out of Derby to the so-called Devonian reef parks of the western Kimberley offers a relatively gentle yet enticing introduction to the Kimberley's landscape, geology, and wildlife.

Heading east out of Derby, the turnoff to Windjana Gorge National Park is about 80 miles (130 km) along the Gibb River Road. Occupying a small section of the rugged limestone **Napier Range**, Windjana once formed part of an enormous barrier reef that stretched

The Bungle Bungles

Of the many strange sights of the Kimberley, perhaps the most bizarre is the massive range of sandstone peaks known as Purnululu, or the Bungle Bungles, rising out of the barren plains 150 miles (240 km) south of **Kununurra**. Viewed from the air – the only way to see the range during the Wet and the easiest way at any time of year – its striped domes resemble thousands of giant beehives.

The alternating layers of green-black and orange are created by lichens and silica protecting the soft white sandstone below. As for the unusual shapes of the 360-million-year-old range, these are the result of millions of years of water erosion.

The Purnululu massif has long been of spiritual significance to Aborigines (*purnululu* means "sandstone" in a local language), who adorned its cliffs and canyon walls with paintings and used its gorges and caves as burial sites. But not until 1879 was it first sighted by a European, explorer Alexander Forrest, and it remained virtually unknown until as recently as 1983, when a television documentary brought it to prominence.

Air tours (above) are a convenient way to view the remote Bungle Bungle range.

Echidna Chasm (right) becomes so narrow that light barely penetrates its recesses.

Though flying over the range, now protected by **Purnululu National Park**, gives you an idea of its scale, it is only at ground level that you can experience the astonishing variety of formations. Walking trails lead to spectacular spots such as **Cathedral Gorge**, where a tranquil water hole is shaded by walls of banded rock, and **Echidna Chasm**, a palm-filled, 300-foot-deep canyon that narrows until you can go no farther. Keep an eye out for euros, wallabies, and bowerbirds around the gorges and green treefrogs among the palms and ferns.

across the western Kimberley 350 million years ago. At the magnificent gorge, limestone walls 320 feet high tower over the **Lennard River**, which rages through the chasm during the Wet but is reduced to a trickle in winter. A trail leads along the eastern side of the gorge past stands of paperbark (known locally as cadjeput), stem-fruited fig, and Leichhardt trees, where hundreds of flying foxes roost by day. Among the many fossils embedded in the gorge walls are the bones of Devonian reef fish and the shells of gastropods (wormlike creatures). Windjana has also yielded the bones of a several-million-year-old ancestor of the saltwater crocodile, which measured around 23 feet in length.

About 2 miles (3 km) past the entrance to Windjana on the main road, a longer trail leads along the cliffs of the Napier Range to the ruins of **Lillimilura Homestead**, noted as the site where Aboriginal tracker and opponent of white settlement, Jundamarra, or "Pigeon," killed a policeman in 1894, thus beginning his career as the region's most infamous outlaw.

It was in present-day **Tunnel Creek National Park** that the police finally caught up with Jundamarra three years later, killing him in a gun battle. The park contains one of the Kimberley's coolest refuges, a half-mile chamber carved through a limestone ridge by Tunnel Creek. Visiting this subterranean system entails wading through pools and scrambling over rocks, flashlight in hand. (The walk should not be attempted during the Wet, when flash floods can occur.) Shine your flashlight into the crevices above you and you are likely to spot one of the five species of bat that reside in the tunnel. Direct your beam sideways and you may pick out the red reflections in the eyes of some relatively harmless but prehistoric-looking freshwater crocs. Midway along the tunnel there is a gap in the roof through which sunlight streams in, and at the far end you can see an inviting rock pool. It was here that Jundamarra met his end.

A boat trip down the **Fitzroy River** at **Geikie Gorge National Park**, near Fitzroy Crossing on the Great Northern Highway, is an equally memorable experience. Wide bands of color mark the gorge walls, ranging from chalky white at the base (indicating the water levels during the Wet), through orange to dark grey at the top. Patches of vegetation, including pandanus palms on ledges and mangroves at the base of the walls, add splashes of green, and the whole scene is mirrored in the still, dark waters of the river.

What is most unusual about Geikie, given that it is over 200 miles (320 km) from the sea, are the saltwater creatures, such as sawfish and stingrays, that inhabit the Fitzroy River here alongside freshwater crocodiles and hefty barramundi. These

Service centers (right) on the Gibb River Road have limited supplies, but most offer friendly service.

Windjana Gorge (below) was once part of an ancient reef system and hundreds of fossils are embedded in its walls.

species spread slowly upstream from the coast over countless generations. Although the ranger-guided river tours are the most popular way of experiencing Geikie, the short walking track that runs along the edge of the gorge provides another perspective. It also allows you to view the resident bird life, including one of the region's specialties, the sandstone

shrike-thrush. In addition, half-day tours run by local indigenous people explain the significance of the gorge in Aboriginal mythology, demonstrate how to obtain food from bush plants, and offer further opportunities for spotting euros (small kangaroos) and rare black-footed rock-wallabies.

Gorge Tour

Those with more time to spare may be tempted to continue eastward along the Great Northern Highway to Halls Creek and the domes of **Purnululu**. For travelers seeking adventure, the Gibb River Road offers challenging four-wheel driving through some of the

region's most rugged and majestic scenery. This is one of Australia's most exciting and demanding off-road routes, and it requires thorough preparation and a sturdy vehicle.

Beyond the turnoff to Windjana Gorge, the road traverses wide plains before climbing past exposed tors to the uplands of the **King Leopold Ranges**, from where you'll have superb views of the surrounding plateau. It's a bumpy ride down a rough five-mile sidetrack in the range to **Lennard River Gorge**, but it's worth the discomfort. From

King George Falls (above), northwest of Wyndham, is one of many dramatic sights that make the Kimberley a photographer's paradise.

From Bell Creek (right), a short trail leads past palm-fringed pools and over slick-rock to the rim of dramatic Bell Gorge.

the end of a short trail, you look down on a thin strip of the Lennard River gripped between two steep, grey cliffs. It's an impressive sight, particularly during or shortly after the Wet when the gorge brims with the waters of three nearby falls. A natural rock staircase leads down to the river, with its secluded swimming holes.

Like Windjana Gorge, **Bell Gorge**, a short drive eastward, has an unmistakably primordial atmosphere. Giant red boulders frame dramatic falls that spill 300 feet down a series of terraced cliffs into a deep pool. Camping at nearby **Silent Grove** or **Bell Creek** can be a magical experience. As the sun sets and the rocks slowly cool, owls call in the dark and the ghostly forms of young dingoes occasionally appear at the edge of the campsite.

At **Adcock Gorge**, red-winged parrots and crowds of vividly marked budgerigars flit between the trees that surround a swimming hole. A taxing clamber to the top of the gorge is rewarded with views over savanna grasslands that seem more "out of Africa" than Australian.

Near the center of the Kimberley plateau, **Manning Gorge** offers bush walks, refreshing pools, and startling scenery. In Lower

Budgerigars (above), much-loved domestic pets the world over, are native to the Kimberley.

Boab trees (right) are not especially tall, but their bulbous trunks may measure more than 80 feet in diameter.

Manning Gorge, flocks of white and black cockatoos congregate noisily, and the reflections of the sky and surrounding palm trees color the water deep blue and green.

Farther east, the landscape is increasingly dominated by mesas and arid plains. Yet here, too, you'll come across large rivers including the Durack, with its sizable populations of saltwater crocodiles, and small waterfalls such as those at **Emma Gorge** in **El Questro Station Wilderness Park**. Nearby **Zebedee Springs** harbors a pocket of lush rain forest and a Jacuzzi-like rock pool framed by tropical palms.

Even a challenging journey along the Gibb River Road does little more than scratch the surface of the Kimberley. For each chasm or waterfall you see, there are probably another 20 hidden away in the enormous cattle stations and national parks that cover the plateau, and many other spectacular sights lie along the remote coastline. But a short visit is sufficient to gain a sense of the region's antiquity, its startling contrasts, its magic, and its splendor.

The Boab Tree

Known by the shortened version of its African name, baobab, the boab is an icon of the Kimberley and the northwestern Northern Territory. Found only in this region, it is a close relative of several other monkey-bread trees that are common in tropical Africa, and it is thought that it owes its presence here to baobab seeds that floated across the Indian Ocean from the island of Madagascar.

Instantly recognizable by its massive, light-grey trunk and its spindly branches, the boab has a grotesque appearance, especially when it sheds its leaves during the dry season. Sometimes the trunks of two or more trees become conjoined, creating an even more bulbous central section from which numerous arms extend.

Boab trees can live for thousands of years, and local Aborigines have long used them as a source of food – the edible fruit is high in vitamin C and protein – and moisture, which the trees retain even in harsh conditions. Some of the finest boabs can be found near Derby. The massive, hollow Prison Boab, on the outskirts of town, was once used to detain criminals en route to jail.

TRAVEL TIPS

DETAILS

When to Go

April to September is the most comfortable period to visit. In October, daily temperatures can reach 95°F (35°C), and later in the year, before the rains start, temperatures of 104°F (40°C) are common. During the wet season (November–March), river and creek crossings become impassable after heavy rains.

How to Get There

Broome International Airport is less than a mile (1.6 km) from Broome township. There are also less frequent flights from Darwin and Perth to Derby and Kununurra. Car and four-wheel drive rentals are available at Broome, Derby, and Kununurra airports.

The route to the Devonian reef parks is well maintained and can be negotiated in a conventional vehicle, but some of the roads are gravel, and a four-wheel drive will offer greater comfort and security. The Gibb River Road is rendered totally inaccessible for much of the wet season. Purnululu National Park can be reached along a rough four-wheel drive track that leaves the Great Northern Highway 157 miles (253 km) southeast of Kununurra.

Special Planning

Large distances separate attractions, and fuel stops are often hundreds of miles apart, so plan your journey carefully. Always carry emergency food and water supplies, spare parts, and a tow rope. Due to the varying quality of the roads, vehicles should be driven at low speed. For hiking, pack a broad-brimmed hat, sunscreen, long pants, and sturdy walking shoes.

Permits and Entry Fees

Entry passes are needed for Purnululu, Windjana Gorge, and Mirima National Parks, and Bell Gorge. Passes can be obtained from the Department of Conservation and Land Management, tourist centers, and ranger stations, or at park entry points.

INFORMATION

Broome Tourist Bureau

Broome Highway, Broome, WA 6725; tel: 08-9192 2222; web: www.ebroome.com/tourism or e-mail: tourism@broome.wt.com.au

Department of Conservation and Land Management (CALM)

P.O. Box 942, Kununurra, WA 6743; tel: 08-9168 4200; web: www.calm.wa.gov.au

Derby Tourist Bureau

1 Clarendon Street, Derby, WA 6728; tel: 08-9191 1426; web: www.comswest.net.au/~derbytb or e-mail: derbytb@comswest.net.au

Kununurra Tourist Bureau

P.O. Box 446; Kununurra, WA 6743; tel: 08-9163 1177.

CAMPING

The best campsites are in Windjana Gorge National Park, Bell Gorge, Manning Gorge, Ellenbrae Station, and Purnululu National Park. Contact the tourist bureaus in Broome, Derby, and Kununurra for more information. Camping fees apply at Purnululu and Windjana National Parks, and at Bell Gorge. They can be paid at visitor centers or to rangers.

LODGING

PRICE GUIDE – double occupancy

$ = up to $49 $$ = $50–$99

$$$ = $100–$149 $$$$ = $150+

Cockatoo Island

P.O. Box 444, Darwin, NT 0801; tel: 08-8946 4455; e-mail: cockatooisland@bigpond.com.au

Unusual luxury accommodations are available on the site of a former mining island off the Kimberley coast. Each of the 24 villas has views of historic mining equipment and the beautiful Buccaneer Archipelago. Meals are included in the price. $$$$

El Questro Station

P.O. Box 909, Kununurra, WA 6743; tel: 08-9169 1777; web: www.elquestro.com.au or e-mail: sales@elquestro.com.au

Set on more than one million acres, El Questro offers four types of lodging: luxury rooms at the homestead, complete with gourmet meals; a holiday retreat at Emma Gorge Resort; air-conditioned family bungalows; and riverside camping. Staff can provide informative tours of the Kimberley's dramatic scenery. $–$$$$

King Sound Resort Hotel

P.O. Box 75, Derby, WA 6728; tel: 08-9193 1044.

Providing 65 motel-style rooms with private baths, this is the best accommodation option in Derby. The hotel has a pool and restaurant. $$

Moonlight Bay Apartments

Carnarvon Street, Broome, WA 6725; tel: 08-9193 7888; web: www.force.com.au/moonlightbay or e-mail: moonlite@tpgi.com.au

These luxury one- or two-bedroom self-contained apartments overlook Roebuck Bay. Facilities include a pool, landscaped garden, and barbecue area. $$$

TOURS & OUTFITTERS

Broome Aviation

P.O. Box 386, Broome, WA 6725; tel: 08-9192 1369; web: www.broomeaviation.com or e-mail: broomeav@comswest.net.au

Half- to full-day air tours cover areas such as the Bungle Bungles, the Devonian reef parks, the Prince Regent River, and the Buccaneer Archipelago. Many of the tours include lunch and informative ranger-led walks.

Geikie Gorge River Tours
Department of Conservation and Land Management, P.O. Box 942, Kununurra, WA 6743; tel: 08-9168 4200; web: www.calm.wa.gov.au

One-hour ranger-guided river tours at Geikie Gorge run four times a day between April and October.

Hot Land Safaris
P.O. Box 232, Derby, WA 6728; tel: 08-9193 1312; web: www.hotland.com or e-mail: enquiries@hotland.com

Camping safaris of the west Kimberley range from two to 12 days and cover lesser-known attractions such as Mornington, Mount Elizabeth, and Mount House Stations as well as better-known sites including Bell and Adcock Gorges. The informative owner-operators conduct the tours in comfortable four-wheel-drive transport and provide full catering.

Kimberley Bushwalks and Camel Safaris
P.O. Box 2509, Broome, WA 6725; tel: 08-9191 7017; web: www.bushwalks.com or e-mail: ttcamels@bigfoot.com

Two- to seven-day camel and bush-walking safaris can be tailored to special interests including bird-watching, food-gathering in the bush (bush-tucker outings, as they are known locally), and medicinal plants. The safaris follow the Fitzroy River's water systems, passing through spinifex scrub country, melaleuca forest, and desert.

Kimberley Thousand Island Charters
P.O. Box 405, Derby, WA 6728; tel: 08-9191 1851.

Boat charters can be arranged for tours, ranging from five to eight days, to various parts of the remote and spectacular Kimberley coast, including the Buccaneer and Bonaparte Archipelagoes.

Excursions

Broome
Broome Tourist Bureau, Broome Highway, Broome, WA 6725; tel: 08-9192 2222; web: www.ebroome.com/ tourism or e-mail: tourism@broome.wt. com.au

This historic pearling port, which has been a

beacon for fortune-seekers since it was established in the 1880s, is one of Australia's most atmospheric towns. Broome has miles of stunning beaches lapped by the turquoise Indian Ocean, dinosaur footprints dating back 130 million years at Gantheaume Point, and an excellent bird observatory at nearby Roebuck Bay.

Mirima (Hidden Valley) National Park
Kununurra Tourist Bureau, P.O. Box 446, Kununurra, WA 6743; tel: 08-9163 1177.

For travelers who don't have the time to visit the Bungle Bungles, this national park on the edge of Kununurra should provide excellent compensation. It comprises a series of rugged hills and gorges as well as Bungle-like striped sandstone formations that are up to 300 million years old. Boab trees grow out of the valley walls, and other trees like woollybutts and bloodwoods are common.

Wolfe Creek Meteor Crater
Halls Creek Tourist Centre, P.O. Box 21, Halls Creek, WA 6770; tel: 08-9168 6262.

Australia's largest meteorite crater and the world's second-largest after the Coon Butte Crater in Arizona, Wolfe Creek was created when a meteorite traveling at some 60,000 mph (100,000 km/ph) crashed into Earth around 300,000 years ago. Known as Kandimalal to the local Aborigines, it is more than half a mile wide and 492 feet deep. The crater is reached via a 70-mile (113-km) dirt road a short distance out of Halls Creek toward Fitzroy Crossing on the Northern Highway.

The Pilbara
Western Australia

CHAPTER 10

n the fiery glow of the midday sun, the sheer rock walls of **Dales Gorge** blaze crimson and vermilion like a savage wound in the heart of **Karijini National Park**. Deep in the gorge, the air is languid and hot – too harsh for most creatures to endure, but ideal for a leathery water dragon basking beside **Circular Pool**. It slumbers, sprawled out on a rock, until the rapid-fire call of a whistling kite sends it scuttling and splashing into the steely water. ◆ A fine fringe of fragile maidenhair ferns and sedges and daisy-chains of water lilies decorate the pool like emerald lacework. Within this sunken garden, life sashays to the gentle *tick-tick-tick* of water spilling over terraced rock. The bright sun casts a spotlight on the impressive stone amphitheater, and a troupe of wanderer butterflies appears, filling the air with fluttering orange-and-brown wings. Droning red wasps and gangly hornets follow, their feet weighted with mud. ◆ But the romantic leads in this impromptu perfor-mance are reserved for a dazzling

A remote region of gorges and grasslands tests your mettle but repays you with some of the continent's most majestic scenery.

company of courting dragonflies and damselflies. One after another, they converge on the pool in search of partners, until it's soon buzzing with amorous azure-blue, daisy-yellow, and vivid pink acrobats. They hover and flit just inches from the water's surface, their translucent wings winking in the sunlight. ◆ The harsh **Pilbara** region of northwestern Australia is renowned for the spectacular, yawning chasms that incise its rolling spinifex plains. It's a landscape of rich colors and contrasts, dazzling wildflower displays, challenging walks, and astounding ancient geology. That the dra-matic gorges and grasslands also harbor lush permanent pools, significant

Weano Gorge provides an insight into the early geological history of our planet: its iron-rich walls formed more than 2½ billion years ago.

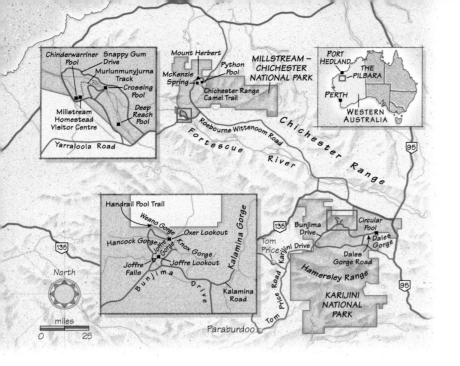

tionary change. The red, iron-rich formations that characterize the park are some of the oldest exposed rock on the Australian continent. They began forming 2½ billion years ago, when most of the Pilbara was bathed in an inland sea. Millions of years of geological activity then compacted, lifted, and buckled the rock, which in turn was sculpted by swift-flowing river channels.

Oxer Lookout, in the north of the park, off **Bunjima Drive**, offers an insuperable introduction to Karijini geology – a vertiginous vista of four gorges converging in a jagged chasm of red rock. Nearby **Joffre Lookout** commands similarly impressive views of semicircular **Joffre Falls**. These lookout ambles are complemented by a variety of more daring scrambles into gorges, such as the three-hour return excursions into **Knox Gorge** and to the base of Joffre Falls.

The transformation of the park's waterfalls and gorges can be dramatic during the summer wet season, when they are flushed by torrential rain. Dry creek beds become surging brown torrents, and floodplains greedily soak up moisture, storing it in vast underground reservoirs that nourish snaking groves of majestic river red gums and shady coolibahs long after the storms have passed. In the slotlike gorges, the water pools for much of the dry winter, sustaining a variety of more sensitive plants and animals. Undoubtedly the best way to delve into their secret underworld is to walk the serpentine tunnels of fractured and sandwiched rock. Follow the one-hour return **Handrail Pool Trail** into the chilly recesses of **Weano Gorge**, a highly polished gash of cathedral dimensions.

A more challenging option is to immerse yourself in **Joffre Gorge** for the day with an

Aboriginal sites, and a plethora of curious arid-adapted plants and animals comes as something of a revelation.

Two neighboring national parks protect a broad swathe of this majestic region. Karijini National Park, four hours south of the coastal town of **Port Hedland**, lies at its blood-red heart. At 1,548,690 acres, it is Western Australia's second-largest and Australia's third-largest national park. It comprises a vast sweep of the **Hamersley Range**, which rises almost 4,000 feet and stretches 250 miles (400 km) across the Pilbara like a voluminous skirt. Smaller **Millstream–Chichester National Park**, to the northwest, encompasses similar terrain but resembles a desert mirage, concealing deep, permanent pools shaded by enigmatic palms. It's an ideal stopover for those returning to the coast from Karijini.

Karijini's Primitive Soul

Gnarled and rusted, the ancient Karijini landscape wears the scars of years of evolu-

Kalutas (opposite) inhabit Karijini's grasslands. Males die after just one breeding season.

Pink mulla mullas and snappy gums (right) grow in profusion around the waterways of Millstream–Chichester National Park.

Crossing Pool (below) is one of several pools in Millstream–Chichester that have sustained people and wildlife for millennia.

inflatable inner tube or air mattress. At 3.7 miles (6 km) long, Joffre is the deepest and one of the wettest gorges in the park, and experiencing it means clambering over boulders, squeezing through narrow tunnels, and paddling or wading through a series of pools. Weather-beaten cliffs tower 100 feet over Joffre's pools like giant bookends, and only the tuneful strains of the pied butcherbird or the raucous calls of white cockatoos accompany the soft rhythm of paddle strokes. There's ample time to appreciate the tenacity of the fleshy rock figs and corky-stemmed iron plants that struggle from fissures in the cliffs or to spot the caves inhabited by tiny bats that emerge at dusk to trawl the air for insects. Exiting from **Hancock Gorge** at day's end, you may even catch a glimpse of the Rothschild's wallaby, a rare resident that relies on its long, brush-tipped tail and thick sole pads for balance and traction on the scree slopes at the gorge's lip.

Fauna Fortresses

Throughout the fierce Pilbara plateau, where the animals are either hunters or hunted, spinifex is the major battlement. And with

12 species of the prickly plant clustered densely throughout the region, it's a defense system of military proportions. Few plants are better adapted to the harsh conditions or as essential to its wildlife. When it's dry and hot outside, the spinifex is a cool retreat, helping the resident reptiles, insects, and mammals conserve moisture. Especially for tiny insects, the mass of intertwined spines serves as a windbreak and safe haven.

For a closer inspection of this vegetation, visitors need stray only a short distance from any road or campground. Spinifex residents are, however, more elusive. Sightings of nocturnal mammals

Female termites (above) develop wings that allow them to leave their nests and establish new colonies.

A pebble-mound mouse (below) piles stones at the entrance of its burrow.

such as the spinifex hopping mouse, red antechinus, and Pilbara ningaui – all small rodentlike creatures – are rare, but walkers sometimes flush plumed pigeons, spinifex birds, and striated grass wrens.

Daylight hours are the time to observe spinifex ants at work as they harvest spinifex seeds, carry them inside their nests to nourish their larvae, then expel the husks in a neat ring around the burrows' entrances. The monuments of the spinifex termites are more impressive – monstrous red mounds, some more than six feet high. The termites also rely on the spinifex for food and construct a maze of underground highways beneath their mounds, some up to 160 feet long, to link the spiky clusters.

Traditional Customs

Most of Karijini's walks can be enjoyed unassisted, but for insights into this timeless landscape you can't beat the commentary

Pilbara Architect

The neatly sculpted mounds of red rocks dotting the spinifex grasslands of Karijini National Park could be mistaken for miniature volcanoes, coughed up from deep within Earth's crust. They are, in fact, the handiwork of a curious native mouse no larger than the ordinary house variety.

The western pebble-mound mouse, one of the Pilbara's most notable but secretive architects, pieces together these hummocks – each up to 20 inches high and covering an area of more than 90 square feet – under the cover of darkness. Remarkably, the nocturnal mouse weighs less than half an ounce but has been seen painstakingly moving stones up to half its weight using only its mouth. The mounds are usually constructed on gravelly slopes, where weathering has produced pebbles of a uniform size.

This rocky portico protects an intricate labyrinth of tunnels, some extending to a depth of 16 inches. Several conical entrance holes lead into a central tunnel, from which branch side tunnels, dead ends, and nesting chambers. Once the mouse wriggles through an entrance hole, rocks slide down to block the path of predators such as snakes, goannas, and birds of prey. The mound also serves as an insulated retreat from the scorching Pilbara temperatures. To ventilate the burrow or control the humidity, the mouse simply moves a rock or two. It can also collect moisture from dew that settles on the stones overnight.

of a true local. On a trail through **Kalamina Gorge**, Aboriginal elder and walking guide Bonnie Tucker scratches a piece of bark from the Kardangba tree (commonly known as the cork tree) and rubs its dark powder onto her chocolate-colored cheek. "We use this powder on newborn babies who are sick or have a temperature," she explains to the enthralled group of walkers. "The babies sleep and then they wake up well. It's also good war paint against sunburn."

Walking through the wide mouth of Kalamina Gorge can indeed be a hot business, but the sun is barely a distraction when the landscape is being interpreted by its traditional custodians. Aboriginal people lived off the land for tens of thousands of years, and the Pilbara is the very source of their ceremonies, stories, and law. Most were forced off their homelands a century ago, with the arrival of European settlers, but are now returning to contribute to the management and promotion of the park. On short guided walks, visitors can also learn where to find the nutty-tasting bardy grubs, an Aboriginal delicacy, and discover how to dig a "soak" in a creek bed to bring fresh water to the surface. Aboriginal people running the park's visitor center also willingly share their proud history.

Liquid Treasure

At **Millstream–Chichester National Park**, local Aborigines recount how the mighty serpent, Walu, carved the course of the **Fortescue River**. Pausing to rest at **Ngarrari** (Millstream), he created the palm-fringed oases for which the park is now renowned.

Millstream's spring-fed pools have supported countless generations of people

The walls of Karijini's crevasse-like canyons are polished smooth by wind and fast-flowing water (left).

Visitors to Millstream are soon awakened to its wonders. At dawn, the skies are splashed yellow and green with the swift wings of budgerigars, and at dusk in summer black and little red flying foxes emerge from their daytime slumber to feed noisily on the rich nectar of the paperbark tree's blossoms. By day, rainbow bee-eater birds drop from the sky like winged opals to chase insects by the pools; by night, the northern quoll, a spotted cat-sized animal, forages for fruit and carrion.

In the harsh summer months, Millstream–Chichester's four main water holes – **Python**, **Deep Reach**, **Crossing**, and **Chinderwarriner** – can be as tepid as baths; immersion is far more comfortable in winter, when the average temperature is an invigorating 68°F (20°F). Canoeing is a terrific way to explore the pools, but swimming is undoubtedly the most

and wildlife. For thousands of years, they sustained Aboriginal groups such as the Yinjibarndi. From the 1860s, they were a reliable water source for European settlers and their stock and for the Afghani camel drivers who serviced the region's remote properties. The source of this liquid treasure is an enormous aquifer contained in the vast block of porous dolomite rock that underlies 772 square miles of the park. Fed by rains falling in the Fortescue River catchment, it has never been known to run dry.

popular pursuit. In Deep Reach, the park's largest pool, there's ample space for a few leisurely laps and rarely a crowd.

As at Karijini, the damp recesses of the waterways are in stark contrast to a harsh backdrop of rocky ranges. The spectacular escarpments of the **Chichester Range** traverse the 494,000-acre park, spilling down to a stony plateau of spinifex and white-barked snappy gums and vast rolling plains. On the ranges, small mammals like the Forrests mouse and fat-tailed antechinus are active

The Millstream Palm

Within the canopy of Millstream's tree-fringed pools lives a rare palm thought to have evolved thousands of years ago. The slow-growing Millstream palm (*Livistona alfredii*) is believed to be a relic of much wetter times, when the region was covered by a lush variety of rain forest plants. This is hard to believe, given that the Pilbara's average annual rainfall today is just 12 inches.

As the region dried out, most other rain-forest species retreated to tropical areas. The palms have survived the arid Pilbara conditions because their prolific root mat can tap deep into the water table. Fibrous trunks also insulate them against fire.

The Millstream palm's fanlike leaves (above) distinguish it from other species growing around the park's waterways.

Sturt's desert pea (below, right) is found in arid areas throughout Australia. Its scarlet flowers open after rain.

The Millstream palm occurs in only six locations in Western Australia, all but one of which are in the Pilbara. At Millstream, palms grow singularly or in small groves along creek lines and the Fortescue River. The palm is distinguished by its fanned, grey-green leaves and smooth trunk, and grows to up to 33 feet. In October, it produces fleshy orange, marble-sized fruits that flying foxes find particularly tasty. When the palm flowers, the sweet nectar of its blooms also attracts honey-eaters and parrots.

only at night, but look to the skies for brown and peregrine falcons, grey goshawks, and wedge-tailed eagles gliding on thermals.

Only spinifex, mulga, and scattered eucalypts usually grow in the drier central-northern section of the park, providing shade and sustenance for red kangaroos, dingoes, and parades of emus. But seeds long dormant in the soil germinate quickly after summer rains, carpeting the plateau with furry pink mullamullas and striking red Sturt's desert peas, soft yellow wattles, everlasting daisies, and orange cockroach bushes.

To probe this rugged northern domain, stock up with water and walk the 4.3-mile (6.9-km) **Murlunmunyjurna Track**, which links the Millstream Homestead Visitor Centre with the Fortescue River near Crossing Pool and meanders through riverine vegetation, spinifex hills, wattle thickets, groves of Millstream palms, and tall paperbark forests. Early morning is the best time to enjoy the contrasting 5-mile (8-km) **Chichester Range Camel Trail**, which crosses the rugged sandstone terrain

Rainbow bee-eaters (right) perch near waterways, ready to pounce on bees and wasps, their favorite prey.

of the Chichester Range following part of an old camel road that links Mount Herbert, McKenzie Spring, and Python Pool – a rock pool fed by a crescent-shaped waterfall. This is an ideal spot for a refreshing swim.

It's easy to feel overwhelmed by the sheer size and grandeur of the Pilbara, so vast are its grasslands and so precipitous its gorges.

But this grand landscape also cradles subtle delights – verdant pools, fragile creatures, and rich folklore. Often parched and always unforgiving, the Pilbara is rarely disappointing.

TRAVEL TIPS

DETAILS

When to Go

The Pilbara is known as the arid tropics. During the summer wet season, between November and March, temperatures soar to 112°F (44°C), and thunderstorms can flood roads and watercourses without warning. The more comfortable time to visit is between April and October, when the average daytime temperature is 77°F (25°C), and there is little rain. Nights are cold, but days are generally fine and mild.

How to Get There

Most commercial airlines fly from Perth to Karratha, Port Hedland, Newman, or Paraburdoo. Rental cars are available at all airports as well as in Tom Price. There is no public transport in either Karijini or Millstream–Chichester National Parks, so visitors will need to rent a vehicle or join a tour group. Driving along the Hamersley Iron Access Road that links Karratha and Tom Price considerably shortens traveling distances to each park. Permits for this private road are free and available from the Karratha Tourist Bureau.

Special Planning

The Pilbara is vast, and visitors may travel several hundred miles without seeing another vehicle. Fill up with fuel when you can, and carry food, water, and medical and mechanical supplies. Pack a broad-brimmed hat, sunscreen, long pants, and sturdy walking shoes. Fuel and food are not available in either park.

Check road conditions with police before setting out. Most roads in Karijini and all roads in Millstream–Chichester are gravel but suitable for conventional vehicles. The only exception is the Millstream Circuit Drive, which can be closed after heavy rains. There are no canoe rentals at Millstream or nearby, so those wishing to paddle should bring their own craft.

A word of warning: mine tailings around Wittenoom still contain dangerous blue-asbestos fibers which may be inhaled if disturbed. Visitors exploring Wittenoom or Yampire gorges should avoid any tailings and keep their car windows closed, particularly on windy days.

Permits and Entry Fees

Entry fees apply in both parks. Park entry passes are available at Department of Conservation and Land Management offices, tourist bureaus, park visitor centers, and ranger stations.

INFORMATION

Karijini Visitor Centre

P.O. Box 29, Tom Price, WA 6751; tel: 08-9189 8121.

Karratha Tourist Bureau

Lot 4548, Karratha Road, Karratha, WA 6714; tel: 08-9144 4600; e-mail: tourist.bureau@kisser.net.au

Millstream–Chichester National Park Visitor Centre

P.O. Box 835, Karratha, WA 6714; tel: 08-9184 5144.

Newman Tourist Bureau

Fortescue Avenue, Newman, WA 6753; tel: 08-9175 2888; e-mail: newmantb@norcom.net.au

Pilbara Regional Office of Department of Conservation and Land Management (CALM)

SGIO Building, Welcome Road, Karratha, WA 6714; tel: 08-9143 1488; web: www.calm.wa.gov.au or e-mail: pilbara@calm.wa.gov.au

Port Hedland Tourist Bureau

13 Wedge Street, Port Hedland, WA 6721; tel: 08-9173 1711; e-mail: phtbinfo@norcom.net.au

Tom Price Tourist Bureau

Central Avenue, Tom Price, WA 6751; tel: 08-9188 1112; e-mail: tptb@norcom.net.au

CAMPING

Camping is permitted only in designated areas. Open fires are not allowed, so bring a portable camping stove or use the gas fireplaces and barbecues provided. Campers are advised to boil collected water before drinking and to be watchful of snakes near water holes. Campsites are available on a first-come, first-served basis.

In Karijini National Park, well-developed campsites are provided at Joffre, Weano, and Fortescue Gorges. All have toilets, gas barbecues, and picnic tables. Drinking water is available from the visitor center and the Weano bore, near the intersection of Bunjima Drive and Weano Road. In Millstream–Chichester, bush-style campsites with pit toilets are provided at Snake Creek, Crossing Pool, and Deep Reach Pool.

LODGING

Travelers visiting Karijini National Park can choose from several campsites, trailer parks, and motels at Tom Price, Paraburdoo, and Newman. The nearest lodging to Millstream–Chichester National Park is at Roebourne or Pannawonica.

Auski Tourist Village

P.O. Box 827, Port Hedland, WA 6721; tel: 08-9176 6988.

This tourist village on the northwestern boundary of Karijini National Park offers a range of lodging, from motel rooms with private facilities to self-contained family units, budget rooms, tent sites, and powered trailer sites. $–$$

Mount Florance Station
PMB 4, Tom Price, WA 6751; tel: 08-9189 8151.

Established around 1880, this cattle station between the two parks has been operated by its current owners since 1910. Basic accommodations are provided in the old corrugated-iron and timber shearers' quarters (May to September only) and in the campground, where there are toilets, showers, and barbecues. $

TOURS & OUTFITTERS

Lestok Tours
P.O. Box 333, Tom Price, WA 6751; tel: 08-9189 2032.

A full-day tour of Karijini's gorges, which includes lunch and a park entry fee, departs from Tom Price from July through September.

Snappy Gum Safaris
P.O. Box 881, Karratha, WA 6714; tel: 08-9185 1278; web: www.kisser.net.au/snappygum/

Tours include a two-day Karijini gorge tour (which includes meals, camping gear, and park entry fees); a Millstream day tour (which includes morning tea and picnic lunch); and a North West Explorer tour (which includes accommodations, meals, and park entry fees) that takes in both Millstream–Chichester and Karijini National Parks.

Red Rock Abseiling Adventures
P.O. Box 559, Tom Price, WA 6751; tel: 0419-961 176; e-mail: r_r_a_a@yahoo.com

Half-day and full-day rappelling (or abseiling) expeditions are available, along with gorge walks and customized day tours.

Excursions

Burrup Peninsula
Pilbara Regional Office, Department of Conservation and Land Management, SGIO Building, Welcome Road, Karratha, WA 6714; tel: 08-9143 1488; web: www.calm.wa.gov.au or e-mail: pilbara@calm.wa.gov.au

One of the world's richest Aboriginal rock-art galleries, resplendent with more than 10,000 rock engravings, lies just a short drive north of Karratha on the Burrup Peninsula. The cultural heritage of the Yapurrara people, now sadly extinct, is preserved in artistic detail in the basalt rocks that litter this finger of land. Some of the engravings, known as petroglyphs, are thought to be thousands of years old.

Miree Pool
Karratha Tourist Bureau, Lot 4548, Karratha Road, Karratha, WA 6714; tel: 08-9144 4600; e-mail: tourist.bureau@kisser.net.au

This permanent freshwater pool on the Maitland River, 25 miles (40 km) south of Karratha, offers a preview of the habitat at Millstream–Chichester National Park. Corellas, honeyeaters, galahs, and ducks are abundant, but visitors should keep their eyes peeled for the star finch, a tropical species usually found only in the Kimberley.

Mount Augustus National Park
Gascoyne District Office of the Department of Conservation and Land Management, Knight Terrace, Denham, WA 6537; tel: 08-9948 1208; web: www.calm.wa.gov.au

Twice the size of Uluru (Ayers Rock) and towering 2,352 feet above the plain, Mount Augustus (or Burringurrah, as it is known to local aborigines) is the biggest "rock" in the world. The Burringurrah Drive – a 30-mile (50-km) loop road – has fine views of the massif's changing faces plus access to gorges, caves, Aboriginal rock art, and walking trails. The park protects lots of wildlife, including blue-winged kookaburras, emus, red kangaroos, and goannas.

Shark Bay
Western Australia

CHAPTER 11

"**S**he's here," one of the rangers announces into her intercom. There's an air of anticipatory excitement as two bottle-nosed dolphins approach the shore at **Monkey Mia Reserve**. Even though the ranger is weighed down by waist-high rubber waders, she runs along the beach. This is the moment the reserve staff has been waiting for: a young female dolphin, now six years old and fully independent, will be offered a fish for the first time. ◆ To the outsider, this may not seem like a momentous event, but to the rangers, the issue of when to offer a young dolphin its first human-caught fish is hugely important. It became particularly significant several years ago, when the rangers discovered that they had begun feeding one of the dolphins too early and it had come to rely on handouts rather than develop its natural hunting skills. ◆ The encounters between dolphins and humans began back in the 1960s, when a local woman, Mrs. Ninni Watts, started feeding the bottle-noses that regularly fol-

This realm of superlatives encompasses the world's largest sea-grass beds, its oldest living species, and some of its friendliest creatures.

lowed her husband's fishing boat to the shore of a campground at Monkey Mia. The dolphins soon became aware of the benefits of paying Mrs. Watts a friendly visit, and a pattern was established that evolved into one of the world's most unusual natural attractions. Today, dolphins visit the shores of Monkey Mia, now a nature reserve, almost daily, and enthralled observers stand shoulder to shoulder with researchers seizing a rare opportunity to investigate the social behavior of wild marine creatures. ◆ From the beginning, the rangers were concerned about the impact of this practice on the dolphins. Would they lose their predatory instinct? Would they contract

Monkey Mia on the Peron Peninsula is the setting of one of the world's most extraordinary encounters between humans and animals.

diseases from humans? More than a decade ago, therefore, staff began to control the feeding strictly, limiting its frequency and the amount of food supplied (currently restricted to one-third of the dolphin's total requirements) and introducing fines for anyone else caught offering fish to the dolphins. Reassuringly, recent research suggests that the current program has had no adverse impact on the dolphins. On the other hand, its benefits are clear: an increased understanding of wild creatures and an awareness of the need to protect them.

Jewel on the Coast

Still a small, remote settlement, Monkey Mia is located more than 500 miles (800 km) north of **Perth**, on the western side of **Shark Bay**, a wide inlet on the northwest coast of Australia. The bay was named by the English adventurer William Dampier during his second voyage to Australia in 1699. Dampier wrote in *A Voyage to New Holland*, "The Seafish that we saw here (for here was no River, Land or Pond of fresh Water to be seen) are chiefly Sharks. There are Abundance of them in this particular Sound, and I therefore give it the Name of Shark's Bay ... 'Twas the 7th of August when we came into Shark's Bay; in which we Anchor'd at three several Places, and stay'd at the first of them (on the W. side of the Bay) till the 11th. During which time we searched about, as I said, for fresh Water, digging Wells, but to no purpose."

Notwithstanding Dampier's rather jaundiced assessment, the bay is a jewel on the Western Australian coast – and the dolphins aren't its only attraction. Shark Bay's location in a transition zone between cold and warm ocean currents and tropical and temperate climates gives it a rich and glorious array of fauna. The seagrass meadows here

Baby green turtles (top) dig their way out of the sand shortly after hatching. Shark Bay has some of Australia's largest turtle colonies.

Visitors (left) marvel as bottlenose dolphins frolic a few feet from the beach.

Lighthouses (opposite) keep shipping clear of the treacherous cliffs that line the coast.

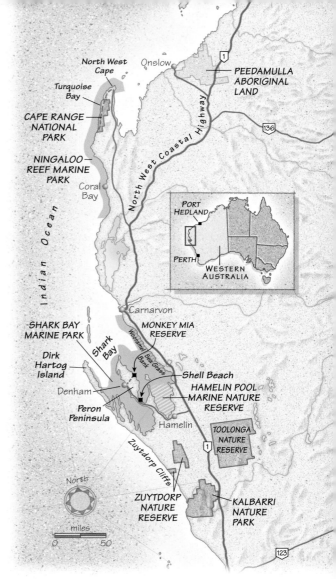

are the largest in the world and home to an estimated 10,000 dugongs – 10 percent of the world's population – and 6,000 marine turtles, including Western Australia's largest community of loggerhead turtles. Onshore, the marginal desert lands, with their sandy soils and their low, scrub-covered hills, are a refuge for endangered species, including 26 types of mammals, 13 kinds of reptiles, and three bird species. More than 700 kinds of wildflowers grow here, and in spring their blooms blanket the usually barren soil.

Moreover, alongside its many spectacular landforms – the precipitous **Zuytdorp Cliffs**, the wild **Peron Peninsula**, and **Dirk Hartog Island**, site of the first recorded landing of a European in Australia – Shark Bay incorporates significant geological curiosities including a beach made entirely of shells and the world's largest colony of stromatolites, Earth's earliest known life-form. The international significance of this remarkable assembly of treasures was acknowledged in 1991, when Shark Bay was declared a World Heritage area.

Dolphins and Dugongs

Standing on the beach is not the only way to make contact with the dolphins of Monkey Mia. Twice daily, two catamarans set off from the town's jetty. This is not conventional cruising: the sails are unfurled and visitors perch on the edges of the deep-sea sailing vessels as they weave their way around the bay locating a wealth of marine life. Dolphins race beside the catamarans, riding the bow waves, and curious dugongs pause to investigate the disturbance as they surface for air. These magnificent creatures, sometimes known as sea pigs or sea cows and once called "mermaids" by sailors, are close relatives of the manatees that inhabit the

Caribbean. Placid and generally timid, they can grow to a length of about 10 feet, live for 70 years, and reach a weight of 880 pounds. Sharks and orcas are their main predators, and in the past decade pods of dugongs have twice been attacked here by orcas.

The waters of Shark Bay are remarkably shallow – the average depth is only 33 to 49 feet – and from above they appear almost transparent. Flights over the bay are therefore highly recommended, particularly those over the **Wooramel Sea Grass Bank** south of **Carnarvon**. As the plane swoops low, you'll appreciate the scale and beauty of the seagrass meadows – in places they resemble

Ranges and Reefs

About 300 miles (480 km) north of Shark Bay, off the remote **North West Cape**, lies Australia's "other" barrier reef. Stretching for 160 miles (260 km) down the western side of the cape to **Coral Bay**, **Ningaloo Reef** has one major advantage over its "Great" counterpart: at many points, including popular Turquoise Bay, it lies less than 100 yards offshore. In such places, the coral forms a magnificent natural lagoon in which even inexperienced snorkelers and divers can safely explore the waters – now part of **Ningaloo Reef Marine Park** – and marvel at the 250 soft and hard coral formations and 500-plus species of marine life, including manta rays, harmless reef sharks, green turtles, strange tropical trumpet fish, and the exotically colored butterfly scorpion fish.

And if you visit around March, you can participate in one of the world's great underwater experiences: swimming with whale sharks. More than 60 feet long and weighing up to 88,000 pounds, these massive but harmless creatures – they are filter feeders and therefore have no teeth – come to the reef to feed on plankton. The presence of a few puny swimmers does little to deter them; indeed, they seem to be curious about, and enjoy the company of, humans. For the swimmers floating amid the coral and small, brightly colored tropical fish, the sudden appearance of a vast grey mass larger than a suburban home is an awesome spectacle.

North West Cape also offers a fascinating land-based nature destination: part of the hinterland is protected by **Cape Range National Park**. Designed to preserve a cross-section of the peninsula's habitats, the park encompasses dry plateau, coastal plains, and mangrove swamps. A number of short walks allow visitors to explore these habitats and view diverse wildlife, including euros (also known as the common wallaroo), red kangaroos, galahs, and emus.

Yardie Creek (above) winds through the Cape Range on its way to the Indian Ocean.

Whale sharks (left) are the world's largest fish. Swimming alongside one is an unforgettable experience.

vast underwater forests cut by delicate, anabranching rivers – and be able to pick out the shadowy shapes of sharks, rays, dolphins, turtles, and dugongs.

Bay of Shells

From a distance, **Shell Beach**, 47 miles (75 km) south of Monkey Mia, appears to be just another stunning Western Australian beach: pure white, gently undulating dunes edged by calm, clear waters. But on closer examination, you become aware that this beach is quite extraordinary: it is made entirely of millions of small, white shells. In places up to 33 feet deep, these are the shells of cardiid cockles. Like the stromatolites found farther down the coast, the cockles thrive in the high levels of salinity created by the protected, shallow bay, while their natural predators are deterred. As a result, the shells have accumulated in immense numbers over the past 4,000 years.

One intriguing result of these deposits has been the formation of a kind of shell-rich sedimentary rock, known as coquina limestone. This has become a popular building material around Shark Bay, and in the town of **Denham** several buildings – including a local restaurant – are built entirely out of coquina limestone blocks. The rough-hewn effect resembles pale sandstone embedded with thousands of tiny fossil shells.

When Earth Was Young

Somehow, coming face-to-face with the world's oldest living things was meant to be more impressive than this. Having made their way across the beach and onto the elevated walkway, a group of travelers are gazing into the waters of **Hamelin Pool Marine Nature**

Reserve, about 30 miles (50 km) southeast of Shell Beach. All they can see are hundreds of bulbous, rocklike shapes: a garden of rocky cauliflowers. Dutifully, they take their photographs, read the placards, and head back to their bus.

The stromatolites of Hamelin Pool may not be one of the world's most dramatic natural phenomena, and understanding what you are looking at requires a leap of the imagination. But once that leap is made, to stand on the walkway watching the heavily saline water lapping against these strange mounds is to marvel at the mysteries of nature.

The pool's bulbous "rocks" are the work of living organisms called cyanobacteria. These microscopic creatures secrete a fine film of mucus that traps sediment. The rocks grow about 0.02 inches each year, and many have been growing for around 3,500 years. Not only that, these cyanobacteria may be Earth's oldest life-forms. The evidence for this – fossils of almost identical cyanobacteria that date to 3½ billion years ago – lies some 500 miles (800 km) to the northeast, at a hot, remote spot known ironically as the North Pole. To stand at Hamelin, therefore, is to stand at the very beginning of Earth's evolution. Here, you can pause and reflect

that these tiny organisms predate the dinosaurs by more than 3 billion years.

Even while evoking our most distant past, Shark Bay's natural wonders can be experienced as an unfolding and evolving world that, for a brief moment, we are allowed to enter. These treasures, from the stromatolites of Hamelin to the dolphins of Monkey Mia, are testimony to the limitless diversity and ingenuity of nature. And if you're wondering how that young dolphin responded to the offer of a fish, she looked at it, played with it for a few seconds, slapped it out of her way, and swam off. Her time for dining with humans is yet to come.

Shell Beach (right) is made entirely of tiny shells deposited by the bay's thriving cardiid cockle colonies.

Stromatolites (below) are constructed by cyanobacteria that are dependent on regular immersion in seawater.

DETAILS

When to Go

The winter months (June to September) are the best time to visit Shark Bay, with comfortable maximum temperatures in the high 70s and low 80s°F (25°–28°C). In summer (December to February), the temperature sometimes rises to more than 110°F (43°C) and remains there for days, while strong southerly winds can blow without interruption for weeks. Visitors who want to enjoy the wildflowers that extend south from Shark Bay should plan to visit the area between late July and November.

How to Get There

Shark Bay is 520 miles (820 km) north of Perth. If you arrive by road, the turn-off to the bay is at the Overlander Roadhouse on the North-West Coastal Highway. From there, it's an 82-mile (130-km) drive to the Bay. Western Airlines, tel: 08-9277 4022, and Skywest Airlines, tel: 08-9334 2288, offer regular air services to Denham from Perth. Feature Tours, tel: 08-9479 4131, and Greyhound Pioneer, tel: 08-9277 9962, operate six bus services a week to the Overlander Roadhouse, and there is a connecting service from the Overlander to Denham and Monkey Mia.

Special Planning

Most of the roads to the principal sights in Shark Bay can be negotiated in conventional vehicles, but for people planning to venture into Cape Range National Park or across to Dirk Hartog Island, a sturdy four-wheel-drive vehicle is a must. If extensive off-road traveling is planned, make sure you carry extra food, water, and spare parts.

Permits and Entry Fees

No entrance fee is charged for entry to the World Heritage Area or any of the local parks.

INFORMATION

Shark Bay Tourist Centre

Knight Terrace, Denham, WA 6537; tel: 08-9948 1253; web: www.sharkbay.asn.au or e-mail: info@sharkbay.asn.au

Department of Conservation and Land Management (CALM)

67 Knight Terrace, Denham, WA 6537; tel: 08-9948 1208; web:www.calm.wa.gov.au

CAMPING

Francois Peron National Park

Department of Conservation and Land Management, 67 Knight Terrace, Denham, WA 6537; tel: 08-9948 1208; web:www.calm.wa.gov.au

Bush camping is permitted at clearly marked sites in this park on the Peron Peninsula. Camping fees apply and should be put into the "honesty box" at the entrance to the park. Open fires are banned; visitors should use the gas barbecues provided.

Monkey Mia Dolphin Resort

Monkey Mia Road via Denham, WA 6537; tel: 08-9948 1320; web: www.monkeymia.com.au or e-mail: sales@monkeymia.com.au

Camping is available at this resort, which also provides a restaurant, a swimming pool, and tennis and basketball courts. $–$$

LODGING

PRICE GUIDE – double occupancy	
$ = up to $49	$$ = $50–$99
$$$ = $100–$149	$$$$ = $150+

Dirk Hartog Island Homestead

Dirk Hartog Island, Shark Bay, WA 6537; tel: 08-9948 1211; web: www.dirkhartogisland.com or e-mail: hartog@space.net.au

This homestead offers comfortable accommodations and all meals on an isolated island that is currently occupied only eight months of the year by two people and a dog. $$$$

Monkey Mia Dolphin Resort

Monkey Mia Road via Denham, WA 6537; tel: 08-9948 1320; web: www.monkeymia.com.au or e-mail: sales@monkeymia.com.au

This low-key resort offers quality lodging from camping and backpacker dormitories to trailers and motel rooms. Facilities include a restaurant, a swimming pool, and tennis and basketball courts. There are daily catamaran tours from the resort, and researchers studying the area's marine life conduct slide presentations nightly. $–$$

Nanga Bay Resort

Nanga Station, Shark Bay, WA 6537; tel 08-9948 3992.

This working sheep station south of Denham overlooks Shark Bay. Accommodations range from simple backpacker rooms to motel-style units. Facilities include a natural artesian spa, a swimming pool, tennis courts, and a restaurant. $–$$

Shark Bay Cottages

13 Knight Terrace, Denham, WA 6537; tel: 08-9948 1206; web: www.sharkbaycottages.com.au or email info@sharkbay-cottages.com.au

Set on Shark Bay, these 14 self-contained cottages have fantastic ocean views. Accommodations range from simple studios to three-bedroom suites. Facilities include a swimming pool, two barbecues, and a boat ramp. For self-caterers, there is a supermarket next door. $

TOURS & OUTFITTERS

Explorer Charters and Cruises

P.O. Box 412, 19 Durlacher Street, Denham, WA 6537; tel: 08-9948 1246; web: www.wantree.com.

au/~explorer/ or e-mail: explorer @wantree.com.au

This outfit offers one- to seven-day diving and wildlife sightseeing tours aboard catamarans in Shark Bay. Destinations include Steep Point, Zuytdorp Cliffs, Dirk Hartog Island, and South Passage. Species that are spotted regularly include dugongs, whales, manta rays, turtles, and dolphins. Cruises can be tailored to suit travelers' interests.

Ningaloo Safari Tours

P.O. Box 203, Exmouth, WA 6707; tel 08-9949 1550; e-mail: ningaloosafari@nwc.net.au

A one-day "Top of the Range Safari" takes in Cape Range National Park, Ningaloo Marine Park, and Osprey Bay, and includes a boat trip along Yardie Creek Gorge, a visit to Shark Tooth Ridge, where many marine fossils can be seen, and snorkeling at Turquoise Bay. Experienced guides provide informative commentary on the area's flora, fauna, history, and geology.

Shark Bay Coach and Tours

13 Dampier Road, Denham, WA 6537; tel: 08-9948 1601.

Daily four-wheel-drive and bus tours leave from Denham and Monkey Mia. Tours include Shell Beach, Goulet Bluff, and the Old Peron homestead site.

Shark Bay Under Sail

P.O. Box 73, Denham, WA 6537; tel: 08-9948 1616; web: www.sharkbay.asn.au/members/UnderSail or e-mail: shanklan@ozemail.com.au

One- to four-day sailing adventures are available. Day trips provide an introduction to Shark Bay; the longer trips are conducted on the luxury 41-foot catamaran *James Scheerer* and allow visitors to view a broad range of wildlife.

Excursions

Kalbarri National Park

Department of Conservation and Land Management, 193 Marine Terrace, P.O. Box 72, Geraldton, WA 6530; tel: 08-9921 5955; web: www.calm.wa.gov.au

Located 35 miles (57 km) east of the town of Kalbarri, this 706-square-mile park is best visited between July and November, when the heathlands provide a spectacular floral display. Twenty-one plant species are unique to the area, including the Kalbarri catspaw and the Murchison hammer orchid. The park also features the twists and turns of the Murchison River and the dramatic beauty of Red Bluff.

The Pinnacles

Department of Conservation and Land Management, Main Roads Department Building, P.O. Box 328, Moora, WA 6510; tel: 08-9651 1424; web: www.calm.wa.gov.au

The Pinnacles, in Nambung National Park, features one of Australia's most surreal landscapes. Ranging from a few inches to 17 feet in height, the thousands of pillars rising out of the desert are the eroded remnants of a formerly thick bed of limestone. Although they were created over millennia, the formations were exposed by shifting sands in relatively recent times.

Wildflower Way

Leeman Tourist Information Centre, Shire Council, Coorow, WA 6515; tel: 08-9952 1103.

If you're driving north to Shark Bay from Perth along the Brand or Midlands Highways between July and November, you'll see astounding displays of the state's thousands of wildflowers on the roadside. For close-up views and informed commentary, visit Alexander Morrison National Park, about 30 miles (50 km) west of Coorow, and the Australian Flower Farm, about 25 miles (40 km) west of Coorow. The farm is reputedly the largest flower farm in the world, and tours are available July to September; tel: (08) 9952 5052. Alternatively, pay a visit to Mount Lesueur Reserve, or Reserve 29073, near Eneabba.

Stirling Range
National Park
Western Australia

CHAPTER 12

Some time around Christmas Day in 1846, British government naturalist James Drummond reached the barely explored **Stirling Range** for the second time. His first visit, three years earlier, had convinced him that the Stirlings were a treasure trove of new and diverse plant species. But now, as the botanist scaled **Mondurup Peak** in the west of the range from his base camp at **Red Gum Spring**, he could hardly contain his excitement: "I ascended by the north east angle and at about the height of 2,000 feet," he wrote, "I found making its appearance a splendid new banksia." ◆ Drummond just had time to note the appearance of the Stirling Range banksia, with its uneven leaves and purplish bronze, cigar-shaped flowers, before he stumbled upon another "exceedingly interesting and beautiful plant, the flowers enclosed by beautiful bracts, white variegated with crimson veins." This was the *Darwinia macrostegia*, or Mondurup bell, a species found nowhere else in the world but on this particular mountain

Against a multihued backdrop of wildflowers, heaths, and craggy peaks, hikers can explore some of the southwest's most challenging trails.

and a few nearby peaks. Drummond was clearly thrilled by his discovery: "These bracts," he continued, "are as elegantly formed as the petals of the finest tulip and they are almost as large, hanging in a bell … I thought I could never gather enough of this charming plant." ◆ It's been more than 150 years since Drummond came across the Mondurup bell, but visitors continue to be drawn to **Stirling Range National Park** as much for its extra-ordinary array of wildflowers and other plants as for the rugged beauty of its isolated peaks. More than 1,500 plant species have been recorded within this 285,682-acre park – more than are found in the entire British Isles – and

Pygmy-possums feed on the nectar produced by the Stirling Range's abundant wildflowers and in turn play a critical role in pollinating the plants.

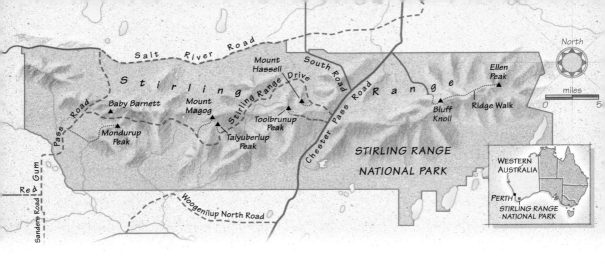

The Stirlings (below) rise from the plains to a height of almost 3,600 feet.

Blushing mountain bells (left) are one of 10 species of mountain bell that bloom on the park's uplands.

The Stirlings (below) rise from the plains to a height of almost 3,600 feet.

In lowland areas (opposite), erosion has exposed blocks of granite and worn them into smooth, round boulders.

at least 87 of these are endemic to the Stirlings. Of the 10 species of pendulous-flowered mountain bell (Darwinias) that inhabit the upper reaches of the park (above 984 feet), only one is found else-where. Also peculiar to the area are a number of species of (mainly red) nemcia peas and some spectacular members of the Proteaceae family, such as the vibrant pink Stirling Range pixie mop.

From afar, it is hard to envisage that this remote and rugged range, which rises forbid-dingly in hues of misty grey and blue from the plains of southwestern

Australia, could contain such a profusion of life. To local Aboriginal groups, who roamed the vicinity of these peaks for around 40,000 years, they were above all a place to fear, as the supreme evil spirit Noatch was believed to dwell there. The Aborigines called the mountains *Koi Kyeunu-ruff*, "place of ever-moving mist and fog," a name that remains apt today, with the summits frequently assailed by swirling clouds. European settlers renamed the range in 1835 in honor of Sir James Stirling, the governor of the nascent Western Australian colony of Swan River, now the city of **Perth**.

Recent geological research suggests that the Stirling Range had its genesis between 540 and 590 million years ago, when a lake bed created by the parting of the Australian and Antarctic plates began to fill with sedi-ments from local rivers. As the Antarctic plate finally broke away, the southwestern section of the continental shelf shifted and was compressed against the northern Yilgarn block. Subsequently, the deposition-al sediment was squeezed between parallel fractures in the crust and forced upward. Then, over millennia, erosion slowly scoured and shaped the sediments.

The result is a single chain of jagged mountains 40 miles long and 12 miles wide (64 by 19 km), with over a dozen summits, including **Bluff Knoll**, the range's highest point at 3,596 feet. The peaks overlook scrubby, heath-covered valleys and are surrounded by flatlands. From a distance, they seem to rise like islands from a vast sea.

Roadside Attractions

Whether you decide to visit the mountains on a tour or under your own steam, it is likely that at some point you'll find yourself on the park's main scenic road, the **Stirling Range Drive**. Running for 26 miles (42 km) from **Red Gum Pass Road** in the west to **Chester Pass Road** in the east, it traverses the western and central areas of the range, following the route of James Drummond's first expedition in 1843.

Initially, the gravel road winds between broad and craggy hills including Mondurup Peak and Baby Barnett. It then heads past picnic spots and several lookouts – including **Mount Magog** with its panoramic views of the range – toward the dramatic eastern end of the Stirlings, where the range's tallest peaks, Bluff Knoll and **Toolbrunup**, are situated. Both can be accessed via the paved Chester Pass Road at the far end of the drive.

Traveling the Stirling Range Drive not only provides an excellent introduction to its intriguing collection of knolls but also acquaints you with the shrubby, prickly habitat typical of their lower slopes. Furthermore, it allows you to view some brilliantly colored varieties of banksia near the roadside, such as the domed scarlet banksia or the bright yellow slender banksia collected by Aborigines

for its bounteous supplies of nectar.

But to get the most out of a visit to the Stirlings, it is essential to climb out of your vehicle and walk some of the park's many trails. This is one of Western Australia's best locations for hiking, with routes ranging from easy half-hour walks to challenging overnight hikes such as the **Ridge Walk**, a strenuous two- to three-day unmarked route that takes in three peaks over 3,300 feet.

While the walks invariably involve some

steep sections, they are definitely worth the effort. Not only do they afford magnificent views; they also offer opportunities for spotting some of the park's 148 bird species as well as the rare mountain bells. You might also encounter one of the two tiny possum species that inhabit the heathland, the western pygmy-possum and the honey possum, both of which feed on nectar and play a significant role in pollinating plants.

Many of the best walks lie just off the Stirling Range Drive. From a parking lot located less than three miles along the road, it's a 15-minute stroll up a rise to the top of **Baby Barnett**, where you'll find an impressive array of wildflowers, including abundant Stirling Range pixie mops, and enjoy fine views toward the eastern end of the range. Two other excellent trails lie about halfway along the drive: the demanding four-hour return hike to the top of **Mount Magog**, from which there are magnificent vistas, and the easier two-hour walk up **Talyuberlup Peak**, which takes in moist gullies, caves, and rock pinnacles. Toward the eastern end of the drive, the moderate climb to **Mount Hassell** reveals further dramatic upland scenery and intriguing rock formations, including a rock stack beneath the peak that resembles an old galleon.

Twin Peaks

It is the Stirlings' two tallest peaks, Toolbrunup and Bluff Knoll, that offer the park's most rewarding short climbs. Of the two, Toolbrunup is the more difficult ascent, heading straight up the side of the 3,450-foot mountain and requiring some scrambling over loose rock near the summit. Its rewards include rare and endemic red-eared firetails in the gullies and woodlands of the lower slopes, and increasingly panoramic views as you climb toward the slate-grey scree slopes near the

Orchid lovers converge on the Stirling Range to view its extraordinary variety of species, including the exquisite phalaenopsis orchid (top), the rare Queen of Sheba orchid (middle), and the striking red-beak orchid (bottom).

Orchid Heaven

While the Stirling Range is justifiably famous for its endemic plant species, another of its major drawing cards is its vast array of orchids. An astonishing 125 members of the Orchidaceae family – around 40 percent of all the orchids found in Western Australia – grow within the park.

Among the most common but nonetheless delightful species are the spider orchids. These range from the most minuscule of spindly petaled dwarf orchids through the yellow and scarlet cowslip to larger species like the elegant white spider orchid. Another prevalent group is formed by the sun orchids, which open only in sunshine; among the most striking is the colorful leopard orchid.

Other species live up to evocative names such as donkey orchid (with yellow "ears" and a mauve "mouth"), bird orchid (green and translucent), and king-in-his-carriage orchid (a splendid maroon, green, and gold hammer orchid). The Stirlings even offer the possibility, within a small window of time between mid-August and early September, of sighting the much-sought-after Queen of Sheba orchid, with its splendid red, yellow, and purple flowers.

The strategies used by orchids to attract pollinating insects are seemingly infinite. The jug orchid, for instance, emits the scent of mushrooms to entice a small gnat, while hammer orchids imitate female wasps in order to attract a male.

The park's orchids are distributed throughout the range, but the best places to look for them are the low-lying wandoo (or white gum) woodlands, where more than half of the species are known to dwell.

peak. Often you'll find yourself sharing those views with a chunky wedge-tailed eagle soaring on thermals just above the summit.

It's a fairly steep 3.7-mile (6-km) return hike to the top of Bluff Knoll, but it's not as difficult as others in the Stirlings thanks to a good footpath that follows the contours of the mountain. From woodland of jarrah and marri trees, the trail rises to an expanse of mallee-heath. In spring, the edge of the footpath is strewn with colorful wildflowers including large orange banksia, hanging shady bells, and golden dryandra. At these lower levels, watch for small purple-crowned lorikeets screeching overhead and two species of black cockatoo, both endemic to south-western Australia: the Baudin's, or long-billed, and the Carnaby's.

From the heathland the path climbs to the summit's rocky outcrops, from where the panorama extends across the range and all the way to the south coast. From the peak itself, those with a good head for heights can peer down a sheer 980-foot cliff face.

The Stirlings may not be one of the continent's tallest mountain ranges, but they are nonetheless a dominating presence in the largely flat terrain that characterizes southwestern Australia. Furthermore, their brooding peaks and imposing ramparts conceal rare beauty of the most delicate and fragile nature, much of it embodied in those extraordinary plant species that, two lifetimes ago, so enchanted an inquisitive British botanist.

The summit of Bluff Knoll (above) offers stupendous views along the range and across the surrounding plains.

Wedge-tailed eagles (left), Australia's biggest birds of prey, occasionally kill large animals such as wallabies.

TRAVEL TIPS

DETAILS

When to Go

The Stirling Range can be visited year-round, but wildflowers are at their best between August and November. During this period the climate is mild, with October having an average daily maximum of 66°F (19°C) and a low of 46°F (8°C). The range's higher peaks are often cold, even in summer, and the area is subject to sudden changes in temperature, as well as driving rain and, occasionally, snow.

How to Get There

Skywest, tel: 08-9334 2288, flies daily from Perth to Albany. Car and four-wheel-drive rentals are available at Albany airport. Stirling Range National Park is about 60 miles (100 km) northeast of Albany and can be reached via the Chester Pass Road. From Perth it's a 197-mile (318-km) drive via the Albany and Great Southern Highways to Cranbrook, 6 miles (10 km) west of the park along the Salt River Road.

Special Planning

Walkers should carry sufficient water and food, warm clothing, and wet-weather gear at all times. As dieback disease (*Phytophthora cinnamoni*) is a problem in the range, hikers are asked to clean their boots and other equipment to avoid introducing any contaminated soil into unaffected areas. Some trails may be closed during wet weather to prevent the spread of the disease.

Permits and Entry Fees

A fee is required for entry into the Bluff Knoll region of the park. To pay the fee, use the self-registration box at the Bluff Knoll Road turn-off along Chester Pass Road.

INFORMATION

Albany Tourist Bureau

Old Railway Station, Proudlove Parade, Albany, WA 6330; tel: 08-9841 1088; web: www.albanytourist.com.au or e-mail: peta@albanytourist.com.au

Department of Conservation and Land Management (CALM)

Stirling Range National Park, R.M.B. 557, Borden, WA 6338; tel: 08-9827 9230.

CAMPING

There is a camping area at Moingup Springs inside the park. A fee applies and is collected at the campsite by rangers.

LODGING

PRICE GUIDE – double occupancy	
$ = up to $49	$$ = $50–$99
$$$ = $100–$149	$$$$ = $150+

Bolganup Homestead

R.M.B. 1340, Mount Barker, WA 6324; tel: 08-9853 1049.

The homestead offers two options: Firmbrook, a three-bedroom apartment that sleeps up to eight people, and Burnley, which has two bedrooms and sleeps up to six. Both are self-contained and have gas stoves, microwaves, and large living areas. The property is close to Porongurup National Park, several wineries, and local shops and restaurants. $$

Karribank Country Retreat

R.M.B. 1332, Porongurup, WA 6324; tel: 08-9853 1022; e-mail: karribnk@albanyis.com.au

Set on 32 acres overlooking the Porongurup Ranges, this is the oldest country retreat in Western Australia. Visitors can stay in two-story chalets, cottages (some of which are mud brick and feature spas and antiques), or rooms with private baths. The self-contained chalets and cottages have verandas with spectacular views. The retreat has a restaurant and is five minutes from local wineries. $$–$$$

Peacehaven Mountain Escape

Millinup Road, Porongurup, WA 6325; tel: 08-9853 2141; e-mail: peace@omninet.net.au

This well-appointed bed-and-breakfast is set on 40 acres of pasture and woodland in an area rich in wildflowers. Breakfast and afternoon tea are included in the price, and other meals can be provided. Peacehaven is within walking distance of Porongurup National Park. $$

The Sleeping Lady Bed-and-Breakfast

R.M.B. 1044, Porongurup, WA 6324; tel: 08-9853 1113; web: www.omninet.net.au/~slady or e-mail: slady@telstra.easymail.au

This secluded lodging has magnificent views of the Stirling Range. Options include bed-and-breakfast accommodations in a queen-sized room with private bath, or a self-contained, two-bedroom cottage with wood heater and full kitchen facilities. $–$$

Stirling Range Retreat

Chester Pass Road, Borden South, WA 6338; tel: 08-9827 9229; e-mail: stirlingrangeretreat@bigpond.com.au

Self-contained chalets, round-earth cabins, and campsites are all in a natural bush setting. The retreat has 103 beds, and facilities include a swimming pool, a kitchen, and a laundry. There are numerous walking trails on the property, and staff members are happy to advise on weather conditions and wildflower walks. $–$$

TOURS & OUTFITTERS

Albany Coastal Safari Tours

7 Milpara Way, Albany, WA 6330; tel: 08-9841 7652.

Operating year-round, this company offers half- and full-day four-wheel-drive tours of the Stirling Range, with a focus on wildflowers. Leaving from Albany, the tours explore the western side of the national park, following the Red Gum Pass and Salt River Roads.

Bush Eco Tours

P.O. Box 183, North Fremantle, WA 6159; tel: 08-9336 3050; web: www.bushecotours. com.au or e-mail: frank@bushecotours.com.au

This ecotour company will tailor two- to three-day trips to the Stirling Range to suit the interests of travelers. Tours depart from Perth or Fremantle.

Coates Wildlife Tours

P.O. Box 64, Bull Creek, WA 6149; tel: 08-9455 6611 or toll-free in Australia 1-800 676 016; web: www.coates.iinet.net.au or e-mail: coates@iinet.net.au

Experienced naturalists lead a range of nature tours to the Stirling Range and other parts of the southwest. Itineraries range from seven to 17 days and include stays at chalets and campgrounds.

Escape Tours

P.O. Box 5555, Albany, WA 6332; tel: 08-9844 1945.

This company runs full-day tours once a week from March to November, or can organize tours especially for individuals or small groups. From Albany, the standard tour takes the Chester Pass Road to the Porongurups and then continues into the heart of the Stirling Range. The itinerary includes frequent stops to look at wildflowers, a visit to Bluff Knoll, and lunch at Moingup Springs.

Excursions

D'Entrecasteaux National Park

Department of Conservation and Land Management, Walpole District Office, South Western Highway, Walpole, WA 6398; tel: 08-9840 1027; web: www.calm.wa.gov.au or e-mail: calmwalp@wn.com.au

Stretching along the southwest coast for 80 miles, from just west of Walpole to just east of Augusta, D'Entrecasteaux features wild and rugged coastal scenery of limestone cliffs, estuaries, inlets, shifting sand dunes, lakes, and rocky headlands. Aboriginal artifacts and camp-sites discovered in the area date back 40,000 years. Between July and September, southern right whales can often be seen migrating along the coast.

Porongurup National Park

Department of Conservation and Land Management, Ranger Station, Bolganup Road, R.M.B. 1310, Mount Barker, WA 6324;

tel: 08-9853 1095; web: www.calm.wa.gov.au or e-mail: charlies@calm.wa.gov.au

Formed 1.1 billion years ago, the Porongurups provide a soft-contoured contrast to the taller, more rugged Stirlings. The range features large granite domes and extensive woodlands of towering karri trees, some of which grow to 200 feet tall. The park is rich in wildflowers and bird life, including wedge-tailed eagles and purple-crowned lorikeets.

Walpole–Nornalup National Park

Department of Conservation and Land Management, Walpole District Office, South Western Highway, Walpole, WA 6398; tel: 08-9840 1027; web: www.calm.wa.gov.au or e-mail: calmwalp@wn.com.au

This 77-square-mile national park encom-passes magnificent tall timber forests and 25 miles (40 km) of sweeping coastal scenery. The Valley of the Giants offers a walk through a grove of centuries-old tingle trees known as the Ancient Empire. The nearby Tree Top Walk stretches 640 yards through the forest canopy at a height of up to 125 feet.

The Flinders Ranges
South Australia

t's remote, but right now **Weetootla Gorge** is anything but peaceful. Why, for instance, is the distinctive noise of a pinball machine throbbing from those reeds? You strain to see across the pool but can't spot the source of this aural assault: the aptly named clamorous reed warbler, a drab bird just over six inches in length, is notoriously shy. Not so flocks of little corellas, the large white cockatoos that argue in throat-tearing yells as they festoon the salmon-and-white mottled limbs of a handsome river red gum. But even the corellas are made melodious by a leaden croak that drops from above, jagging at the red rock walls of the gorge. Look up: it's the white-faced heron changing pools.　◆　The real music of Weetootla Gorge, in **Gammon Ranges National Park**, is in the thin notes of the tiny spring-fed stream that meanders among the gorge's rocks. In these **Jagged ridges and dramatic escarpments shelter diverse environments, abundant wildlife, and magnificent Aboriginal rock art.** arid hills, water is all-important. It's near rock-cradled oases like Weetootla that you meet many of the animals of the **Flinders Ranges** on their own terms. Exercise patience and wait … for the wrens, the honeyeaters, five species of robin in shades ranging from rose-red through crimson to black and white, 16 multihued species of parrot, the euro (a kangaroo of the hills), or the cautious yellow-footed rock wallaby, the ranges' rarest marsupial.　◆　The **Flinders Ranges** begin about 125 miles (200 km) north of **Adelaide**, the South Australian capital, and thrust up into an increasingly arid outback for 260 miles. For 120 miles (190 km) they form a classic range: a main spine with parallel digressions that add the plural "s" to Flinders Ranges. At **Wilpena Pound**, all coherence stops. Like the whorls of a thumbprint, the ridges loop, enclose,

On the cliffs of Wilpena Pound, a climber focuses on the task at hand, seemingly oblivious to the astonishing scenery behind him.

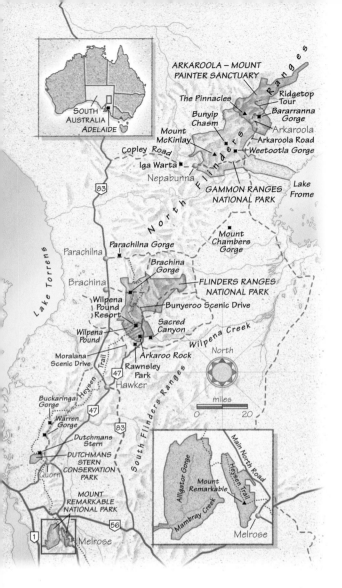

ARKAROOLA – MOUNT PAINTER SANCTUARY

The Pinnacles
Ridgetop Tour
Bunyip Chasm
Bararranna Gorge
Mount McKinlay
Arkaroola
Arkaroola Road
Copley Road
Weetootla Gorge
Iga Warta
Nepabunna
GAMMON RANGES NATIONAL PARK
Lake Frome
North Flinders Ranges
Parachilna
Parachilna Gorge
Mount Chambers Gorge
Brachina Gorge
Brachina
FLINDERS RANGES NATIONAL PARK
Lake Torrens
Wilpena Pound Resort
Bunyeroo Scenic Drive
Sacred Canyon
Wilpena Creek North
Wilpena Pound
Moralana Scenic Drive
Arkaroo Rock
Rawnsley Park
Hawker
Buckaringa Gorge
Warren Gorge
Dutchmans Stern
DUTCHMANS STERN CONSERVATION PARK
Quorn
MOUNT REMARKABLE NATIONAL PARK
Melrose

SOUTH AUSTRALIA
ADELAIDE

Heysen Trail
South Flinders Ranges

miles
0   20

Alligator Gorge
Mount Remarkable
Heysen Trail
Main North Road
Mambray Creek
Melrose

harbor places for exploration and discovery, as well as a get-away-from-it-all serenity.

From Coast to Outback

Emus pace between the stately river red gums of **Mambray Creek**, site of the ranger headquarters at **Mount Remarkable National Park**. The manic eyes of these flightless birds – Australia's largest – are at odds with their retiring nature. The emu is just one of 100 bird species from desert, forest, and sea that assemble in this 62-square-mile reserve, which lies a two- to three-hour drive north of Adelaide. Walk the forested valleys to see species such as the arresting crimson rosella, a parrot of moist forests; higher up, in semiarid scrub, you can spot creatures from drier environments, like the brilliant scarlet-chested parrot.

There are no alligators in **Alligator Gorge**, the most visited spot in the park, but prehistoric-looking tree goannas up to 6½ feet long occasionally stalk over the water-worn terraces between the gorge's sheer red faces. Although it wouldn't serve as a goanna's snack, the diminutive variegated fairy wren is often more visible: the blue, purple, and russet male glows like a jewel in the scrub. Watch, too, for the dipping flight of the emerald-green mallee ringneck parrot and the red-billed, red-rumped diamond firetail finch.

You make the transition from the gorge's depths to the heights of 3,159-foot **Mount Remarkable** via **Melrose** township, sleepily inviting at the mountain's eastern foot. It's a steep, four-hour walk from the village through eucalypt woodlands to the peak and its views over the park, the shining arm of **Spencer Gulf** to the west, and the long march of the Flinders Ranges to the north.

Quorn, about 30 miles (50 km) north of the park, is a town that hasn't shaken off a railway heritage that effectively ended when the last commercial train drummed through in 1956. This township was once

fragment, or spear off into the hazy blue distance. On the ranges' far northeastern tip, at **Arkaroola**, the landscape disintegrates into a chaos of steep hills and rough-cut gorges that abruptly metamorphoses into the vast plains of central Australia.

Once, these ranges jutted 20,000 feet into the sky. Weather and eons have worn them down, in keeping with the rest of ancient Australia, and furnished the hills with a spectacularly diverse combination of plants and animals – 283 species of birds have been recorded in the region – that sustained local Aborigines for at least 15,000 years. Like a long rocky island in the plains, the Flinders

linked to every major capital city by a ribbon of rail. In 1942, General Douglas MacArthur passed through Quorn in retreat from the Japanese-held Philippines. He made his famous promise to recapture the islands at Terowie, 80 miles down the line. The Pichi Richi Railway Preservation Society, on the outskirts of Quorn, has the carriage MacArthur traveled in, along with an array of meticulously restored rail memorabilia. Panting steam trains carry sight-seers on a scenic route down **Pichi Richi Pass** between May 1 and October 30.

You won't find a scarlet robin or laughing kookaburra farther north than nearby **Dutchmans Stern Conservation Park**. Look west, north, and east from the 2,690-foot

Scorpions (opposite) use their huge claws to seize and kill prey. Their stinging tail provides an additional weapon.

The hike to St. Marys Peak (left), the highest point in the Flinders, takes at least a full day.

The precipitous cliffs of Wilpena Pound (below) rise nearly 1,000 feet above the plains.

Stern – named for its resemblance to the steering end of an 18th-century Dutch sailing vessel – and you gaze into the beginnings of the outback. Not that you would guess it amid the gentle scenery of **Warren** and **Buckaringa Gorges**, a few minutes' drive north of the park. Reedy creeks and camping sites in glades of northern cypress pine make these ideal spots for lunch or an overnight camp.

The Long and Winding Trail

Parachilna Gorge (above) provides a picturesque climax to the winding, 930-mile-long Heysen Trail, one of Australia's best hikes.

Yellow-footed rock-wallabies (below) bound nimbly over stone and scrub in the Flinders.

Parachilna Gorge, in the central Flinders, marks the northern extremity of a walking track that winds not only over the next horizon but clear down to **Cape Jervis**, south of Adelaide – a distance of some 930 miles (1,500 km). Only a hardy few have tackled the entire length of the **Heysen Trail**. Most use this well-marked and strategic route – it passes through every major preserve in the southern and central Flinders – for day walks or short multiday expeditions.

The Heysen Trail can take you into areas you might otherwise merely wonder at: the long north ridge of Mount Remarkable, the valley beneath the ramparts of the **Elder Range**, near Hawker, and the otherwise-inaccessible area north of the **Aroona Valley** in the central Flinders. A series of detailed 1:50,000 maps covering the entire trail is available from the South Australian Department of Recreation and Sport. The department can also help with information on the cyclist's version of the Heysen Trail, the 500-mile (800-km) **Mawson Trail**. Starting in Adelaide, this equally well-planned track finishes at **Blinman**. The route avoids vehicles by using a network of fire trails and road reserves. Good preparation is necessary, and sturdy mountain bikes should be used.

Heart of the Ranges

From **Hawker**, a handy service town where you can hitch a ride on a camel and arrange an exploration of traditional Aboriginal culture, the Flinders' best-known feature looms on the northwestern horizon – **Wilpena Pound**, centerpiece of 366-square-mile **Flinders Ranges National Park**. The ridges framing this 22,000-acre natural basin with 550-million-year-old rock made it a natural corral for pioneering cattlemen, who added the English term for a stock enclosure to the Aboriginal "Wilpena." To tribal Aborigines, the walls of Wilpena were the frozen bodies of two great serpents, or *akurra*, that slid down from the north along routes marked by the sinuous ridges of the **Heysen** and **ABC Ranges**. Pretty **Wilpena Creek** was a preferred camping place for Aboriginal tribes, as it is now for tourists, and the boles of the immense river red gums along the creek have been hollowed by generations of Aboriginal cooking fires. Until the cattle came, initiation ceremonies were held in the pound to induct children into adulthood and adults into the tribes' binding laws. Paintings and petroglyphs of tribal beliefs and totems are preserved in atmospheric natural galleries at **Arkaroo Rock** and **Sacred Canyon**.

Trails to suit all schedules and abilities begin at **Wilpena Pound Resort** and **Rawnsley Park**. Be alert in springtime: the native wildflowers of the Flinders seldom bloom in eye-catching profusion, but they are unforgettable once their subtlety is discovered. Look for the scarlet burst of Flinders Ranges bottlebrush, the red yawp of cockies tongue, and the yellow pom-pom flowers of the abundant wattles. Glance up, and you may catch a pair of wedge-tailed eagles swinging on a thermal or a black falcon quivering over a ravine.

Much that is beautiful about the central Flinders can also be seen from a vehicle.

Reserve **Moralana Scenic Drive**, southwest of Wilpena Pound, for the late afternoon, when the sun silhouettes the march of river red gums along Moralana Creek and fuels the glow that seems to emanate from the pound's rock face. **Bunyeroo Scenic Drive** follows the ranges to the north, first passing through open grasslands where kangaroos and emus graze, and river red gums where corellas, galahs, and red-rumped parrots may adorn a single tree like rowdy confetti. Beyond the grasslands, the road climbs to reveal a panorama of the ranges before wending through pretty Bunyeroo Gorge and forests of cypress pine to **Brachina Gorge**.

The genesis of these mountains is revealed at Brachina, where a well-signposted nine-mile geological trail leads you past rocks laid down between 640 and 520 million years ago – long before life gained a foothold on land. At dusk in the gorge, keep your eyes on the northern cliffs; you may spot yellow-footed rock-wallabies descending to drink at the gorge's pools.

Legends of the North

According to Aboriginal myth, the cleft in the eastern end of **Mount Chambers**, 80 miles (126 km) northeast of Wilpena Pound Resort, was cut by a boomerang hurled by the ancestor white-winged fairy wren. The wren's second boomerang came

to rest as the mountain's cap. Other legends, no longer understood, are depicted on the walls of the magnificent gorge that cuts the mountain: look for rock engravings in the first tributary gorge on the left. Kangaroos, once a valued food source for the nomads, now laze at the main gorge's entrance.

For a deeper appreciation of a culture that has endured through the rise and fall of more prominent civilizations, head for the **Nepabunna** or **Iga Warta** Aboriginal

The pleasing symmetry of Wilpena Pound (right) can be fully appreciated from its quartzite ridges.

communities, on the Copley road, and ask whether a guide can take you into the surrounding indigenous lands. There are no set tours, but depending on your interests you can sample native food plants, view rock engravings, learn about the Dreaming – or do all three.

The territory of the northern Flinders tribe, the Adnyamathana, was centered on 3,448-foot **Mount McKinlay**, a statuesque solitary peak in the heart of 495-square-mile Gammon Ranges National Park. Much of this harsh but spectacularly beautiful environment can be seen from the challenging four-wheel-drive track looping around the park's core. Walking is best, however, if you're to discover the subtleties hidden among the towering ridges of rock.

Weetootla Gorge, the location of the park's two marked trails, offers some of the easiest walking and most diverse scenery. For other walks, you'll need a detailed bush-walking guidebook, a topographic map, and plenty of water. Good preparation is necessary even for a short walk, such as the two-hour rock-hop up the headwaters of Weetootla Creek to the water-worn gash of **Bunyip Chasm**. Clambering up dry waterfalls on the approach, you encounter ferns

The cool waters of Bararranna Gorge in Arkaroola Sanctuary (above) provide a welcome refuge from the desert heat.

At Iga Warta (left), an Aboriginal community, visitors can view a fascinating range of rock art.

left over from an age when Australia was covered in dripping rain forests. Higher up, the gorge abounds in grass trees – sprouted, Aborigines say, from the shattered remains of a woman who fell from the cliffs while greedily eating the plant's tasty white core.

The only regular accommodation in the northeastern Flinders is at the **Arkaroola Sanctuary**, the headquarters of the privately owned **Arkaroola–Mount Painter Sanctuary**. Travel within the sanctuary is strictly by four-wheel drive. The magnitude of this astonishing tract of mountains and ravines unfolds on the sanctuary's guided **Ridgetop Tour**, a drive along precipitous tracks to a high crest with 100-mile views across the eastern plains and the shimmering salt pan of **Lake Frome**.

Pull on a good pair of boots to explore the well-marked walks that fan around the village. Birds abound: 168 species have been spotted in the region, including 14 birds of prey, eight honeyeaters, and the red-backed kingfisher, its nape the deep, clear green of Arkaroola's plentiful water holes. Yellow-footed rock-wallabies live on the largest of the **Pinnacles** – two once-molten lava plugs that formed 450 million years ago – and several species of dragon lizards sun themselves on rocks along the tracks. The red-barred dragon,

found only in the northeastern Flinders, is most readily encountered in spectacular **Bararranna Gorge**. The crimson stripes on the dragon's abdomen mimic the bloody cuts slashed on the chests of young male Aborigines being initiated into manhood – a coincidence that links these magnificent ranges, its wild creatures, and its human inhabitants into a spiritual whole.

A miner relaxes in a subterranean dwelling in Coober Pedy (right).

Pale mounds of sand (below) attest to generations of hopeful prospectors.

Subterranean Town

Looking like the habitat of some giant prairie dog, the holed and hummocked landscape of **Coober Pedy** is in fact a powerful testament to the lure of instant riches – especially riches that flicker with the cold flame of opal. The name of this town, a five- to six-hour drive north of **Port Augusta**, was derived from the Aboriginal *kupa piti*, meaning "whitefellas burrow." The name is apt: searing summer temperatures and a lack of building timber drove early miners into the 75°F (24°C) comfort of the mine shafts.

Today, much of what happens in Coober Pedy occurs beneath a landscape so barren that it featured in the end-of-the-world scenes of the movie *Mad Max III*. A number of imaginatively eccentric underground homes are open to visitors, as are underground motels, churches, museums, art galleries, and a post office. The peculiarities of Coober Pedy's living arrangements often overshadow the fact that this is the world's preeminent source of opal. Since 1915, when 14-year-old Willie Hutchison walked back into his prospector father's camp carrying fragments of the luminous stone, the great lottery of opal mining has lured fortune hunters to Coober Pedy. The joyous gamble of sinking a shaft into the ground in the hope of striking a vein has cross-cultural attractions: about 45 nationalities are represented in the town's permanent population of 3,500.

Several tour operators take visitors through working mines, and those with the urge to try their hand can apply for a Mines Department prospecting permit and within a few days be digging their own burrows. Use caution when exploring the field: not only are there numerous unmarked shafts, but trespassers on claims can be heavily fined.

TRAVEL TIPS

DETAILS

When to Go

The fire-ban season, from November to April, coincides with the hottest time of the year, when temperatures in the northern Flinders can shoot above 110°F (43°C) and stay there for days. Most people choose to visit the Flinders in the autumn, winter, or spring months. If good rains have fallen in the latter two seasons, the water holes are usually full and wildflowers abundant.

How to Get There

A small commuter airline, Augusta Airways, tel: 08-8642 3100, flies weekdays from Adelaide to Port Augusta, 12½ miles (20 km) from the Flinders Ranges. The town is also serviced by two long-distance passenger trains – the Sydney–Perth *Indian-Pacific* and the Adelaide–Alice Springs *Ghan*, tel: 88 213 4592. Prearranged car rentals are available at the airport. Several tour coach lines visit the Flinders as part of longer trips, but for real freedom an automobile is essential.

Coober Pedy is a five- to six-hour drive north of Port Augusta. Greyhound Pioneer operates a daily bus service from Adelaide; tel: 132 030 (toll-free in Australia).

Special Planning

Most key areas of the southern and central Flinders can be negotiated in conventional vehicles, but for the northern region a sturdy four-wheel-drive vehicle is a must. If extensive off-road traveling is planned, carry spare parts and emergency food and water. Heavy rain will make some main roads in the north impassable. Check road conditions with the Department of Transport hot line: 1300 361 033. Pack comfortable clothing that can be layered to suit changing weather.

Permits and Entry Fees

Entry fees apply to the Flinders' parks. Passes and permits may be purchased from National Parks and Wildlife South Australia offices throughout the region. For information, call 08-8648 4244.

INFORMATION

Flinders Ranges and Outback Tourism/Wadlata Outback Centre
41 Flinders Terrace, Port Augusta, SA 5700; tel: 08-8641 0793 or 08-8642 4511; e-mail: wadlata@wadarid.mtx.net

Flinders Ranges National Park
Wilpena Visitor Centre, Wilpena, SA 5434; tel: 08-8648 0048.

Gammon Ranges National Park
Balcanoona Ranger Station, P.M.B. via Copley, SA 5434; tel: 08-8648 4829; e-mail: gammon@dove.net.au

Mount Remarkable National Park
P.M.B. 7, Mambray Creek via Port Pirie, SA 5540; tel: 08-8634 7068; e-mail: mambray@dove.net.au

Pichi Richi Railway
Railway Terrace, Quorn, SA 5433; tel: 08-8395 2566 (recorded information); web: www.prrps.com.au or e-mail: pcapps@prrps.com.au

CAMPING

Bush camping is permitted in most areas of the Flinders Ranges national parks, but visitors must first obtain a permit, available from National Parks and Wildlife South Australia offices. Car campsites are clearly marked. Don't camp in creekbeds – flash floods can occur – or beneath large gum trees, as they can spontaneously shed heavy limbs. Fire bans are in place in summer months, and year-round bans exist in some parks. Commercial campgrounds offer a range of facilities throughout the Flinders.

LODGING

Accommodations on farms and stations (similar to American ranches) are available throughout the Flinders, an option that gives visitors access to people, places, and heritage that would otherwise go unnoticed. Several stations offer private tours and demonstrations of pastoral life. There is also a full range of accommodations, including hotels, motels, and caravan parks, in the Flinders towns of Melrose, Port Augusta, Quorn, and Hawker. Contact Flinders Ranges and Outback Tourism for details.

Angorichina Tourist Village
P.M.B. via Port Augusta, SA 5710; tel: 08-8648 4842.

Established in 1927 as a sanitarium, this beautifully sited village, in the heart of the Flinders Ranges, switched to its current operation in 1973. A range of budget accommodations – including a 51-bed dormitory, four self-contained cabins, three self-contained units, campsites, and on-site trailers – are available for those happy to cook their own meals. Facilities include showers, a well-stocked general store, and a fuel outlet. $

Arkaroola Tourist Village
Via Port Augusta, SA 5700; tel: 08-8648 4848; web: www.arkaroola.on.net or e-mail: admin@arkaroola.on.net

This village offers a variety of accommodations, including three standards of motel lodges, self-contained cottages, a trailer and camping park, and backpacker budget lodging. Amenities include a restaurant, a bar and barbecue area, a swimming pool and shopping center, and an observatory. $–$$

Wilpena Pound Holiday Resort
C.M.B. Wilpena Pound, SA 5434; tel: 08-8648 0004; web: www.wilpenapound.on.net or e-mail: wilpena@adelaide.on.net

Originally established in 1947, this resort is set in attractive surroundings at the mouth of Wilpena Pound and makes an ideal base for exploration. The recently rebuilt motel and separate chalets offer 60 rooms, 10 of which are self-contained. Amenities include a restaurant and swimming pool, barbecue areas, and a visitor center. Additional accommodations are available in the resort's trailer park and campground alongside Wilpena Creek. $–$$

TOURS & OUTFITTERS

Aboriginal Tours at Iga Warta
Iga Warta via Copley, SA 5732; tel: 08-8648 3717.

Informative tours and talks on northern Flinders tribal culture, the Dreaming, and bush tucker (food collected from the bush) are conducted by Aboriginal guides.

Aboriginal Tours at Nepabunna Community
Nepabunna Community via Copley, SA 5732; tel: 08-8648 3764.

Local guides offer tours covering northern Flinders tribal culture, the Dreaming, and bush tucker. Inquire on arrival.

F.R.A.Y. Aboriginal Cultural Tours
P.O. Box 187, Hawker, SA 5434; tel: 08-8648 4122; web: www.hawker.mtx.net

Multiday tours of Dreaming landscapes, culture, and bush tucker are offered. Reservations are essential.

Excursions

Lake Eyre National Park
National Parks and Wildlife South Australia, P.O. Box 102, Hawker, SA 5434; tel: 08-8648 4244.

One-sixth of Australia drains into the two branches of Lake Eyre, yet only three or four times each century does enough rain fall to fill this 3,860-square-mile would-be inland sea, at which time it attracts an amazing array of bird life. At other times it is a blinding plain of shimmering salt. Donald Campbell used it in 1964 to set a land-speed record of 403.1 mph in his rocket car, but modern-day travelers are asked not to drive on the surface. The park is accessible only by four-wheel-drive vehicle.

Warraweena Private Conservation Park
P.O. Box 269, Kingston S.E., SA 5275; tel: 08-8675 2770.

A group of conservationists bought this former sheep station in 1997 and have opened it to anyone wishing to explore its classic Flinders Ranges terrain. Bush walkers can roam 137 square miles of creeks and forests, and climb 3,562-foot Mount Hack. There are several colonies of yellow-footed rock-wallabies, and bird watchers have spotted at least 53 bird species including emus, crimson chats, and white-winged wrens. Huts are available; nominal fees apply.

Winninowie Conservation Park
P.M.B. 7, Mambray Creek via Port Pirie, SA 5540; tel: 08-8634 7068.

On the shores of Spencer Gulf, Winninowie attracts a bewildering mix of 124 bird species from desert and sea, including wrens, chats, thornbills, oystercatchers, terns, and egrets as well as several migratory species that regularly stop off on their way from Europe and Asia to Antarctica. The park's flats feed mangrove stands rich with marine life, and Aboriginal shell middens mark an ancient shoreline more than a mile inland.

Kangaroo Island
South Australia

CHAPTER 14

The soft, needlelike fronds of the she-oaks stir as the ocean breeze rolls over **Lathami Conservation Park**. Fallen remnants of earlier growth carpet the floor, soaking up the sounds of your footsteps. Beneath the dense forest canopy, it's as cool and dark as twilight. As you crouch behind a roughened trunk, you notice movement out of the corner of your eye. Edging forward, your eyes start to focus on a patch of grey, but whatever it is, it spots you first and bounds away. ◆ Creeping farther into the forest, keeping low to avoid the larger branches and to scan the undergrowth for marsupials, you emerge into a grassy clearing. The breeze is in your favor: the animal's nose twitches but it can't capture your scent, and its eyesight isn't acute enough to distinguish your form. The ears swivel from side to side, attempting to pick up your breathing. Then, from the Tammar wallaby's pouch, a smaller head pops up. The youngster topples out and struggles uncertainly onto its over-

Few places let you encounter diverse wildlife – especially at close range. This is one of them.

sized legs. Suddenly, an ear-piercing screech erupts from above as a glossy black cockatoo swoops down onto a casuarina tree. The traumatized joey hops back into the safety of its mother's pouch, and within seconds both have vanished into the bush. ◆ Scenes such as this unfold daily on **Kangaroo Island**, located 7 miles (11 km) off the coast of South Australia, 68 miles (109 km) south of the state capital, Adelaide. Isolated from the mainland for thousands of years, Kangaroo Island – Australia's third-largest island – has developed into a species-saving sanctuary for countless plants and animals. This landmass was never colonized by the dingo, Australia's "native" dog, believed to have been introduced from Asia some 4,000 years

Koalas are so abundant on Kangaroo Island that some have been relocated. Solitary animals, these marsupials spend most of the day sleeping.

ago. Nor, despite the arrival of Europeans in the mid-19th century, has it been invaded by more recently introduced European species such as the red fox and the rabbit, which have devastated indigenous wildlife and habitats on the mainland. In addition, more than one-third of the island is now protected by 19 national and conservation parks and five wilderness protection areas, and authorities have worked closely with private landowners to create wildlife corridors that help maintain the animals' home ranges and hence their biological diversity. A haven for wildlife, Kangaroo Island is consequently a paradise for nature lovers.

Among the island's success stories are the Tammar wallaby, which is threatened with extinction on the mainland but thrives here, and the grey Kangaroo Island kangaroo, a subspecies of the eastern grey kangaroo and a stockier animal than its mainland cousin, with shorter limbs, darker fur, and slower movements. Rare Australian sea lions, New Zealand fur seals, pygmy-possums, and the echidna, which is elusive on the mainland but seen here

regularly, have also benefited from the island's isolation. Bird life includes abundant sea eagles, black swans, sacred ibises, pelicans, fairy penguins, galahs, and crimson rosellas, as well as rare residents such as the glossy black cockatoo, stone curlew, and endemic sooty dunnart. The island even provides a last refuge for a bee. The Ligurian bee, introduced from Italy in 1881, is now found nowhere else.

Many Australian species, including the ring-tailed possum, platypus, bush turkey, and Cape Barren goose, were brought to the island so they would endure here even if mainland populations dwindled. Most of these newcomers have had little impact on the island's ecology – with one notable exception. In the early 1920s, 18 koalas were shipped over from Victoria; by the 1990s, thriving on the absence of predators and disease and an abundance of their favorite manna gum trees, the population had swelled to around 4,000. Soon they were beginning to eat themselves out of house and home – a large colony could quickly strip the leaves off an entire forest – and by 1996 some were reported to be starving to death. The South Australian government considered a proposal to cull the animals but rejected it following an international outcry, opting instead to trap and neuter as many as possible while deporting others to the mainland.

Around the Coast

Lathami Conservation Park, on the north shore, provides a tantalizing introduction to the island's ecology. The park, which as yet has limited facilities, plays an important role in protecting the endangered glossy black cockatoo. Measuring 20 inches in length and with dusky brown-black plumage, a wide band of red across its long tail, and a crestless head, the cockatoo tends to be elusive. But you may come across the artificial nest boxes set up by dedicated local volunteers, who comb the forests and scrub annually, counting adult cockatoos, juveniles, and nesting cavities in tree trunks. The last census registered nearly 260 adults and 40 chicks. Conservationists have also planted thousands of saplings in recent years, particularly those of the casuarina, the cockatoos' only food supply.

The greatest concentration of wildlife on Kangaroo Island is found at **Flinders Chase National**

Wildflowers (right) bloom on the cliffs of Cape du Couedic as waves pound the shore.

Young kangaroos (opposite, above) practice fighting. Adult males may battle to the death for mating rights over females.

Cape Barren geese (opposite, below) were hunted almost to extinction in the early 20th century, but now thrive.

Park. Established in 1919, it encompasses the entire west coast and a total of 17 percent of the island's landmass. The park is home to 443 species of native plants – including acacias, banksias, tea trees, several kinds of eucalyptus, and more than 50 species of orchids – and some 130 species of birds. A number of reptiles also thrive here, including black tiger snakes and pygmy copperheads, as well as the heath goanna, a fearsome-looking monitor lizard that grows to around 5½ feet in length. Many animals are so tame that

Close Encounters

Beyond the sand dunes, dark shapes loom on an expanse of white-sand beach, some of them swaying in time to the waves that crash on the shore. Screeching seagulls soar overhead, and the air is heavy with the odor of fish and seaweed. Walk into **Seal Bay Conservation Park**, on the southern shore of Kangaroo Island, and you enter the domain of the Australian sea lion. Once hunted mercilessly for its blubber, this is now the world's rarest member of the seal family, with a world population of only 12,000. Home to 600 individuals, Seal Bay is not merely one of the best places to observe these majestic creatures – it is the only place in the world where they tolerate human visitors.

There are two ways of viewing the colony: strolling on your own along a raised boardwalk that winds through the dunes or joining a ranger-led walk along the shoreline. Guides constantly monitor the behavior of the animals and keep visitors at an appropriate distance.

At any one time, the beach and dunes may be studded with up to 100 animals. The adult males, with their distinctive cream manes, are more massive than the females. Unlike most seal species, which breed annually, Australian sea lions reproduce every 18 months, with most of the colony's females giving birth around the same time. Adults usually spend three days at sea feeding before returning to rest for three days, while their pups – small, dark parcels of wriggling fat – are often left to fend for themselves. When a mother returns to land, she is utterly exhausted but hauls herself across the beach, howling for her young. Reunited with her offspring, she slumps down on the sand, and almost at once the relieved youngster snuggles to her chest and begins to suckle contentedly.

Sea lions (above) feed mainly on fish and squid. In turn, they are preyed upon by sharks.

Fairy penguins (below) nest in burrows. They are the only penguins that breed on the Australian mainland.

of the Wilderness Protection Area before looping west past coastal caves. Allow four hours for the return trip.

Seal Caves and Penguin Rookeries

The island's most impressive coastal scenery is found at **Cape du Couedic** at the southern tip of Flinders Chase, where millions of years of crashing waves have created curious structures, such as the aptly named **Remarkable Rocks**. Here, giant boulders, colored orange by lichens and leached iron and sculpted by wind and sea, balance on top of a massive granite dome. Nearby, the hollowed-out limestone promontory called **Admirals Arch** is the eroded remains of a giant sea cave. Standing beneath the arch amid the skeletal remains of stalactites, you can observe some of the island's 4,000-strong colony of New Zealand fur seals frolicking in the rock pools below.

Caves are the main attraction in neighboring **Kelly Hill Conservation Park**, where coastal heaths and dunes conceal an extensive system of 140,000-year-old limestone chambers. The system was first discovered in the 1880s by a stockman when his horse,

fences have had to be set up around picnic grounds to give visitors some respite from their frequent approaches.

North of the **Rocky River**, where patient observers may catch a glimpse of the elusive platypus, eucalypt woodlands shroud a rugged plateau. To the south, the land is thick with stands of stunted mallee, a low-growing eucalypt, which blend into heathland near the limestone cliffs of the coast. Most of the park's trails are short walks through coastal heath and scrub. One exception is the challenging **Ravine des Casoars** wilderness hike. It leads southwest from a parking lot off the **Playford Highway** into the eucalypt forests

Kelly, fell into a sinkhole. Tours of the caves, with their extraordinary calcite formations in myriad shades of orange, red, and brown, are conducted daily, and the park can also organize adventure caving trips on request.

Heath goannas (left) are carnivores. They can move surprisingly fast and even stand on two legs.

The Remarkable Rocks (below) have been shaped by wind and water and colored by lichens and minerals.

Farther east, birders will be drawn to **Murray Lagoon**, on the northern edge of **Cape Gantheaume Conservation Park**. The largest lagoon on the island, it is an important habitat for thousands of waterbirds, including ducks, swans, and waders. The **Timber Creek Trail** offers an easy one-hour stroll along the lagoon shores.

No island tour is complete without a visit to the fairy penguin rookeries near the settlements of **Penneshaw** and **Kingscote**. Also known as the little penguin, this is the smallest of the 18 species of penguin. Weighing only 2.2 pounds and standing just 13 inches high, it has short, black, flipperlike wings, a snow-white front, and pale, webbed feet with long black toenails. The best time to observe these birds is at dusk, when they return to

land after a hard day's fishing. Guided walks depart each evening from the towns' interpretive centers. Viewing in the company of a ranger means not only that you receive an informed commentary; it also helps park authorities prevent inadvertent damage to the birds or their habitat.

Staggering out of the surf, the penguins form a comical procession. Wagging their wings for balance, they waddle up the shore, ignoring the onlookers, before plunging into their burrows and disappearing from sight. It's experiences like this that highlight the significance of Kangaroo Island, both as a sanctuary of inestimable value for an extraordinary range of species and as an incomparable destination for ecotravelers.

TRAVEL TIPS

DETAILS

When to Go

The best time to visit Kangaroo Island is between November and March (though accommodations can be difficult to find over the Christmas holiday). July and August tend to be rainy, and winter can be cold, though often milder than on the mainland around Adelaide. Although the island has plenty to offer year-round, wildlife is generally most visible during the winter and in summer, during the cooler times of the day; September through October is the best time to view the island's delightful wildflowers.

How to Get There

Kendell Airlines, tel: 08-8231 9567, offers daily services from Adelaide to Kingscote, the island's principal town. The flight takes about 25 minutes. An Airport Shuttle Service, tel: 08-8553 2390, meets all flights and can transport visitors from Kingscote Airport to their Kingscote accommodations. Car rentals are available at the airport.

For those who prefer to travel by sea, Kangaroo Island SeaLink, tel: 08-8553 1122, operates two oceangoing vehicle and passenger ferries from Cape Jervis, on the tip of the South Australian mainland, to Penneshaw on Kangaroo Island. There are several departures daily, depending on demand. The trip takes around 40 minutes, and there is a connecting bus service from Adelaide to Cape Jervis.

Special Planning

At 96 miles long and up to 34 miles wide (155 by 55 km), Kangaroo Island is bigger than many visitors expect. Those wanting to explore the island at a leisurely pace should plan to stay at least two days. Though paved roads link the main towns and attractions, the island's minor roads are gravel and can be slippery. Visitors using unpaved roads should reduce speed and drive with caution.

At times, cool ocean breezes make windproof clothing necessary, while central areas of the island occasionally experience temperatures of 95°F to 104°F (35°–40°C). Come prepared with layered clothing.

Permits and Entry Fees

Entry fees apply to the island's national parks and reserves. Visitors may pay individual tour and entrance fees as they go, or they can purchase an Island Parks Pass from any of the island's National Parks and Wildlife South Australia offices or sites, or from the Gateway Visitor Information Centre in Penneshaw.

INFORMATION

The Kangaroo Island Gateway Visitor Information Centre

P.O. Box 336VG, Penneshaw, SA 5222; tel: 08-8553 1185; web: www.tourkangarooisland.com.au or e-mail: tourki@kin.on.net

National Parks and Wildlife South Australia, Kangaroo Island

Regional Office, P.O. Box 39, Kingscote, SA 5223; tel: 08-8553 2381.

CAMPING

Camping is allowed only at designated sites; the major location is at Rocky River in Flinders Chase National Park. Permits are essential and are available from park offices.

LODGING

Graydon Holiday Lodge

16 Buller Street, Kingscote, SA 5223; tel 08-8553 2713.

This lodge has seven fairly basic self-contained, two-bedroom units sleeping up to six. It's a minute's stroll to the waterfront and a five-minute walk to the center of Kingscote. There are barbecue and laundry facilities on the premises. $$

The Open House

70 Smith Street, Parndana, SA 5221; tel: 08-8559 6113; e-mail: walls@arcom.com.au

Of the four homey rooms here, two have double beds, one has a queen-sized bed, another has two singles, and the last is a family room sleeping up to four. The owners are friendly, and meals are eaten around a communal table with plenty of wine. $$–$$$

Ozone Hotel

P.O. Box 145, Kingscote, SA 5223; tel: 08-8553 2011; web: www.ozonehotel.com or e-mail: general@ozonehotel.com

The Ozone gets its name from the aroma of the sea, which virtually laps at its door. The hotel's 36 rooms are comfortable and large, some with good views of the bay. There is a restaurant with an à la carte menu, a casual bistro serving good meals, two bars, a game room, a pool and sauna, and a laundry. $$

Wanderers Rest

P.O. Box 34, American River, SA 5221; tel: 08-8553 7140; web: www.wanderersrest.com.au or e-mail: wanderers@kin.on.net

Set on a hillside with panoramic views across the sea to the mainland, this nine-room hotel offers large, comfortably furnished

rooms with balconies and private showers. Facilities include a pool and spa in the garden and a game room. A full breakfast is included in the price, and packed lunches are available. Dinner is optional and is served in the communal dining room. Children must be 12 or older, and smoking is not allowed. $$

TOURS & OUTFITTERS

Adventure Charters of Kangaroo Island
P.O. Box 169, Kingscote, SA 5223; tel: 08-8553 9119; e-mail: wildlife@kin.on.net

The knowledgeable and gregarious Craig Wickham conducts one-day safaris to all the major sites. Tours include flights to and from Adelaide.

Kangaroo Island Odysseys
P.O. Box 494, Penneshaw, SA 5222; tel: 08-8553 1294; e-mail: annah@kin.on.net

This company offers personalized soft-adventure, wildlife, and nature tours by four-wheel-drive vehicle lasting from one to four days.

Kangaroo Island Wilderness Tours
P.O. Box 84, Parndana, SA 5220; tel: 08-8559 2220; e-mail: kitours@ozemail.com.au

These highly informative one-day tours in small four-wheel-drive vehicles seating a maximum of six people include park entry fees and an excellent lunch. Two-, three-, and four-day trips, with all meals and accommodations included, are also available.

Excursions

Coffin Bay National Park
Department for Environment, Heritage, and Aboriginal Affairs, P.O. Box 22, Port Lincoln, SA 5606; tel. 08-8688 3111.

Set 440 miles (700 km) west of Adelaide, this beautiful park preserves 75,038 acres of coastal wilderness on the Great Australian Bight. Many species of seabirds, including reef herons and white-bellied sea-eagles, nest here, and the park is also home to brumbies (wild horses). In spring and summer, wildflowers carpet the heathlands.

Coorong National Park
National Parks and Wildlife South Australia, Coorong District Office, P.O. Box 105, Meningie, SA 5264; tel: 08-8575 1200.

This giant wetlands area, which hugs the coast for 90 miles (145 km) starting 83 miles (133 km) south of Adelaide, is one of Australia's most impressive waterbird sanctuaries. It is home to 238 species including the Australian pelican, black swan, and  royal spoonbill, and it protects the breeding sites of many of the world's 300 or so remaining hooded plovers. The lakes regularly support up to 120,000 waders and a large population of Cape Barren geese during summer.

Encounter Bay
Victor Harbor Visitor Information Centre, P.O. Box 11, Victor Harbor, SA 5211; tel: 08-8552 5738.

The former whaling center of Victor Harbor on Encounter Bay, 51 miles (82 km) south of Adelaide, is today a prime base for visitors intent on catching sight of southern right whales. Once hunted almost to extinction, the whales have started to recover, and pods of up to 40 now visit the bay between June and September each year. Dolphins, seals, and penguins are also active in the area, and little penguins can be viewed on Granite Island.

The High Country
Victoria

C H A P T E R
15

All around, the landscape is wild and forbidding. Sheer basalt bluffs – folded and uplifted and worn down over eons by wind and rain – rise above an extensive plateau of ground-hugging shrubs and bare rock. A cold wind bowls down from the exposed slopes and ridges, rippling the jackets of a group of weary but exhilarated walkers. From the distance comes the roar of a mountain stream rushing away through a narrow gorge.　◆　The walkers tramp onward across the **Bogong High Plains**, nearing day's end on the **Australian Alps Walking Track**, one of Australia's premier hiking trails. The bluffs give way to rolling hilltops coated with a frost of flowering daisies. Tiny white-browed scrub-wrens and red-breasted flame robins dart past, low to the ground. A crowlike pied currawong eyes the walkers from its perch on a hollow log, its sweet, musical call somehow at odds with its menacing black beak.　◆　The ground becomes boggier and clumps of alpine marsh marigolds appear amid hummocks of sphagnum moss. A spur-winged plover calls to its mate in a piping voice from a shallow depression filled with icy water and flanked by rushes and sedge. Far above, a kestrel hovers. Finally, the walkers reach **Cope Hut**. The accommodation is spartan, with no electricity and few creature comforts, but the walkers are grateful for their simple beds.　◆　Australia's highest mountains, the **Australian Alps** run parallel to the southeastern coast of the continent, stretching from **Canberra**, the national capital, in the north down through southern New South Wales (where they are known as the Snowy Mountains) and westward across the Victorian **High Country** to the

Hikers exploring Australia's highest range encounter a fascinating array of specialized animals from alpine lizards to rare marsupials.

In winter, when the upland walking trails are blanketed with snow, it's mainly skiers and climbers that venture onto the Bogong High Plains.

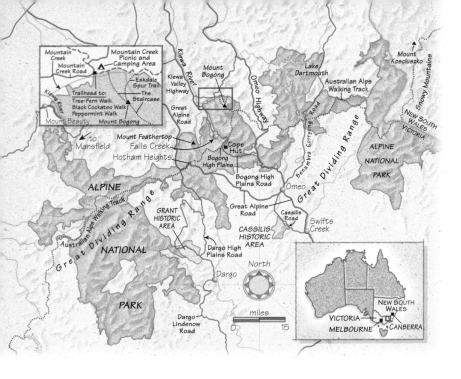

Map labels: Mountain Creek, Mountain Creek Picnic and Camping Area, Mountain Creek Road, Eskdale Spur Trail, The Staircase, Kiewa Valley Highway, Mount Bogong, Kiewa River, Lake Dartmouth, Mount Kosciuszko, Australian Alps Walking Track, Snowy Mountains, Omeo Highway, Trailhead to: Tree-Fern Walk, Black Cockatoo Walk, Peppermint Walk, Kiewa River, Great Alpine Road, Mount Beauty, Mount Bogong, to Mansfield, Mount Feathertop, Falls Creek, Hotham Heights, Cope Hut, Bogong High Plains, Bogong High Plains Road, Benambra Corryong Road, Great Dividing Range, NEW SOUTH WALES, VICTORIA, ALPINE NATIONAL PARK, Omeo, Great Alpine Road, ALPINE, Australian Alps Walking Track, Great Dividing Range, GRANT HISTORIC AREA, Great Alpine Road, Cassilis Road, CASSILIS HISTORIC AREA, Swifts Creek, NATIONAL, Dargo High Plains Road, North, PARK, Dargo, miles, 0, 15, Dargo-Lindenow Road, Dargo Lindenow Road, NEW SOUTH WALES, VICTORIA, MELBOURNE, CANBERRA

correspondingly varied plant and animal life. In all, the Australian Alps support more than 40 species of native mammals, about 200 species of birds, 30 types of reptiles, 15 species of frogs, 14 kinds of native fish, and countless insects.

Historic Trails

Alpine National Park encompasses 2,490 square miles of Victoria's share of the range. This is the state's largest park – it stretches along the **Great Dividing Range** from the outskirts of Mansfield in the west to the New South Wales border in the east, and it incorporates the state's tallest mountains: **Mount Bogong** at 6,516 feet and **Mount Feathertop** at 6,306 feet.

Walking trails criss-cross much of the park, taking visitors from the lowlands to the highest plains. Most were formed by settlers who first moved into the area in the 1830s. By the 1880s, the springtime cattle drive up the mountains had become a well-established practice, and stockmen had built numerous huts, many of which still dot the area. Even today, grazing is permitted in parts of the park. Some 3,000 cattle are walked up along the stock routes into the Bogong High Plains just before Christmas and left to feed on the grasses for the remainder of the summer. Around Easter, when the weather turns cold, the annual muster begins.

northeastern fringe of **Melbourne**. The mountains are diminutive by world standards – the tallest peaks barely rise above 6,500 feet – but loom large in a country characterized by flat terrain.

The highest parts of the range are much cooler and wetter than the rest of Australia, and they remain under snow for about four months of the year. Such conditions, combined with the mountains' geographical isolation, present major challenges to plant and animal life and have resulted in a high degree of specialization – a significant number of the Alps' plants and animals occur nowhere else. The lower slopes and sheltered valleys encompass diverse habitats, including dense forests and open, grassy woodlands.

The wide variety of vegetation across the range, along with changing weather conditions, give rise to

Gang-gang cockatoos (left) winter on the plains, returning to the Alps in summer to nest in tree hollows.

On the lower slopes and tableland areas of the Alps, the trails lead through grassy woodlands inhabited by fan-tailed cuckoos and yellow-faced honeyeaters, and open forests of mountain swamp gum and narrow- and broadleaved peppermint. In spring, these forests are vibrant with the yellow blooms of Ovens wattle. Above, on the wetter montane slopes, higher rainfall results in thicker vegetation. Eucalypts such as brittle gum, blue gum, and mountain grey gum stand proud above a dense understory of tree ferns.

To sample this varied scenery, hike the trails that depart from the **Mountain Creek Picnic and Camping Area** at the base of Mount Bogong, where boisterous gang-gang cockatoos and crimson rosellas forage for visitors' scraps. The 1¼-mile (3-km) **Tree-Fern Walk** heads east along a creek before crossing a footbridge and linking up with the Mountain Creek four-wheel-drive track. At this point, you can return to the picnic area via the four-wheel-drive track or continue eastward along **Black Cockatoo Walk**, named for the large parrots that excavate holes in the tree trunks in search of moth larvae. This trail also rejoins the Mountain Creek track.

Peppermint Walk traces a semicircle on the southern side of the four-wheel-drive track. It meanders through peppermint forest

On high peaks (left), few plants grow and walkers often have to scramble over bare rock.

Horseback-riding tours (below) offer adventure and intriguing insights into the lives of the region's pioneers.

before skirting a ferny creek and leading back to the picnic area. Watch out for swamp wallabies and eastern grey kangaroos near the creek. If you are lucky, you may spot a common wombat waddling through the peppermint trees. These forests are also home to small nocturnal mammals that remain hidden by day, including the rare smoky mouse, the long-nosed bandicoot, and carnivorous marsupials such as the brown and Swainson's antechinus, and the tiger quoll, sometimes referred to as the native cat.

The 2½-mile (4-km) **Eskdale Spur Trail** climbs higher through forests dominated by alpine ash, also known as woollybutt

Higher still, above 4,500 feet, you reach the alpine zone, where even in summer the temperature barely rises above 50°F (10°C) and the severe winters prevent any tree growth. In places, the cold air regularly drains into basinlike valleys, creating unusual treeless bowls ringed by snow gums.

The best way to experience this environment is to hike part of the **Australian Alps Walking Track**, a fully signposted 400-mile trail that runs almost the entire length of the range from Walhalla in Victoria's south to Tharwa near Canberra. The most popular section stretches 15½ miles (25 km) across the Bogong High Plains, from Cope Hut, near Falls Creek, to Mount Bogong. That may not seem a great distance, but count on three days and two nights to complete the one-way trip. You can break your trek by camping out in the bush or in one of the basic huts, but you need to be completely self-sufficient and prepared for cold weather.

because of its rough, fibrous bark. Scan the trees early in the morning or at dusk and you may spot common brushtail and ringtail possums, or, if you're very lucky, a rare Leadbetter's possum. Measuring only 12 inches, half of which is its tail, this small marsupial is found only in this region.

Creatures of the Heights

Above 3,800 feet, the scenery changes abruptly, and you find yourself tramping through sparse forests of stunted and twisted snow gums, carpeted with low-growing shrubs, grasses, and herbs. In early and midsummer, the white flowers of the mint bush and rare light-blue ufrasias bloom in profusion.

A joey (top) peers from its mother's pouch, where it will remain for about 300 days.

Bogong moths (right) undertake a remarkable summer migration from eastern Australia to the High Country.

Flight of the Bogong

The Bogong moth is hardly a beauty – but boy, does it taste good. For millennia, this two-inch, light brown to dark grey moth, with its distinctive arrow-shaped marking, was an important food source for the region's indigenous peoples.

Today, millions of bogong moths still emerge from burrows in the ground across the pastureland of eastern New South Wales and southern Queensland, where as caterpillars they fed on broad-leaved weeds and cereal, linseed, and vegetable crops. At the height of summer, when temperatures are uncomfortably hot, they take to the air in thick, dark clouds and head for the High Country. Those that make it to the mountains congregate around the area of Mount Bogong, where they seek cool caves and crevices in the rock. There they rest in thick clusters, each moth with its head under the wings of the one in front, until the fall, when they begin the return journey.

Countless generations of Aborigines trekked to the mountains every year from far and wide to collect and feast on the moths and to mark the occasion with ceremonies. Using a smoldering piece of brushwood, they would knock the moths into a container made of bark or kangaroo skin, or a net made of kurrajong fiber. The Bogongs were then roasted in hot ashes to separate the bodies from the wings and legs, and the fleshy parts were mashed up to make nutty-tasting "moth meat."

A dusting of snow drapes the mountaintops (right). Visitors must be prepared for sudden weather changes.

Only one mammal, the rare mountain pygmy-possum, is restricted to the alpine and subalpine zone. This resilient creature, one of the smallest of all marsupials, is also the only marsupial that stores food to last it through winter. It was thought to be extinct and known only from fossils, until a live specimen was discovered in 1966. Only about 3,000 survive in the Bogong area, and they remain vulnerable to foxes and cats. Other members of the alpine mammal community include the bush rat, which lives in a grass-lined burrow beneath a rock or log, and the broad-toothed rat, once widespread throughout southern and southeastern Australia but now found only in scattered areas.

Even on the highest peaks, you'll come across lizards and snakes basking in the summer sunshine. Remarkably, the Victorian High Country has some of the highest densities of reptiles recorded anywhere in Australia, with tree dragons, skinks, the southern blue-tongue lizard, and the copperhead snake being particularly common. Many lizards spend the winter massed together in hollow logs or hibernating under boulders deep beneath the snow.

A detour off the track, known as **The Staircase**, leads to the summit of Mount Bogong. Though this trail is only five miles long, parts of it are steep, especially the last half-mile, and with little more than rocks covering the summit, it's quite exposed. It's worth the effort, however, for the magnificent panorama, extending across the high ridges and down to the distant plains, encompassing almost the whole of this extraordinary alpine wilderness.

TRAVEL TIPS

DETAILS

When to Go

During winter, the average daily temperature is 28°F (–2.2°C). In summer, it rises to 50°F (10°C), but be prepared for nights that drop below freezing and days that reach highs of up to 104°F (40°C). The High Country is famous for its skiing; the ski season runs from the end of June to the end of September. Bush walkers should head to the High Country between late October and early April.

How to Get There

Albury Airport, just over the border in New South Wales, is a 90-minute drive from the High Country. Flights from Melbourne to Albury take 45 minutes; from Sydney the flight is about 75 minutes. Car rentals and a shuttle bus to Falls Creek are available at the airport. The drive to Falls Creek from Melbourne takes around four to five hours. The drive from Sydney takes eight hours. Between early June and late September, flights are available from Melbourne and Sydney to Hottram Heights.

Special Planning

Warm clothing is essential year-round. During winter, driving can be hazardous and snow chains must be carried. In summer, temperatures soar by day and dip below freezing at night, so hikers should come prepared with a tent, camping stove, sleeping bag, and plenty of water.

Permits and Entry Fees

No entrance fees are charged, and no special permits are required.

INFORMATION

Bright Visitor Information Centre

119 Gavan Street, Bright, Vic 3741; tel: 03-5755 2275; e-mail: brightbc@netc.net.au

Falls Creek Information Centre

1 Bogong High Plains Road, Falls Creek, Vic 3699; tel: 03-5758 3490; web: www.skifallscreek.com.au or e-mail: fallsinfo@fallscreek.albury.net.au

High Country Information Centre

Bogong High Plains Road, Mount Beauty, Vic 3699; tel: 03-5754 4531 or 1800 808 277 (in Australia).

Mount Hotham Resort Management

Great Alpine Road, Mount Hotham, Vic 3741; tel: 03-5759 3550; web: www.mthotham.com.au or e-mail: mhar@netc.net.au

CAMPING

Bush camping is permitted throughout the park, but fires are not allowed on Mount Feathertop and Mount Bogong. The Mountain Creek Picnic and Camping Area is at the base of Mount Bogong. Most hotels and all the information centers supply maps of the camping areas. Though the huts along the High Country trails can be used for temporary shelter, walkers must carry camping gear with them. For environmental guidelines, call Parks Victoria, tel: 03-5755 1577, or 131 963 in Australia.

LODGING

Attunga Alpine Lodge and Apartments

10 Arlberg Street, Falls Creek, Vic 3699; tel: 03-5758 3255; web: www.attungalodge.com.au or e-mail: enquiries@attungalodge.com.au

Attunga offers both deluxe and standard lodge rooms sleeping up to four people, as well as self-contained apartments sleeping between six and eight. Attractions include a bar, fabulous views, and a sauna and swimming pool. $$–$$$

Feathertop Lodge

Parallel Street, P.O. Box 259, Falls Creek, Vic 3699; tel: 03-5758 3232; web: www.ski.com.au/feathertop or e-mail: feathertop@fallscreek.albury.net.au

This pleasant old-fashioned ski lodge is nestled among the gum trees and offers good views from several of its 13 rooms, which are functional yet cozy. Facilities include a bar, library, sauna, swimming pool, and restaurant. $$–$$$

Mount Buffalo Chalet

Mount Buffalo National Park, Vic 3740; tel: 03-5755 1500 or 1-800 037 038 (in Australia); web: www.mtbuffalochalet.com.au or e-mail: buffaloc@netc.net.au

Built in 1910, this enormous rambling wooden guesthouse has 97 rooms decorated in a 1930s style. Front rooms offer extensive views across the valley below. There's a large lounge room with an open fireplace, restaurant, sauna and spa, tennis courts, and bar. In summer, the chalet offers canoeing, mountain biking, and rappelling. $$$–$$$$

Summit Ridge Alpine Lodge

6 Schuss Street, Falls Creek, Vic 3699; tel: 03-5758 3800; web: www.fallscreek.albury.net.au/sumridge or e-mail: sumridge@fallscreek.albury.net.au

This upmarket property has pleasant rooms, a large lounge

and dining room on the ground floor, and a small library on the second. $$$–$$$$

TOURS & OUTFITTERS

Bogong Horseback Adventures

P.O. Box 230, Mount Beauty, Vic 3690; tel: 03-5754 4849; web: www.bogonghorse.com.au or e-mail: sbaird@albury.net.au

Trail rides tour the national park in summer and visit the Kiewa Valley year-round.

Ecotrek

P.O. Box 4, Kangarilla, SA 5157; tel: 08-8383 7198; web: www.ecotrek.com.au or e-mail: ecotrek@ozemail.com.au

Five treks are offered, including an eight-day Bogong Alpine Traverse leaving from Melbourne, with four nights' camping and three nights in ski lodges; an eight-day Alpine Ramble based at Falls Creek ski lodge; and a five-day "Walking in the Crosscut Saw" trek. A six-day summer alpine bicycle tour is also offered.

Pyles Coaches

233 Kiewa Valley Highway, Tawonga South, Vic 3698; tel: 03-5754 4024; web: www.buslines. com.au/pyles or e-mail: pyles@mtbeauty. albury.net.au

This company provides regular bus transport to Falls Creek from Melbourne and Albury. In the summer months, it also conducts informative four-wheel-drive tours of the High Country, with an emphasis on destinations of historical and geographical interest.

Excursions

Brindabella National Park

National Parks and Wildlife Service, P.O. Box 1189, Queanbeyan, NSW 2620; tel: 02-6299 2929; web: www.npws.nsw.gov.au

Brindabella is the northernmost park in the Australian Alps. Encompassing 46 square miles, it is particularly significant as a travel corridor for native animals. Vulnerable species such as the powerful owl, common bent-wing bat, yellow-bellied glider, and koala occur here, while other rare or uncommon species, including the peregrine falcon and the alpine tea-tree, are found at the park's northern limits.

Kosciuszko National Park

National Parks and Wildlife Service, P.O. Box 2228, Jindabyne, NSW 2627; tel: 02-6450 5600; web: www.npws.nsw. gov.au or e-mail: frvc@npws.nsw. gov.au

Kosciuszko is one of the country's best-known parks, attracting around three million visitors each year. It contains the mainland's only glacial lakes, as well as limestone caves, grasslands, heaths, woodlands, and Australia's highest mountain – 7,308-foot Mount Kosciuszko. Unusual wildlife includes the mountain pygmy-possum and the endangered northern corroboree frog. Spring brings a profusion of exquisite wildflowers, including many alpine species.

Mount Buffalo National Park

P.O. Box 72, Porepunkah, Vic 3740; tel: 03-5755 1466.

Imposing granite tors, tumbling waterfalls, snow gums, and colorful wildflowers are some of the prime natural features of this 120-sq.-mile park. There are more than 56 miles (90 km) of well-marked trails, ranging from short nature walks to more challenging treks. The 45-minute walk to Eurobin Falls is a fine introduction and offers visitors a chance to see swamp wallabies grazing among the ferns.

Cradle Mountain–
Lake St. Clair
National Park
Tasmania

C H A P T E R 16

aught in the bright beam of a hiker's flashlight, the nocturnal eastern quoll twitches its moist red nose before bounding up the ghostly trunk of a snow gum. Though preferring to hunt at ground level, this cat-sized carnivorous marsupial with glossy black fur and white spots is an agile climber, and the hiker has a hard time keeping it in view.   ◆   From the safety of a high branch, the quoll pauses to study the group of observers standing in the tussock grass and sedge at the tree's base. Its jaws open slightly, revealing sharp canine teeth – perfect for disposing of birds, insects, rabbits, and small marsupials. A wriggling movement from beneath its belly and a row of glowing red eyes indicate that it is a female with young. At three months old, the babies are too big for the pouch and dangle precariously from their mother's teats. Just to reach this stage they've fought a battle for survival: the quoll produces up to 30 rice-grain-sized young but can feed only six. Two months from now, these quolls will be almost fully grown

A challenging trail traverses an incomparable mountain kingdom where platypuses inhabit icy pools flanked by ancient native pines.

and completely independent; at 10 months, they themselves will begin to breed.   ◆   The eastern quoll was once common across much of eastern New South Wales, Victoria, and southeastern South Australia. But like Australia's other quoll species, it was harried and hunted by settlers determined to rid the country of native animals with a liking for poultry. Eastern quoll populations were further decimated by parasites contracted from domestic cats, habitat loss, and predation by foxes, and eventually the species became extinct on the mainland. It now survives only on the island of Tasmania, where it finds a refuge in the island's large areas of fox-free wilderness.

Richea plants abound on the rich quartzite soils of Cradle Valley. Many of Tasmania's plants are Gondwanan relicts related to species in New Zealand and South America.

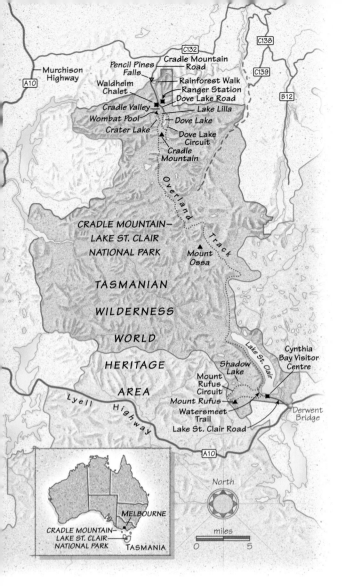

Tasmanian mountain shrimps (left) evolved during an ice age over 200 million years ago. They are endemic to the island.

made it a haven for numerous species that have died out or struggled to survive in other parts of Australia. As a result, it is home to a broad range of plant and animal species found nowhere else on Earth.

Much of the island's extraordinary ecology is protected by the Tasmanian Wilderness World Heritage Area, which encompasses around one-fifth of the entire state – from the central highlands to the southwest coast – and incorporates five national parks. Easily the most accessible of these parks is **Cradle Mountain–Lake St. Clair National Park**, one of Australia's most spectacular wilderness areas. Its distinctive upland landscape blends typical alpine features, such as tarns, cirques, glacial valleys, and jagged peaks, with lush and varied vegetation including stands of alpine ash, stringybark, and yellow gums, temperate rain forest dominated by myrtle beech, and forests of native pines. Many of the plants, such as pandanus and celery top pine, are Gondwanan relict species closely related to other flora found in southern New Zealand and Chile.

Cradle Mountain–Lake St. Clair's rugged scenery had its origins in sediments of silt and sand that accumulated in the area some 1.1 billion years ago. These layers were gradually eroded, exposing strata that are still visible in some parts of the park today. Following an ice age around 290 million years ago, much of the area became part of a flooded river plain, and deposits of limestone, siltstone, and sandstone were laid down. Molten dolerite from deep within Earth's crust then rose through cracks in the rock and pooled in certain areas. The surrounding sediments were subsequently worn away, revealing the distinctive columnar rocks that characterize the park's peaks. During two further ice ages, glaciers scoured the range, forming valleys and lakes, and depositing debris and sediments.

Glacial Wilderness

Opportunities for exploring this intriguing environment abound at **Cradle Valley**, in the north of the park. Several day walks depart from near the park headquarters, including

Tasmania's location, its relatively small human population, the remoteness and ruggedness of many of its natural areas, and its variety of environments – ranging from alpine moorland to vast stretches of eucalypt woodlands and temperate rain forest – have

Eastern quoll babies (left) huddle in a den. Adult quolls continue to hunt in winter, even on snow.

Look here, too, for the Tasmanian mountain shrimp. Found only on the island, this two-inch crustacean is unlike any other shrimp in that it has a straight back rather than a hump and a body divided into 14 sections. Unchanged for more than 200

the easy 0.3-mile (500-meter) **Rainforest Walk** across a small buttongrass plain and alongside a beautiful myrtle forest with a damp and dimly lit moss-covered floor.

The buttongrass plains of the highlands are often studded with water-filled hollows. Peer into these stagnant pools and you might come across a yabbie, a red-to-pale-blue freshwater crayfish, four to six inches long, that inhabits small underwater burrows.

This thylacine skull (above, right) clearly shows the animal's powerful jaws.

Last pictured in captivity (below), the thylacine is thought to be extinct, though sightings are occasionally reported.

million years, the Tasmanian mountain shrimp is almost identical to fossils found in Europe and North America.

The Rainforest Walk continues through eucalypt forest, where walkers are often

Last of the Tigers?

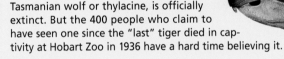

The Tasmanian tiger, also known as the Tasmanian wolf or thylacine, is officially extinct. But the 400 people who claim to have seen one since the "last" tiger died in captivity at Hobart Zoo in 1936 have a hard time believing it.

A lightly built, dog-sized marsupial, the tiger was common throughout mainland Australia and New Guinea until about 4,000 years ago, when competition from the dingo resulted in its extinction. It continued to thrive for a time in Tasmania, but with the introduction of sheep to the island in 1824, a bounty was placed on the tiger's head by farmers. By 1910, thylacines were so rare that zoos around the world were attempting to breed them. Unfortunately, no captive births ever occurred.

Many Tasmanians are convinced that the tiger lives on in the island's dense forests. They explain the limited number of sightings and lack of visual evidence as a result of the creature's timidity and nocturnal lifestyle, and they point out that its preference for dense forest and the camouflage offered by its dark brown vertical stripes would also make it difficult to spot.

The most recent sighting of this elusive marsupial predator occurred in January 1995, when a Parks and Wildlife Service officer saw one in eastern Tasmania. Unfortunately, he wasn't carrying a camera. In 1999, the Australian Museum in Sydney announced that it plans to clone the Tasmanian tiger from a specimen preserved in alcohol with its DNA intact.

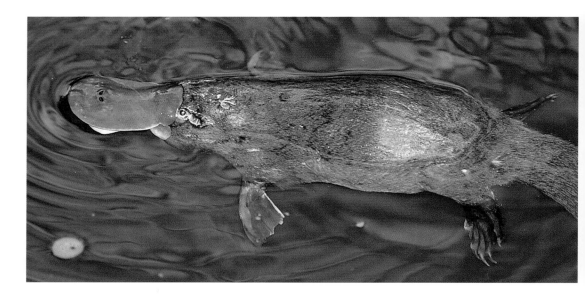

startled by the raucous shrieks of large flocks of black cockatoos or stopped in their tracks by the green rosellas (which are endemic to Tasmania), yellow wattlebirds, and crescent honeyeaters that flit between the flowering trees in spring, feeding on their nectar. The trail ends at **Pencil Pines Falls**, a dramatic 40-foot waterfall surrounded by a forest of pencil pines.

Around the waterways, keep an eye out for the duck-billed platypus. Elusive in other parts of Australia, the platypus is a fairly common sight in Cradle Valley. A bizarre creature, it resembles an otter with a beaver's flat tail, a bare snout shaped like a duck's beak, and webbed feet with long claws. The male is also armed with vicious spurs on its hind limbs, through which it can eject a powerful toxin. The platypus is one of only three monotremes – mammals that lay eggs – in the world (the other two are echidnas). The female incubates the eggs in a burrow, then feeds the young on milk exuded through the skin pores of a mammary patch on her abdomen.

It's not unusual to find the odd rufous wallaby, distinguished by its short ears and tail, grazing alongside the trails here. Ringtail and brush-tailed possums, sugar gliders, broad-toothed rats, and marsupial mice also make these forests their home, though you are unlikely to spot them as all are nocturnal. One nighttime stalker that occasionally hunts by day is the second of Tasmania's two quoll species. Rare on the mainland, the spotted-tailed quoll is relatively abundant in Cradle Valley and is often seen around the forest fringe. Identified by its fawn-colored, white-spotted fur, it's the largest of the quolls: a male can weigh as much as 7.7 pounds, more than 50 percent heavier than males of other quoll species.

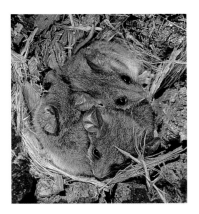

The platypus (opposite) has sensors in its bill that detect electrical charges generated by prey.

Little pygmy-possums (right) are the smallest pygmy-possums, measuring just 2½ inches, excluding the tail.

The park's temperate rain forests (below) are swathed in a thick growth of mosses and lichens.

To experience the ice-carved rockscape and alpine vegetation that typify the park's upland areas, take the three-mile trail to **Lake Lilla** and **Dove Lake** that departs from **Waldheim Chalet**. An easy, three-hour amble, the walk initially follows gravel tracks and boardwalks to the quiet shores of pretty little **Wombat Pool**, located high on a ridge. It then descends through snow gums to Lake Lilla, and onward through mixed eucalypt forest to Dove Lake. Walkers are rewarded with a splendid view across the lake to Cradle Mountain. Sharp-eyed observers may spot water rats – semi-aquatic creatures with white-tipped tails – in and around both lakes.

Ideal for a day when the clouds are hanging low is the **Dove Lake Circuit**, which takes around two hours to complete. The trail skirts the lakeshore, then passes through alpine forest and under the steep slopes of Cradle Mountain before returning to the Dove Lake car park. Along the first part of the walk, you're likely to be mobbed by wallabies looking for a snack. Don't be tempted to feed them, as certain human foods can cause blindness in these lactose-intolerant marsupials.

Several day walks also depart from the **Cynthia Bay Visitor Centre** near **Lake St. Clair**, at the southern end of the park. The most popular is the **Watersmeet Trail**, a one-and-a-half-hour loop that passes through eucalypt forest and temperate rain forest and skirts a beach where platypuses are often observed. For a longer adventure, visitors can catch a ferry to the top of the lake and return along the five-hour lakeside trail or take the three-hour return trail to picturesque **Shadow Lake**, nestled in a cirque. For superb views of the Lake St. Clair area as well as parts of the Franklin–Gordon Wild Rivers National Park to the south, follow the **Mount Rufus Circuit**, a six-hour return hike to the summit of the 4,649-foot mountain of the same name.

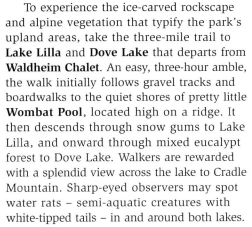

Ways of the Devil

For many of us, the name "Tasmanian devil" conjures up a snarling, spinning, cartoon creature. The living counterpart of the Warner Brothers creation isn't big and brown and doesn't travel like a tornado, but it is partial to rabbits and does have a fearsome reputation.

The largest living marsupial carnivore, the Tasmanian devil is the size of a small, stoutly built dog and has a distinctively large head, powerful jaws, and strong teeth. Its jet-black fur is usually marked with white on the chest and sometimes the rump. Though scabs and scars attest to its quarrelsome nature, it is harmless to humans.

Once found throughout Australia, the species disappeared from the mainland following the arrival of the dingo and is now restricted to Tasmania, which remains dingo-free. With their characteristic loping gait, devils emerge from their lairs after dark to hunt wallabies, possums, and wombats, which they kill with a powerful and tenacious bite to the head or chest. Their strong sense of smell also allows them to find and scavenge any dead animals, ranging from beached fish to roadkill (including rabbits).

Devils often feed in groups – a noisy affair accompanied by jostling, ritualized displays of teeth, and varied vocalizations ranging from soft barks and snorts to monotone growls and eerie screams. Tasmania's smaller carnivores, the quolls, often wait patiently beside a wombat carcass until a devil arrives to crunch its way through the particularly tough hide. As soon as the devil moves away, the quolls nip in to claim their share.

Tasmanian devils (left) travel up to 5 miles (8 km) a night in search of prey.

The Overland Track (below) is one of Australia's most exciting and challenging long-distance trails.

Going the Distance

For serious hikers, the highlight of any visit to Cradle Mountain is the **Overland Track**, one of Australia's best-known and most popular long-distance walks. Stretching 53 miles from **Cradle Valley** to **Cynthia Bay** on Lake St. Clair, the trail takes five to eight days to complete (depending on how many side trips you take) and allows you to experience the full gamut of Cradle Mountain's habitats. Rudimentary huts located every 11 miles (18 km) or so divide the trail into five sections and provide basic accommodations. There are also several bush camping sites along the route, mostly around the huts.

The first part of the trail, to **Crater Lake**, is easy going and can be undertaken as a day hike. Allow two hours for the 2¼-mile (4-km) return trip to the lake and another two hours if you intend to climb **Cradle Mountain**. From the parking lot at Waldheim Chalet, the trail runs along a boardwalk across an open valley, then climbs a lightly timbered spur with a fine view of Cradle Valley. From here, follow the signs to Crater Lake, which was not, as the name implies, formed by volcanic activity but by glacial action. The lake is surrounded by cliffs up to 800 feet high, which are usually reflected in the water's still surface. In fall, the cliffs are clothed in the bright orange and bronze leaves of Tasmania's only endemic deciduous tree, the small, straggly fagus or deciduous beech.

At the boulder-strewn base of Cradle Mountain, walkers can take the first of several side trips – the one-hour hike to the mountain's summit. The climb uphill requires some tricky boulder-hopping, and the peak is famous for its sudden weather changes. But the view from the top is spectacular, encompassing several lakes and much of the plateau below.

From Cradle Mountain, the Overland Track wends its way south over sodden moorland and rocky ridges, past glacial lakes and swathes of dense forest. Around the midpoint, those fond of a challenge can attempt the three-and-a-half-hour side trip to the top of **Mount Ossa**. At 5,305 feet, this mountain is Tasmania's highest peak, and there are dramatic views from its summit across forests of Tasmanian beech and pencil pines.

The epic hike reaches its climax at Lake St. Clair, Australia's deepest. From the top of

Climbing Cradle Mountain (left) involves crossing fields of weathered boulders and can be tough going.

Lake Dove and Cradle Mountain (below) were shaped by glaciers, which retreated 20,000 years ago.

the lake, you can catch a ferry or follow either of two trails to Cynthia Bay. Both skirt shorelines fringed with boulders and sandy beaches, and backed by eucalypts and pencil pines.

By this stage, most walkers are exhausted but also exhilarated and humbled by the majesty of the park's astonishing scenery. What's more, they have acquired a sense of serenity, of peace and calm, that will stay with them for weeks – a sense that only wilderness can bring.

TRAVEL TIPS

DETAILS

When to Go

Visitors to Cradle Mountain–Lake St. Clair National Park should be prepared for cold and wet weather at all times. In January, at the height of summer, the maximum daily average temperature in Cradle Valley is just 62°F (17°C), while it gets close to freezing overnight. In July, expect a maximum daily temperature of 40°F (4.4°C) and an average low of 31°F (–1°C). On average, it rains seven days out of 10, snows 54 days each year, and the sky is completely clear on only one day out of 10. The trekking season extends from October to April. Between June and October, it's sometimes possible to cross-country ski within the park.

How to Get There

There are regular flights from the Australian mainland to Hobart, Launceston, and Devonport. Vehicle rentals are available at the airports. Motorists enter the park via the Lyell Highway from Hobart, via Deloraine or Poatina from Launceston, and via Sheffield or Wilmot from Devonport. TWT Tassie Link, tel: 03-6334 4442, runs buses to Cradle Mountain from Hobart, Launceston, Devonport, and Strahan.

Special Planning

Conditions can change rapidly, so warm clothing, wet-weather gear, and good boots are essential year-round. The Overland Track is particularly busy in January, when as many as 100 walkers set out each day, and it can be difficult to find a camp-site or a bed in a hut.

Permits and Entry Fees

Permits are required for vehicles and individuals entering the park. They are available from the Cradle Mountain Visitor Centre, tel: 03-6492 1133.

INFORMATION

Cradle Mountain Visitor Centre
P.O. Box 20, Sheffield, Tas 7306; tel: 03-6492 1133; web: www.tourism.tas.gov.au

CAMPING

Cradle Mountain Tourist Park

The only camping in the Cradle Valley area is at Cradle Mountain Tourist Park, tel: 03-6492 1395. There are several marked camp-sites along the Overland Track. Bush camping is not permitted elsewhere in the park.

LODGING

Cradle Mountain Highlanders
P.O. Box 220, Sheffield, Tas 7306; tel: 03-6492 1116; web: www.cradlehighlander.com.au or e-mail: cradle.mt@bigpond.com.au

Located just 1 mile (1.6 km) from the entrance to the national park, these self-contained cabins offer varying degrees of luxury, from spa cabins to simpler family huts. $$–$$$

Cradle Mountain Lodge
G.P.O. Box 478, Sydney, NSW 2001; tel: 03-6492 1303 or 800-225-9849 (toll-free in U.S.); web: www.poresorts.com.au

The 96 comfortable, self-contained cabins at this award-winning lodge all have a pot-bellied stove, an electric heater, a private shower, and a small kitchen. More upmarket cabins have carpets, a spa tub, and a balcony, and some have a separate bedroom. Resort facilities include a dining room, guest lounge, bars, a tavern, and a café. Marsupials, including possums, wombats, Tasmanian devils, wallabies, and quolls, wander throughout the grounds. $$$–$$$$

Lemonthyme Lodge
Off Cradle Mountain Road, Moina via Sheffield, Locked Bag 158, Devonport, Tas 7310; tel: 03-6492 1112; web: www.lemonthyme.com.au or e-mail: lemonthyme@trump.net.au

The largest log cabin in the Southern Hemisphere contains eight sparsely furnished rooms with shared bathrooms. There are also five self-contained two-bedroom cabins, and 14 luxury cabins (seven with spas). All meals are served in a rustic dining room in front of a log fire. $$–$$$$

Waldheim Cabins
Cradle Mountain Visitor Centre, P.O. Box 20, Sheffield, Tas 7306; tel: 03-6492 1110; web: www.parks.tas.gov.au or e-mail: cradle@dpiwe.tas.gov.au

These cabins, run by the Parks and Wildlife Service, are just 3 miles (5 km) from Cradle Mountain Lodge, and are close to the start of many of the park's trails. The eight simple, affordable cabins sleep between two and eight people, and include basic cooking facilities and heating. $$

TOURS & OUTFITTERS

Craclair Tours
P.O. Box 516, Devonport, Tas 7310; tel: 03-6424 7833; web: southcom.com.au/~craclair or e-mail: craclair@southcom.com.au

An eight-day Overland Track tour, including camping and hut accommodations, is offered between October and mid-April. Trips leave Devonport every Sunday and Wednesday.

Cradle Mountain Huts

P.O. Box 1879,
Launceston, Tas 7250;
tel: 03-6331 2006;
web: www.cradlehuts.
com.au or e-mail:
cradle@tassie.net.au

Six-day walking tours
leave every day from
Launceston between
November and May.
This operator has well-
equipped and comfortable huts
on the track featuring showers, a
main living area, a kitchen, and
twin-share accommodations. A
three-course meal is provided
every night.

Seair

P.O. Box 58, Wynyard, Tas 7325;
tel: 03-6492 1132; e-mail:
seaair@bigpond.com.au

Scenic flights tour the World
Heritage Area. The 25-minute
flight takes in Cradle Mountain,
Barn Bluff, Fury Gorge, and Cradle
and Dove Lakes. The popular 50-
minute tour flies over the whole
World Heritage Area, following
the Overland Track from Cradle
Mountain to Lake St. Clair. The
65-minute excursion includes a
flight over the Franklin River,
Frenchmans Cap, Lake Burbury,
and the Eildon Ranges.

Tasmanian Expeditions

110 George Street, Launceston,
Tas 7250; tel: 03-6334 3477 or
1-800 030 230 (in Australia);
web: www.tas-ex.com or e-mail:
tazzie@tassie.net.au

Treks include a three-day walking
tour around Cradle Mountain,
leaving from Launceston and
staying at Waldheim Cabins; an
eight-day hike
along the Overland
Track with six
nights camping;
and a six-day trip to
Cradle Mountain–
Lake St. Clair and
Walls of Jerusalem
National Parks,
including three
nights camping
and three nights
in a cabin.

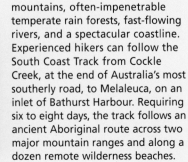

Excursions

Franklin–Gordon National Park

*Parks and Wildlife Service,
P.O. Box 62, Strahan, Tas
7468; tel: 03-6471 7122;
web: www.parks.tas.gov.au*

Encompassing the wild Franklin
and Gordon Rivers, jagged
peaks, and huge areas of pristine temperate rain forest, this
giant park covers 1,698 square miles. A challenging three- to
four-day circuit trail via the dramatic 4,734-foot white quartzite
dome of Frenchmans Cap departs from the Lyell Highway west
of Derwent Bridge. The Franklin offers some of Australia's most
exciting whitewater rafting, while a more sedate day trip on
the tranquil Gordon River departs from Strahan.

Freycinet National Park

*Parks and Wildlife
Service, Private Bag,
Bichenow, Tas 7215;
tel: 03-6257 0107;
web: www.parks.
tas.gov.au or e-mail:
fionaho@dpiwe.
tas.gov.au*

Encompassing 65 square miles on the east coast of Tasmania,
Freycinet is famous for its craggy peaks, spectacular white
beaches, wetlands, heathlands, and dry eucalypt forests. Seals
and dolphins are regularly sighted from land, and migrating
humpback and southern right whales pass close to shore
between May and August. On the popular 6-mile (10-km)
trail to beautiful Wineglass Bay, visitors may spot wallabies,
possums, wattlebirds, and sea eagles.

Southwest National Park

*Parks and Wildlife Service, Station Road, Dover, Tas 7117;
tel: 03-6298 1577; web: www.parks.tas.gov.au*

One of the wildest parts of Australia, this park includes rugged
mountains, often-impenetrable
temperate rain forests, fast-flowing
rivers, and a spectacular coastline.
Experienced hikers can follow the
South Coast Track from Cockle
Creek, at the end of Australia's most
southerly road, to Melaleuca, on an
inlet of Bathurst Harbour. Requiring
six to eight days, the track follows an
ancient Aboriginal route across two
major mountain ranges and along a
dozen remote wilderness beaches.

The Blue Mountains
New South Wales

CHAPTER **17**

A disjointed avian chorus greets the sunrise as the gorge's rough-hewn sandstone cliffs turn from deep magenta to gold. A kookaburra's maniacal laugh, a whipbird's explosive whistle, the sad squeal of a black cockatoo, and the liquid notes of a superb lyrebird follow one another as though the birds were calling in turn. ◆ Two hikers, their breath rising in gilded clouds through the frosty air, sit on the edge of a precipice that drops hundreds of feet to scrub-cloaked scree. Somewhere in the gorge's inky depths, 1,600 feet below their boots, a creek whispers. ◆ For a moment the hikers are duped by the birdsong. But by the third repetition, the kookaburra's laugh is sounding bogus. Then it strikes them: the caller is not a kookaburra at all. Every one of these sounds is coming from the lyrebird. This inveterate mimic often issues a stream of other birds' calls interspersed with its own. And its mimicry doesn't stop there: it has also been heard imitating frogs, dogs, cats, chainsaws, phones, automobile starter motors, and camera motor-drives.

Lofty escarpments, fern-filled canyons, and dense eucalypt forests characterize one of the continent's most spectacular and accessible wilderness areas.

◆ Although the superb lyrebird is common along the southeast coast of Australia, the **Blue Mountains** of southeastern New South Wales are one of its great strongholds, so much so that the region's early settlers named it the Blue Mountains pheasant. ◆ The hikers have come to savor the dawn at **Kanangra Walls**, a magnificently rugged gorge rimmed by walls of sandstone in **Kanangra–Boyd National Park**, in the heart of the mountains. With four other national parks – **Blue Mountains, Wollemi, Nattai,** and **Gardens of Stone** – Kanangra–Boyd protects 3,860 square miles of ancient plateaus,

A walkway links two of the Three Sisters, a trio of sandstone pillars that juts out into the Jamison Valley near the town of Katoomba.

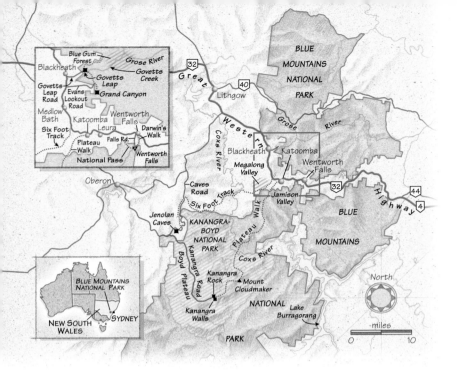

up to 20,000 years by the time the first Europeans arrived in 1788. Yet for more than 20 years, the labyrinthine landscape had the new arrivals baffled, and it wasn't until 1813 that an expedition found a way across the plateau, along a single continuous ridge. A road quickly followed.

Today, a highway and a railway line follow the route of that first road. Strung along this transportation artery are 26 towns and villages, with a combined population of about 75,000. This 60-mile (100-km) urban strip hardly makes a dent in the landscape's savage beauty, but it provides a safe platform from which to appreciate the stupendous setting and to strike out along trails and tracks on foot or mountain bike, or down a cliff on the end of a rope.

spectacular gorges, towering cliffs, plunging waterfalls, and wide, blue-hazed valleys.

There are places here where no human has set foot. Yet, amazingly, the wilderness starts on the western edge of Sydney. From the city center, the mountains look like gentle hills. That's one of their deceptions. Another is that they are not mountains at all but the remnants of a plateau that over eons has been scoured by rivers and creeks. Nor are the "mountains" really blue: their name derives from the blue-tinted haze that often hangs over them, made up of tiny eucalypt-oil droplets emitted by the vegetation.

Aborigines had been crossing the mountains on well-trodden tracks for

Into the Valleys

Begin exploring the Blue Mountains by doing what naturalist Charles Darwin did when he

Blue gum trees (right) line the Grose River near Blackheath. This majestic forest narrowly escaped logging in 1931.

At Wentworth Falls (right), a network of trails extends along the cliffs and down into the Jamison Valley.

visited in 1836. At the village of **Wentworth Falls**, he walked one of the region's first trails to the rim of the **Jamison Valley** and was staggered by the sight that greeted him. "Suddenly & without any preparation, through the trees, which border the pathway, an immense gulf is seen at the depth of perhaps 1,500 feet beneath one's feet," he wrote. Today a network of walking trails, many dating from the 1800s and early 1900s, allows maximum enjoyment of this view south across **Blue Mountains National Park**. You can even follow in the footsteps of the great naturalist himself – on **Darwin's Walk**, an easy one-hour (each way) trail that leads from near the railway station through native bushland to the cliff edge.

One of the outstanding walks here is the **National Pass** trail, named in celebration of the federation of Australia in 1901. The "pass" follows a ledge in the middle of the cliff for nearly four miles, either beginning or ending at the cascades that give the village its name. Whichever end you start at, you can't fail to feel you're flying over the wondrous landscape. Currawongs swoop past at eye level, and pink-and-grey gang-gang cockatoos float over the crinkled green like shadows, their rusty-hinge calls echoing outlandishly. Of the Blue Mountains' 400 animal species, birds are the most conspicuous.

When you're at the falls, look out for a small botanical survivor. The fine spray that drenches the cliffs creates the perfect environment for the rare dwarf pine. Only about 300 specimens remain, and they are all found here. These pines are a relict of the time when Australia was part of the supercontinent of Gondwana, from which it separated about 60 million years ago.

Pockets of Gondwanan vegetation survive throughout the mountains in inaccessible gullies and gorges, and in patches of temperate rain forest that cluster along tumbling creeks. You can get an inkling of what those moister Gondwanan times were like when you descend into the **Grand Canyon**, at **Blackheath**.

Sandstone walls tower 330 feet above the canyon floor, keeping the atmosphere cool and damp. Giant tree ferns catch occasional shafts of sunlight, and in the mossy depths the spotted-tailed quoll, a catlike marsupial, hunts bush rats. Keep a lookout here for yellow-throated scrub wrens, golden whistlers, and yellow robins.

Once out of the canyon, you'll find yourself in a wide valley beneath towering crags. You can continue the circular trip, which takes three to four hours, or carry on into the

gorge of the **Grose River**. While journeying along the ridges on either side of this impressive gorge, Daruk Aborigines would descend into its fertile depths to gather food and camp. Evidence of their visits – grooves in rocks where axes and spears were sharpened, engravings, and the remains of campfires – is everywhere. Several of the steep tracks that hikers use today were undoubtedly routes that the Daruk trod.

On lush flats near the Grose River's junction with **Govetts Creek**, blue gum trees

The superb lyrebird (above) is named for the male's tail feathers, which open to form a shape like a lyre.

Wollemi pines (below) grow in remote valleys of the Blue Mountains; their precise locations are kept secret.

Prehistoric Pine

The Wollemi pine is one of the rarest trees in the world. Found in the wild only in **Wollemi National Park**, it is a member of the ancient conifer family Araucariaceae. These trees were widespread between 200 and 65 million years ago but were dying out in the Northern Hemisphere by the time the dinosaurs disappeared. They held on in Gondwana, and survivors can be found on fragments of the former supercontinent, including South America, Australia, and some Pacific islands.

Until 1994, the Wollemi pine, which grows to 130 feet, was known only from fossils and did not have a name. That year, ranger David Noble rappelled into a gorge in a remote region of the park and found trees unlike any he had seen before. It took scientists weeks to identify them, and when the discovery of an entirely new genus and species was announced, it astounded botanists around the world. The tree was given the scientific name *Wollemia nobilis*, for the park and David Noble.

Counts established that only 38 adult trees and about 200 young ones were growing at two sites, whose exact locations remain a closely guarded secret. However, within weeks of the discoveries, Australia's Royal Botanic Gardens had begun propagating the species at one of its nurseries. Early in 1999, a private company won a contract to cultivate the trees and sell them to the public, with profits going toward research into the pine. Thirteen young Wollemi pines can now be viewed at **Mount Tomah Botanic Gardens** in the Blue Mountains.

grow ramrod-straight to 165 feet or more. This is **Blue Gum Forest**, which was rescued from logging by conservationists in 1931 and incorporated into Blue Mountains National Park in 1959. Eucalypts dominate here as they do throughout the Blue Mountains. The region has the world's greatest variety of eucalypt species: of 700 species worldwide, 92 are found here. The environs of the town of **Katoomba**, with 65 species, may have the world's greatest concentration.

Jenolan Caves (left) consist of at least 300 limestone chambers, many of which are linked by narrow tunnels.

Climbers (right) enjoy the challenges posed by the plateau's extensive and varied sandstone escarpments.

You can get down to Blue Gum Forest and out again in a day, but it's best to camp overnight and savor the scenery and wildlife. The flats abound with birds. One of the most beautiful, the superb fairy wren, flits like a jewel through the shrubbery. At dusk, swamp wallabies graze in clearings, and at night ringtailed possums scuttle in the trees above your tent as the *boo-book* call of the southern boo-book owl echoes through the forest. If you're lucky, you may catch sight of Australia's largest nocturnal aerial hunter, the powerful owl, which preys mainly on possums.

Beyond the Walls

For a longer walk through varied countryside, try the **Six Foot Track**, on the other side of the ridge. Allow three days for this 26-mile (42-km) trail from Katoomba to **Jenolan Caves**. The caves were such a popular tourist destination in the 1800s that the state government ordered this bridle track built in 1884 to replace the circuitous train and horse route. Named for its original width, it weaves through the farmland of the **Megalong Valley** to the **Coxs River**, which you cross on a pedestrian suspension bridge.

From Jenolan Caves, it's a 45-minute drive along a well-maintained gravel road to Kanangra Walls. The road crosses the **Boyd Plateau**, a granite tableland covered with subalpine vegetation that includes heath, snow gums, temperate rain forest, mossy swamps, and snowgrass. Leave your vehicle at the car park and follow the **Plateau Walk** across the heathland behind the cliff. Here, crimson rosellas skim overhead like multicolored missiles, while honeyeaters sip nectar from banksias. At **Kanangra Rock** you'll have superb views of the walls, gorge, and the unforgettable scenery beyond.

Experienced hikers can try the challenging 15-mile (24-km), two-day return trip from Kanangra Walls to **Mount Cloudmaker**. The mountain often lives up to its name, and walkers should always be prepared for rain and cold. It's possible to continue the hike beyond Mount Cloudmaker all the way to Katoomba, a trip that requires thorough preparation and at least three days. However short or long your trail and whichever route you take through the Blue Mountains, you're sure to be amazed by the wildness of this landscape and to marvel that it exists so close to a major city.

TRAVEL TIPS

DETAILS

When to Go

The Blue Mountains can be explored year-round, with spring and fall being the most comfortable seasons. During the winter, the average maximum temperature in the Upper Mountains is 41°F (5°C), while in summer the maximum is 64°F (18°C). The Lower Mountains have a much warmer climate; the average maximum temperature is 61°F (16°C) in winter and 84°F (29°C) in summer.

How to Get There

Kingsford Smith Airport in Sydney is about 68 miles (110 km) from Katoomba, the Blue Mountains' main town. Car rentals are available at the airport for the two-hour drive along one of two routes: the Great Western Highway or Bells Line of Road. Regular CityRail services link Sydney's Central Station and Lithgow. Numerous coach companies conduct day trips to the Blue Mountains, and CityRail offers a number of rail-coach tour options.

Special Planning

The best way to see the Blue Mountains is on foot along one of the many walking trails. Many areas of the park are very wild, and hikers entering them should be experienced and self-reliant. Wear a hat and sunblock, and take warm clothing and wet-weather gear, even in summer. Although the more popular lookouts are well-fenced and safe, those in more remote places may have no fencing, and some cliff edges are not as solid as they appear. Those planning a walk during a period of high fire danger should stick to rain-forest gullies near settlements and heed fire restrictions.

Although four-wheel-drive vehicles and mountain bikes are allowed in the national parks, they are not permitted in all wilderness areas. For information, call the National Parks and Wildlife Service, tel: 02-4787 8877.

For disabled visitors, the *Blue Mountains Access Guide* booklet lists wheelchair-accessible sites and facilities in the mountains. It is available from the Access Committee, Blue Mountains City Council Community Services, tel: 02-4780 5788.

Permits and Entry Fees

Entrance to the national parks is free. Only those wishing to camp at Euroka Clearing, in the Glenbrook area, will need a permit. It is advisable to book two weeks ahead through the National Parks and Wildlife Service's Richmond office, tel: 02-4588 5247.

INFORMATION

Blue Mountains Visitor Information Centre

Echo Point Road, Katoomba, NSW 2780; tel: 1300 653 408; web: bluemountainstourism.org.au

National Parks and Wildlife Service

Blue Mountains Heritage Centre, Govetts Leap Road, Blackheath, NSW 2785; tel: 02-4787 8877; web: www.npws.nsw.gov.au

CAMPING

There are hundreds of designated car-camping and bush-camping areas. In very wild areas, visitors may camp more or less anywhere as long as they follow guidelines designed to protect the local environment, which are available from the National Parks and Wildlife Service.

LODGING

PRICE GUIDE – double occupancy

$ = up to $49 $$ = $50–$99
$$$ = $100–$149 $$$$ = $150+

Bungaree Earth Cottages

P.O. Box 97, Wentworth Falls, NSW 2782; tel: 02-4757 3096.

Bungaree is an Aboriginal word that suggests closeness to the land and sensitivity to the environment. Located near Wentworth Falls in 23 acres of Blue Mountains forest, these three mud-brick cottages are self-contained and have solar power. Their discrete bushland settings provide peace and privacy; two cottages are wheelchair-accessible. $$

Hydro Majestic Hotel

Medlow Bath, NSW 2780; tel: 02-4788 1002; web: www.hydro-majestic.com.au or e-mail sales@hydromajestic.com.au

Built in 1904, the Hydro Majestic is the Blue Mountains' most famous hotel. Set on an escarpment, it offers sweeping views of the Megalong and Kanimbla Valleys. The hotel's 63 rooms, all with private baths and fully restored, offer a variety of options, including spas and furnishings in Edwardian and Art Deco styles. Facilities include two all-weather tennis courts, a swimming pool, and a croquet lawn. The hotel staff can arrange activities such as mountain biking, rappelling, and bush walking. $$$$

Jenolan Cabins

Porcupine Hill, 42 Edith Road, Jenolan Caves, NSW 2790; tel: 02-6335 6239.

Located five minutes' drive from Jenolan Caves, these cabins offer 360-degree views over Blue Mountains National Park, Kanangra–Boyd National Park, and Jenolan Caves Reserve. Each cabin is self-contained, accommodates six people, and has a well-equipped kitchen, a dining room, a lounge room with large

picture windows,
a cathedral ceiling,
and a log fire. $$

TOURS & OUTFITTERS

Cox's River Escapes

P.O. Box 81; Leura,
NSW 2780; tel:
02-4784 1621 or
015-400 121; web:
www.bluemts.com.
au/CoxsRiver/ or e-mail:
coxrivesc@hermes.net.au

The company offers guided four-wheel-drive and walking tours of the Cox's River, Jenolan Caves, and surrounding areas. Tours range from three hours to three days in length, and can be tailor-made to suit visitors' needs. Activities include bush walking and swimming.

Fantastic Aussie Tours

283 Main Street, Katoomba,
NSW 2780; tel: 02-4782 1866.

Bus tours and four-wheel-drive tours explore the Blue Mountains and destinations such as Jenolan Caves, the Plug Hole, Zig Zag Railway, and Mount Tomah Botanic Garden. Adventure trips include horse-riding, rappelling, four-wheel-drive safaris, and caving.

Tread Lightly Eco Tours

100 Great Western Highway,
Medlow Bath, NSW
2780; tel: 02-4788
1229; e-mail:
treadlightly@
hermes.net.au

Guided bush
walks emphasize
wildlife, bush food,
Aboriginal culture,
and ecology. The
half- to full-day
walks are designed
for people at all
levels of fitness.

Excursions

Colo River

National Parks and Wildlife Service, Blue Mountains Heritage Centre, Govetts Leap Road, Blackheath, NSW 2785; tel: 02-4787 8877; web: www.npws.nsw.gov.au

At 984 feet deep and 50 miles (80 km) long, the sandstone Colo Gorge is reputed to be the longest such gorge in Australia. In summer the best way to see it is by floating down the river on an air mattress. Wildlife abounds: the river is home to eels, perch, gudgeon, and frogs, while terrestrial denizens include eastern grey kangaroos, red-necked wallabies, echidnas, and lyrebirds.

Glow-Worm Tunnel

National Parks and Wildlife Service, Blue Mountains Heritage Centre, Govetts Leap Road, Blackheath, NSW 2785; tel: 02-4787 8877; web: www. npws.nsw.gov.au

This 1,312-foot former railway tunnel, 19 miles (30 km) from Lithgow in Wollemi National Park, has been colonized by the larvae of the fungus gnat. The larvae build snares of silken threads studded with sticky droplets to trap flying insects such as mosquitoes, luring their prey with a blue glow produced in their abdomens. The glow-worms are so abundant that looking up is like viewing a starlit sky.

Yerranderie

Yerranderie Ghost Town, P.O. Box 420, Milsons Point, NSW 1565; tel: 02-4659 6165.

In the early 1900s, this historic ghost town in the Burragorang Valley near Warragamba Dam was a bustling silver-mining settlement of 2,000 people. It is now owned by Val Lhuede, who has devoted her life to preserving and restoring the site as a destination for bush walkers and adventurous motorists. There are camping facilities as well as basic accommodations in charmingly restored buildings.

Corner Country
New South Wales

CHAPTER 18

Rounded, wind-polished pebbles, each gleaming with a red-brown coating of iron and manganese oxides, litter the lands that stretch wide and flat as an ocean to the line of low, table-topped hills on the far horizon. On the dirt road that cuts across the plain, a vehicle slows to cross the sandy bed of another dry creek; clumps of dark green, stiff-foliaged acacia line the banks, their roots searching out hidden moisture. ◆ Well camouflaged in the sparse shade lies a small group of red kangaroos. For added comfort, each has scooped a depression in the soft, pale sand to accommodate an ample hip and well-muscled thigh. Leaning on an elbow, the roos lounge on their sides like picnickers after a long lazy lunch, dozing away the heat of the day. ◆ The vehicle worries a gentle-faced doe, and she is soon on her feet, her half-grown joey at her side. Both stand in a watchful pose, holding their forearms like swimmers ready to dive and twitching their great ears. Minutes pass. Finally, satisfied that there

Expansive and hauntingly beautiful landscapes harbor a wealth of wildlife and an intriguing human history stretching back 20,000 years.

is no danger, the female ambles back to the others. A second, younger joey, now bold, peeps from her bulging pouch. ◆ This is **Corner Country**, a remote, broad sweep of red dunes, flat-topped hills, sandy creek beds, and stony plains, so named because the pin-straight borders of three states, New South Wales, Queensland, and South Australia, meet here in a giant T-junction. Less than a day's drive north of **Broken Hill** in western New South Wales, it is situated on the edge of the great sun-baked deserts of Central Australia, in one of the driest regions on Earth. ◆ The frontier township of **Tibooburra** is the Corner's only settlement; north and east of this outpost

Vast expanses of sand, stone, and spinifex characterize much of the Corner Country. The animals and plants that survive here are hardy specialists.

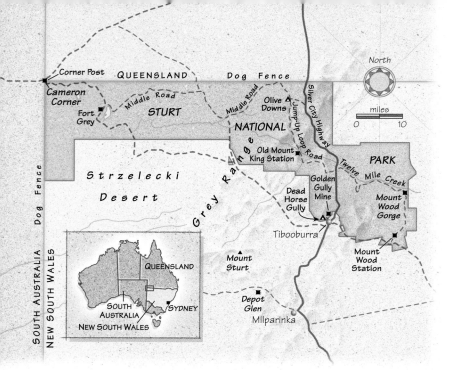

the sole reason for the town's existence, but it has since served several generations of pastoralists and, more recently, adventurous travelers. Facing each other across the short paved section of road that is the town's main street are its two pubs: the Tibooburra Hotel, always referred to as the "Two Storey" and the highest building for hundreds of miles, and the Family Hotel, famous for the murals on its walls by well-known Australian artist Clifton Pugh and other bush painters.

From Tibooburra, you can strike out into the park along dirt roads to the north, east, or west. Heading north on the **Silver City Highway**, **Dead Horse Gully** campground lies 0.6 miles (1 km) from the town, just inside the park boundary. Here, a self-guided walk (about one hour round-trip) winds between granite outcrops, leathery-leafed beefwood trees – fragrant in spring with spikes of cream-colored flowers – and saltbush, and provides views across granite tors and the old goldfields. Nearby **Golden Gully Mine** is a reconstruction of an 1880s

lies **Sturt National Park**, formed in the early 1970s by the amalgamation of six sprawling sheep farms (known locally as stations) and named for the first European explorer to reach this area, Charles Sturt. Today, the park is once again the domain of the red kangaroo, emu, wedge-tailed eagle, and fearsome-looking but harmless lizards. Although little has changed here in the past 200 years, you'll also come across traces of intrepid explorers, pioneer pastoralists, and gold-hungry miners, as well as echoes of the area's lost Aboriginal groups who lived in harmony with these harsh lands for millennia.

Jump-Up Country

The low granite hills surrounding Tibooburra gave the town its name: the word means "many rocks" in the language of the local Wangkumara Aboriginal people. Gold found in these rocky gullies in the 1880s was

Desert plants (right) respond very rapidly to rains, carpeting the plains with blossoms.

mine scene featuring original equipment.

About 15 minutes farther north, **Jump-Up Loop Road** branches off to the west. Named for the long, flat-topped hills – known locally as jump-ups – that are the park's most distinctive geological feature, the loop provides access to some of the most scenic parts of the park. (Count on three hours to complete the circuit and return to Tibooburra.) Near the ruins of **Old Mount King Station**, avenues of stately river red gums line the channels of **Twelve Mile Creek**, which hold permanent pools in all but exceptionally dry periods. Watch here for larklike pipits gleaning caterpillars from leaves and tiny fairy wrens flitting among low branches. The pools regularly attract huge numbers of kangaroos, including herds of stockily built euros (also known as wallaroos) and eastern greys. During prolonged droughts, even the mighty red kangaroos forsake the plains to congregate here.

The human inhabitants of the Corner (above) have devised their own ways of coping with the region's climatic extremes.

The Silver City Highway (right), named for the mining center of Broken Hill, is the region's major roadway, but much of it is unpaved.

Another common visitor to the creek is Australia's largest bird, the flightless but fleet-footed emu. You may spot a harried male bird directing his flock of chicks in a deep, rumbling voice. In a remarkable role reversal, the parenting work of the female is finished once the eggs are laid, and it is left to the male, the smaller of the couple and recognizable by his white collar, to incubate the eggs. Such is his devotion to duty that for the 60 days or so it takes for the eggs to hatch, he rarely leaves his nest of trampled grass. To conserve energy, he lowers his metabolic rate, becoming almost torpid. The striped chicks

stay with the father for six months, snuggling together each night beneath his feathers.

As the road nears **Olive Downs** campground, take time to savor the spectacular views to the south and west of the **Grey Range** jump-up, which juts 500 feet above the plain. The mesas of the Corner are capped with an ancient soil layer that long ago hardened into a rocky crust. This crust is more resistant to the forces of wind and water than the softer strata below are, but as erosion gnaws at the lower layers, it slowly collapses and crumbles. Rocky debris from the undercut crust lies scattered over the plains, where it has been weathered into shining pebbles called "gibbers." At Olive Downs, the Wanyiwalku and Malyangapa people quarried outcrops to make blades, scrapers, and other tools.

The park's stony plains are an ideal reptile habitat. In warmer months, you are likely to encounter bearded dragons and shinglebacks soaking up the sun among the pebbles, and you may even spot a sand goanna, which can measure up to five feet in length. It normally walks on all fours, but when pursuing prey or fleeing danger, it will rear up and dash along on two legs, a habit that has earned it the nickname "racehorse goanna."

From the camping area, a 1.8-mile (3-km) self-guided trail takes walkers to the top of a mesa for uninterrupted views over gibber plains. You'll often see wedge-tailed eagles, wheeling overhead on powerful updrafts. Look for their nests – large, untidy bundles of twigs – in the tops of mulga trees.

Shinglebacks (left) are often seen basking on the ground or rocks. These skinks may live for 15 to 20 years.

Monarch of the Arid Plains

Restricted to arid and semiarid parts of Australia, the red kangaroo is the largest living marsupial. A heavily muscled, russet-colored male can stand seven feet tall and weigh more than 175 pounds, while the smaller and slighter blue-grey doe (sometimes called a blue-flier) weighs in at about 90 pounds. In Sturt National Park, the species occurs in greater concentrations than ever before – a result of the protection afforded from hunters and predators (particularly dingoes) and the permanent water supply provided by the former sheep stations' ground tanks.

Yet even when dependent on the whims of the natural water supply, red kangaroos are well equipped to handle the vagaries of the outback climate. By a process known as delayed implantation, a female can keep a fetus in suspended development until her current joey leaves the pouch. If food and water are in short supply, she can even delay the birth until the situation improves.

A joey leaves the pouch at seven or eight months but still runs with its mother, putting its head inside the pouch to suckle. Usually, the doe has a younger joey inside the pouch as well as the one at heel, and produces two types of milk to suit their respective needs.

Red kangaroos (above) normally inhabit a territory of about 250 acres.

Echidnas (below, left) break open ant and termite nests to feed on the insects inside.

Sand goannas (bottom) stay in their burrows during the hottest part of the day.

Pastoral Heritage

In seasons following good rains, the road east from Tibooburra weaves through tall Mitchell grass, but normally gibber plain predominates. These lands were once part of **Mount Wood Station**, and today an outdoor museum near the farm buildings includes a replica of a shepherd's hut and examples of the equipment used a century ago to pump water and scour wool.

In the timbered areas along the rocky gully of nearby **Mount Wood Gorge**, you may be lucky enough to come upon an echidna, ambling along with lurching gait in search of a termite nest. Should it sense your

presence, it may begin to dig furiously, sinking backward into the leaf litter and soft soil, or, if the ground is rocky, roll itself into a tight ball, a defensive maneuver designed to protect its vulnerable, spikeless underside from the teeth or beak of a predator.

From the gorge, you can backtrack or continue onward to the Silver City Highway, which will return you to Tibooburra. The 60-mile (100-km) round trip takes about two hours.

For many visitors, the region's biggest attraction is the 90-mile (140-km) drive to **Cameron Corner**, where the state boundaries meet. The dusty, often corrugated track retraces much of the route taken in 1845 by Charles Sturt as he and his party trekked the plains in a vain search for the great inland sea that they and many others believed lay at the center of the continent.

For the first 45 miles (70 km), the route traverses gibber plains; then red dunes appear and gradually increase in size until, near Cameron Corner, they form a natural roller coaster that rises and falls by 33 feet or more. Sturt found the desert scenery "awfully fearful," recording

Emus (above) are nomadic and will travel long distances to find water.

Burrowing frogs (left) survive drought by burying themselves in the sand inside a water-filled cocoon of skin.

in his journal that "a kind of dread came over me as I gazed upon it. It looked like the entrance into Hell." Today's visitors can enjoy the stark beauty of its vivid color contrasts and endless emptiness without the understandable apprehension of the far-flung explorers.

In 1880, surveyor John Cameron, having reached this isolated intersection of state lines, planned to mark the spot with a stone cairn; the dunes, however, yielded little in the way of building material, and he had to make do with a wooden post. The marker you'll see today, the **Corner Post**, dates from 1969 when Cameron's lines were resurveyed and the accuracy of his calculations confirmed.

To reach the post and the famous Corner Shop, which serves cool drinks, snacks, and fuel, you pass through the world's longest fence. Built in the 1880s to keep rabbits out of Queensland, and later strengthened and raised to six feet to keep dingoes out of New South Wales sheep country, it extends 3,489 miles (5,615 km) in an enormous "L" from Queensland to the edge of the Great Australian Bight in South Australia. Responsibility for the fence falls to the fiercely named Wild Dog Destruction Board, and it is kept in good repair by boundary riders who live in isolated cottages along its length.

Dreams and Dust

Some 25 miles (40 km) south of Tibooburra, just off the western side of the highway, a cluster of imposing but deserted stone buildings and a still-open-for-business outback pub are all that remains of the settlement of **Milparinka**, founded in the 1880s following the discovery of gold. From here, a well-signposted dirt road leads 7½ miles (12 km) west to **Depot Glen**, where Sturt and his party faced their greatest challenge.

Having used the long inland rivers to reach the interior, at Menindee, east of Broken Hill, the party headed off into the unknown with sheep and cattle, hauling the boat they planned to launch on the inland sea. But instead of lush pastures, they trudged into lands parched by one of the driest spells on record. At Depot Glen you can sit where they set up camp beside the quiet, olive-green pools, the only reliable water for hundreds of miles. Unable to retreat and afraid to proceed any farther, they remained chained to the dwindling waters throughout the hot, dry summer of 1844–45.

To keep his men occupied, Sturt had them build the cairn that is still visible on the red hill nearby; it subsequently became a memorial to James Poole, Sturt's second-in-command, who died of scurvy during the enforced stay and is buried beneath a beef-wood tree a mile or so to the east. Depot Glen water hole is worth a late afternoon visit for its chattering, darting bird life, but as you clamber past forbidding ridges of jagged

shale, it is the area's history that hangs heavy in the air, and you can almost feel the weary desperation of the trapped men.

Rains eventually allowed the party to push farther north (and return safely to Adelaide). Their next base was at **Fort Grey**, in the west of the park. The tree blazed by Sturt still stands there, and there is a camping area for those who wish to follow in the footsteps of the explorers. At the time of Sturt's stay, this shallow basin had been transformed by rainfall into an oasis of "verdure and richness," prompting the explorer to claim, "I never saw a more beautiful spot." Even when there's barely a trace of green to be seen, many a modern-day traveler will concur.

Mutawintji National Park

Its name, meaning "green grass and water" in the language of the Wilyakali people, says it all. For thousands of years, the hidden gullies, pastures, and rock pools of **Mutawintji**, located 85 miles (130 km) northeast of Broken Hill in the **Byngnano Range**, have provided a haven in times of drought for the animals and humans of the surrounding saltbush plains.

The generations of Aboriginal peoples who gathered here during the past 20,000 years or so left a remarkable artistic legacy in the form of innumerable stencils, paintings, and engravings in caves and on cliffs and overhangs. They made the stencils by placing an object against the rock face and spitting thick paint around the edges. Many are of human hands, but some depict boomerangs, woven nets, and other everyday objects. As Europeans moved their flocks across the region, tools such as blade shears and even a clay pipe were added to the visual archives. Engravings were created with the use of a rock hammer and sharp stone to punch an outline on a flat rock; the interior was then hollowed out in reverse relief.

Mutawintji is of great spiritual significance to its traditional owners. Access to some areas is restricted, and visitors to the rock-art sites must be accompanied by an accredited ranger. The park's abundant wildlife includes wedge-tailed eagles, fairy martins (look for their bottle-shaped mud nests hanging from the cave roofs), shingleback lizards, bearded dragons, euros, and flocks of screeching corellas and galahs.

Little Half Dome (above, right) is one of the most distinctive rock formations in Mutawintji National Park.

A brown falcon (right) scans the grasslands at Mutawintji for prey such as reptiles and small mammals.

TRAVEL TIPS

DETAILS

When to Go

The most comfortable seasons to travel to this region are fall, winter, and early spring, roughly from April to October. During this period, the average daily temperature ranges from 64°F to 83°F (18°–28°C), while nights are chilly, with temperatures getting down to 41°F (5°C) in July. During summer, the temperature soars, and the area is notorious for being the hottest part of New South Wales. In January, Tibooburra has an average daily maximum temperature of 96°F (36°C).

How to Get There

Broken Hill, the major hub for travel to the Corner, is 718 miles (1,158 km) west of Sydney at the intersection of the Barrier and Silver City Highways. There are regular flights to Broken Hill from Sydney, Melbourne, and Adelaide. Buses to Broken Hill run from Sydney, Adelaide, and Mildura; the town is also served twice a week by the Sydney–Perth *Indian-Pacific* train. Car rentals are available at Broken Hill airport. Sturt National Park is 204 miles (330 km) north of Broken Hill via the Silver City Highway.

Special Planning

Travelers venturing into Corner Country are advised to carry extra food, spare tires, and plenty of water. Access roads are normally suitable for conventional vehicles but may become impassable after rain. To check road conditions, contact the New South Wales National Parks and Wildlife Service's Tibooburra District Office, tel: 08-8091 3308. Drivers should watch out for kangaroos and livestock wandering onto roads.

Permits and Entry Fees

No permits or entry fees are applicable.

INFORMATION

Broken Hill Regional Tourist Association

P.O. Box 286,Broken Hill, NSW 2880; tel: 08-8087 6077; web: www.murrayoutback.org.au or e-mail: tourist@pcpro.net.au

National Parks and Wildlife Service

Broken Hill District Office, 183 Argent Street, Broken Hill, NSW 2880; tel: 08-8088 5933; web: www.npws.nsw.gov.au

New South Wales National Parks and Wildlife Service

Tibooburra District Office, Briscoe Street, Tibooburra, NSW 2880; tel: 08-8091 3308; web: www.npws.nsw.gov.au

CAMPING

There are National Parks and Wildlife Service campsites at Mount Wood Station, Olive Downs, Fort Grey, and Dead Horse Gully. Camping fees should be paid using the self-registration boxes at the campsites.

LODGING

PRICE GUIDE – double occupancy

$ = up to $49	$$ = $50–$99
$$$ = $100–$149	$$$$ = $150+

Family Hotel and Family Lodge Motel

Briscoe Street, Tibooburra, NSW 2880; tel: 08-8091 3314.

Noted for its historic murals, the Family Hotel has nine simple rooms with shared facilities, and a restaurant. The lodge, directly opposite the hotel, offers 10 motel-style rooms that are self-contained and air-conditioned, and have televisions. $–$$

Granites Motel Caravan Park

Tibooburra Post Office, Tibooburra, NSW 2880; tel: 08-8091 3305.

The Granites has 10 motel-style units, four cabins (two with private facilities), and one trailer. All accommodations have cooking facilities and are air-conditioned. $

PJ's Underground

Dugout 72, Turleys Hill, White Cliffs, NSW 2836; tel: 08-8091 6626.

PJ's underground establishment has five rooms with tea and coffee facilities and bar refrigerators. The price includes breakfast, and other meals are available. Facilities include a spa room, a crafts showroom, and a mine offering conducted tours. $$

Tibooburra Hotel

Briscoe Street, Tibooburra, NSW 2880; tel: 08-8091 3310.

Known as the "Two Storey," this historic establishment offers 14 rooms with shared facilities, and a restaurant. $

White Cliffs Hotel

White Cliffs, NSW 2836; tel: 08-8091 6606.

Located in the center of town, the hotel has seven simple rooms. The dining room is open seven days a week, and the pub has an outback atmosphere. $

White Cliffs Underground Dugout Motel

Smiths Hill, White Cliffs, NSW 2836; tel: 1-800 021 154 (toll-free in Australia).

Maintained at a comfortable air-conditioned temperature regardless of surface conditions, the motel has 30 spacious underground rooms with queen-sized beds and shared bathrooms. Facilities include a swimming pool and restaurant. $$

TOURS & OUTFITTERS

Crittenden Air

P.O. Box 346, Broken Hill, NSW 2880; tel: 08-8088 5702; e-mail:

crittair@pcpro.net.au

This company runs charter flights and three standard tours. On the "Bush Mail Run," travelers accompany the flying postman as he delivers mail to outback stations. The "Tibooburra Aerial Tour" flies to Cameron Corner, taking in Sturt National Park, Tibooburra, and Milparinka Historic Courthouse. The "White Cliffs Tour" travels to White Cliffs over Mutawintji National Park and includes an inspection of opal fields and underground living quarters.

Go Bush Tours

128 Marconi Circuit, Kambah, ACT 2902; tel: 02-6231 3023; web: www.gobushtours.com.au or e-mail: info@gobush.com.au

Leaving from Canberra, this company's 14-day tour of outback New South Wales and remote southwestern Queensland visits Tibooburra, Cameron Corner, Innamincka, and Broken Hill. The tour takes a maximum of eight passengers and includes cabin and tent accommodations.

Mutawintji Heritage Tours

Mutawintji Local Aboriginal Land Council, P.O. Box 459, Broken Hill, NSW 2880; tel: 08-8088 5933.

On Wednesday and Saturday between April and November, the Land Council conducts tours of the Mutawintji Historic Site, one of the best collections of Aboriginal rock art in New South Wales. Reservations are not required.

Silver City Tours

380 Argent Street, Broken Hill, NSW 2880; tel: 08-8087 3144; web: www.ruralnet.net.au/~wincen or e-mail: wincen@ruralnet.net.au

Tours ranging from half-day to six-day adventures take in sites of historical, natural, and cultural interest around Broken Hill, including Mutawintji National Park, Menindee Lakes, and Kinchega National Park.

Excursions

Broken Hill

Broken Hill Regional Tourist Association, P.O. Box 286, Broken Hill, NSW 2880; tel: 08-8087 6077; web: www.murrayoutback.org.au or e-mail: tourist@pcpro.net.au

Surrounded by desert, the "Silver City" is the largest outback town in New South Wales and home to the world's richest deposits of zinc, silver, and lead. The town's two working mines are not open to the public, but there are tours of old mines, including Delprat's Mine and the Historic Day Dream Mine. Also worth visiting are the numerous art galleries, the Royal Flying Doctor Base, and the School of the Air.

Kinchega National Park

National Parks and Wildlife Service, Broken Hill District Office, 183 Argent Street, Broken Hill, NSW 2880; tel: 08-8088 5933; web: www.npws.nsw.gov.au

Rich in Aboriginal sites and European relics, Kinchega is 69 miles (111 km) southeast of Broken Hill. Set in this dry landscape are the Menindee Lakes, which consist of freshwater overflow from the Darling River and hold three times as much water as Sydney Harbour. Home to brolgas, black swans, pelicans, spoonbills, corellas, swamphens, and peregrine falcons, the lakes are a waterbird-watcher's paradise.

Silverton

Broken Hill Regional Tourist Association, P.O. Box 286, Broken Hill, NSW 2880; tel: 08-8087 6077; web: www.murrayoutback.org.au or e-mail: tourist@pcpro.net.au

Located 15½ miles (25 km) northwest of Broken Hill, this ghost town may be familiar to those who've seen *The Road Warrior* or *A Town Like Alice*, which were both filmed here. A former silver-mining center, the town began to empty out in 1889 when the mines closed. Its cinematic fame has provided a number of its buildings with a new lease on life, including the Silverton Hotel (once again open for business) and the jail (now a museum). Camel rides are available, departing from the hotel.

Lamington
National Park
Queensland

CHAPTER 19

n the everlasting shade of the subtropical rain forest, the dark boles of booyong trees rise like pillars to support the roof of foliage high above. Nearby, the trunk of a towering carabeen tree flares out at the base, forming extravagant buttresses. Thick lianas coil down from the branches, and strands of lawyer vine trail menacingly, their hooked tendrils waiting to snare an unwary visitor. ◆ The air is heavy and humid on this steamy summer day, and just as you pause to extract an arm from a vine's prickly embrace, there is an explosive clapping of wings. A wonga pigeon, flushed from cover, rises quickly from the ground and flies to the safety of a branch. Settling, the bird turns its back to present drab-colored wing feathers and immediately merges into the forest. ◆ Above you is the rain forest's hanging garden of orchids and bird's-nest, elkhorn, and staghorn ferns; beyond is the green canopy that shields this primeval scene from sun and wind. The crowns of the trees seem to touch, but there are gaps that

Some of Australia's most colorful birds – along with marsupials, reptiles, butterflies, and rare plants – thrive in these ancient forests.

serve as aerial pathways for speeding flocks of fruit pigeons and the small hawks and owls that hunt them. Soon your gaze returns to the ground, tracing the aerial roots of a strangler fig downward to the deep, moist carpet of rotting leaves on the forest floor. Somewhere in the forest, a green catbird calls, its wails like the cries of a lost infant. ◆ Walk into an Australian rain forest and you travel back 60 million years, to a time when Australia was splitting from the supercontinent of Gondwana and beginning its long drift north. As the continent moved into more arid climes, its once-extensive rain forests dwindled. Today, rain forests cover less than 1 percent of

Emerging from the rain forest that blankets the Lamington Plateau, the waters of Coomera Falls plunge more than 200 feet into the valley below.

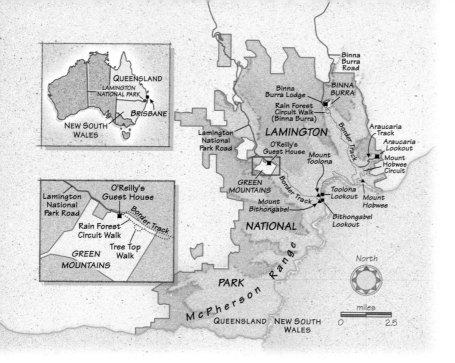

QUEENSLAND
LAMINGTON
NATIONAL PARK
BRISBANE
NEW SOUTH
WALES

Binna
Burra
Road

Binna
Burra Lodge

BINNA
BURRA

Rain Forest
Circuit Walk
(Binna Burra)

Lamington
National
Park Road

LAMINGTON

O'Reilly's
Guest House

Mount
Toolona

Araucaria
Track

Araucaria
Lookout

Mount
Hobwee
Circuit

Border Track

GREEN
MOUNTAINS

Mount
Bithongabel

Border Track

Toolona
Lookout

Mount
Hobwee

NATIONAL

Bithongabel
Lookout

North

PARK

McPherson Range

miles

0   2.5

QUEENSLAND   NEW SOUTH
WALES

O'Reilly's
Guest House

Lamington
National
Park Road

Rain Forest
Circuit Walk

Border Track

Tree Top
Walk

GREEN
MOUNTAINS

pouched frog and for mammals near the edge of extinction like the Hastings River mouse. They also host a bewildering array of invertebrate and insect life, including the continent's third-largest butterfly, the magnificent black-and-green Richmond birdwing.

Dedicated in 1915, Lamington covers more than 54,000 acres of the **McPherson Range**, an eastern spur of the **Great Dividing Range**. Countless streams have cut into Lamington's volcanic plateau, and their crystal-clear waters cascade down some 500 waterfalls before rushing through boulder-filled gorges to the low country. In addition to rain forests, Lamington encompasses eucalypt forests of tallowwood and blackbutt, bloodwood and scribbly gum, and small tracts of mountain heathland where spring wildflowers bloom in profusion.

Rain Forest Trails

All of Lamington's environments can be experienced on approximately 100 miles (160 km) of marked trails in the northern

Australia, and most are protected in World Heritage-listed national parks. **Lamington National Park** in southeastern Queensland preserves part of the largest remnant of subtropical rain forest in Australia, as well as patches of cool temperate rain forest, warm temperate rain forest, and so-called dry rain forest. Lamington is one of Earth's rarities, a lost world where species have been able to persist virtually unchanged for millions of years.

Today, the subtropical and cool temperate rain forests alone harbor more than 170 species of rare and threatened plants and provide habitat for rare birds such as the rufous scrub-bird and Albert's lyrebird, as well as for endangered amphibians like the

The carpet snake (above), one of the few pythons that climbs trees, kills its prey by constricting and suffocating it.

Crimson rosellas (right) add splashes of contrasting color to the park's verdant hues.

sector of the park. (The southern sector is a wilderness area visited only by experienced hikers.) Most depart from the historic lodges at the two park entrances. **O'Reilly's Guest House** at **Green Mountains** was built by the five O'Reilly brothers, who arrived here from New South Wales in 1911. They opened the guesthouse in the 1920s after most of the plateau had been reserved as a national park. **Binna Burra Lodge** was set up in 1933 by Arthur Groom and Romeo Lahey, pioneers of the Queensland national parks movement.

For an introduction to Lamington's subtropical rain forests, follow either of the **Rain Forest Circuit Walks** at Binna Burra or Green Mountains. In the early morning or at dusk, look for the red-necked pademelon, a medium-sized brown wallaby, sometimes seen bounding across a trail. You might even hear the *thump, thump* of a pademelon's hind foot as it warns others of your approach. Tame pademelons feed regularly next to the two lodges.

The subtropical rain forest is a place of bird-song. Listen for the repetitive *wonk, wonk, wonk* of the wonga pigeon and the sharp crack of the male whip-bird urgently followed by the female's double-note reply. The loud and melodious song of the

Albert's lyrebird often echoes through the forest; you may also hear the *wheeooo* of the satin bowerbird from some high perch and, around the edges of the plateau, the gentle tinkling of bellbirds drifting up from the valley below. A fluttering of wings high in the canopy normally indicates flocks of topknot pigeons searching for native fruits, while the garrulous chattering is likely to come from crimson rosellas. These and other canopy

The Border Track (right) leads hikers along the edge of Lamington's volcanic plateau, revealing sweeping views across the Tweed Valley.

The eastern water dragon (left) has changed little during its 20-million-year tenure in Australia.

species usually remain well hidden, but the **Tree Top Walk** at Green Mountains, with its elevated walkway, gives you a chance to match the sounds to the birds.

The thick roof of leaves is continuous throughout much of the forest, but here and there sunlight pours down. This indicates that a great tree has fallen, tearing open the canopy. The change is dramatic: beneath the opening sprouts a tangle of fast-growing and short-lived pioneer plants, including wild tobacco, corkwood bleeding heart, and the stinging tree – one of Lamington's hazards. Its dinner-plate-sized leaves are covered with tiny spines that can inflict hours of severe pain.

A movement in the leaf litter may reveal the presence of one of Lamington's most bizarre residents. The spiny crayfish, a bright blue-and-white crustacean with reddish markings, lives in the plateau's pools and streams and grows to more than nine inches in length. In hot, damp weather, the crayfish will leave the water and scavenge for rotting animal and plant matter on the forest floor. Approach one of these creatures and it will brandish its big claws and hiss loudly.

The bark of every tree in the rain forest is darkened by a covering of mosses, lichens, and algae, all working relentlessly to break down organic matter and release nutrients. The process of decay is assisted by many kinds of fungi. Among the most interesting are the luminous fungi, which can be seen in dark corners of the rain forest at night, glowing with a ghostly greenish-white light.

Night walks provide intriguing insights into the park's nocturnal community. A view of the evening sky may reveal grey-headed or red flying foxes setting out to forage. Scanning the trees with a flashlight may

Bowerbird Burglars

During your visit to Lamington, keep an eye on your valuables if they are small and blue – even your blue Australian 10-dollar notes. Otherwise, you could fall victim to the satin bowerbird, a distinctive resident of Australia's east-coast rain forests and an accomplished avian thief.

In spring, the male bird, which has shiny blue-black plumage and is about the size of a pigeon, builds a platform of sticks on the ground. It uses twigs to construct an impressive arch, or bower, then decorates the arch with any natural or man-made object it can find – preferably something blue. Typical ornamentation includes flowers, feathers, snail shells, and any scraps of blue paper, plastic, or glass that the bird can steal from a nearby cabin or tent.

Once the stage is set, the courtship performance begins. Going all-out to impress passing females, the bird runs through the bower, raising and lowering its wings, thrusting out its breast feathers, and making loud *churring* noises.

Satin bowerbirds often build their bowers close to buildings, so these performances are easily observed. Those of a more colorful relative, the regent bowerbird, are seldom so public. This striking, orange-gold-and-black bird tends to hide its more modest bower deep in the forest. In contrast to its attention-hungry cousin, it is also more egalitarian, allowing females to join in the activity.

A male satin bowerbird (below) adds another blue object to an already impressive collection.

The Tree Top Walk (opposite, top) allows visitors to explore the rain-forest canopy.

Strangler fig roots (opposite, bottom) enclose a void where a host tree once grew.

offer a glimpse of a dainty sugar glider, a small marsupial with winglike flaps of skin on the side of its body that allow it to glide from tree to tree in search of sweet blossoms.

On the Border

The backbone of Lamington's trail system is the 13½-mile (22-km) **Border Track** linking O'Reilly's and Binna Burra, which can be completed in a day if side trips are omitted. The trail leads to the plateau's southern edge, opening up a vast panorama over the **Tweed Valley** of New South Wales, with the peak of **Mount Warning** at its center. This magnificent scene was formed by the Mount Warning shield volcano, which erupted 22 million years ago, creating a giant dome-shaped mountain. Millions of years of erosion carved out the huge caldera of the Tweed Valley, forming a ring of peaks: the McPherson, **Tweed**, and **Nightcap Ranges**.

The Border Track accesses the best of Lamington's cool temperate rain forests. Near the **Bithongabel** and **Toolona** lookouts, Antarctic beech trees grow up to 60 feet tall and 3 feet in diameter. The living root stock of one of these venerable giants is thought to be 5,000 years old. Lamington is the northern limit of this ancient Gondwanan species, which also grows in southern South America. With their gnarled forms, their exposed root systems, and the mosses, lichens, and ferns that grow from their boles, the beech trees conjure up a scene from *The Lord of the Rings*.

A detour along the **Mount Hobwee Circuit** will take you to **Araucaria Lookout**, where hoop pines grow. Another remnant of Gondwanan life, these tall, straight trees, which reach 230 feet high, belong to the ancient araucaria family of conifers and are even older than the beech trees. The symmetrical crowns of these "dinosaur trees" often rise high above Lamington's green covering of forest, marking this as a place where the primeval world lives on.

TRAVEL TIPS

DETAILS

When to Go

Lamington has a pleasant climate year-round. The drier months from May to November are the most comfortable time to visit, with daily maximum temperatures between 54°F and 77°F (12°–25°C). In summer, storms are common, making tracks slippery and causing sudden drops in temperature. In winter (June to September), days are sunny but often chilly, with temperatures near freezing overnight.

How to Get There

There are regular flights to Brisbane and Coolangatta, and vehicle rentals are available at both airports. Lamington National Park is a one-hour drive from Coolangatta and 90 minutes from Brisbane. From Brisbane or Coolangatta, take the Pacific Highway to Nerang and follow the signs to Beechmont. Binna Burra Mountain Lodge, tel: 07-5533 3622, operates daily bus service to its resort from the Surfers Paradise Transit Centre, Nerang Railway Station, Coolangatta Airport, and various points in Brisbane. The Mountain Coach Company, tel: 07-5523 4249, has daily service to O'Reilly's Guest House from Coolangatta Airport and the Gold Coast. Allstate Scenic Tours, tel: 07-3285 1777, services the area from Brisbane.

Special Planning

As the area is sometimes subject to sudden weather changes, travelers should bring warm clothing, wet-weather gear, and sturdy shoes. A water bottle, flashlight, map, compass, first-aid kit, and extra food are recommended for hikes. Visitors should be wary of the park's cliffs, venomous snakes, stinging trees, ticks, and leeches.

Walking off the track is not prohibited but is advisable only for experienced hikers who are equipped with a compass and large-scale map (1:25,000 scale). Visitors who wish to venture away from the trails, or to camp out, must advise the ranger, tel: 07-5544 0634, and complete a Bushwalker Safety Form.

Permits and Entry Fees

Campers must obtain a permit from the ranger station, tel: 07-5544 0634.

INFORMATION

Environmental Protection Agency

Naturally Queensland Information Centre, Ground Floor, 160 Ann Street, Moggill, Qld 4000; tel: 07-3227 8186; web: www.env.qld.gov.au

Queensland Parks and Wildlife Service

55 Priors Pocket, Moggill, Qld 4070; tel: 07-3202 0200; web: www.env.qld.gov.au

Queensland Parks and Wildlife Service

Lamington National Park Ranger Station, O'Reilly's (Green Mountain) entrance to Lamington National Park; tel: 07-5544 0634; web: www.env.qld.gov.au

CAMPING

Camping in the park is permitted at designated campsites, and camping fees apply. Numbers are limited to protect the environment and prevent overcrowding, and advance booking is recommended. Call the ranger station, tel: 07-5544 0634. Wilderness campsites are not open between December 1 and January 30, and campsites may be closed in the case of a fire threat or to allow regeneration.

Camping in parties of more than 15 people is discouraged, and the maximum number of hikers per party is six. Campers should carry a portable stove as open fires are not permitted, except where firewood is supplied at main campsites.

LODGING

PRICE GUIDE – double occupancy

$ = up to $49 $$ = $50–$99

$$$ = $100–$149 $$$$ = $150+

Binna Burra Mountain Lodge

Beechmont via Nerang, Qld 4211; tel: 07-5533 3622 or toll-free in Australia 1-800 074 260; web: www.binnaburralodge.com.au or e-mail: binnabur@fan.net.au

Set amid rain forest at the entrance to the national park, this is one of Australia's longest-running nature-based resorts. Accommodations range from luxurious wooden cabins with panoramic views of the Numinbah Valley to a campsite with safari-style tents and trailer and tent sites. Facilities include a game room, library, craft shop, and restaurant with sweeping views of the Coomera Valley. A resident ornithologist can help visitors find and identify the many birds that live around the property. $–$$$$

O'Reilly's Guest House

Lamington National Park Road via Canungra, Qld 4275; tel: 07-5544 0644 or toll-free in Australia 1-800 688 722; web: www.babs.com.au/qld/oreillys.htm or e-mail: reservations@ oreillys.com.au

This historic rain-forest retreat offers three styles of accommodations. The Bithongable Rooms have high ceilings, exposed beams, and private balconies overlooking the McPherson Range. The Elabana Rooms feature red-cedar shutters, furniture crafted from Queensland maple, and timber queen-sized beds. The Toolona Rooms offer simpler accommodations with shared

facilities. Two packages are available. The "traditional" package includes all meals, guided rainforest walks, four-wheel-drive and spotlighting trips, bush bands, and audio-visual presentations. The "eco experience" package covers most of these activities but includes only morning and afternoon snacks and a late supper. $$$–$$$$

TOURS & OUTFITTERS

Adventure Technology

P.O. Box 745, Newport Beach, NSW 2106; tel: 02-9973 2547; e-mail: info@adventure technology.com.au

Join a group of scientists studying biodiversity and herbivory in Lamington National Park's rain forest. Lodging is at O'Reilly's Guest House, and the tour includes a short course in rain-forest ecology.

Bush 'n' Back Four-Wheel-Drive Tours

P.O. Box 2259, Nerang, Qld 4211; tel: 07-5596 5318; web: www.bushnback.com.au

Departing from the Gold Coast, day tours of the park offer visitors a chance to hand-feed native parrots, take a refreshing swim in a mountain stream, and stroll along the Tree Top canopy walkway. A barbecue lunch is included.

Go Tours

7 Davenport Street, Southport, Qld 4215; tel: 07-5591-2199; web: www.gotours.com.au or e-mail: gotours@fan.net.au

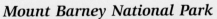

Night tours from the Gold Coast take four to five hours and include a meal, a chance to observe southern-hemisphere constellations, and the opportunity to see nocturnal native animals such as echidnas and brush-tailed possums. They also visit the park's glow-worm caves.

Excursions

Border Ranges National Park

New South Wales National Parks and Wildlife Service, P.O. Box 174, Kyogle, NSW 2474; tel: 02-6632 1473; web: www.npws.nsw.gov.au

Covering 123 square miles of the McPherson Range on the New South Wales side of the border, this park protects the western rim of the Mount Warning caldera, with its rain forests and patches of Antarctic beech. The Tweed Scenic Drive, a loop road from Murwillumbah to Kyogle and Lismore, provides access to points of interest within the park, including excellent viewpoints on the caldera rim.

Girraween National Park

Queensland Parks and Wildlife Service, Girraween National Park via Ballandean, Qld 4382; tel: 07-4684 4157; web: www.env.qld.gov.au

This 47-square-mile park contains a landscape of immense granite domes and tors, many of which are Aboriginal sacred sites, leading up to Castle Rock and 4,157-foot Mount Norman. Its eucalypt woodlands and open forests contain a remarkable variety of flowering shrubs including wattles, peaflowers, wild cherry, mintbush, and boronia. The park's fauna includes red-necked wallabies, wallaroos, red-brown finches, and eastern yellow robins.

Mount Barney National Park

Queensland Parks and Wildlife Service, Ipswich-Boonah Road, Boonah, Qld 4310; tel: 07-5463 5041; www.env.qld.gov.au

To the west of the McPherson Range, this 50-square-mile park encompasses the Mount Barney massif with its two major peaks and seven smaller ones. There is rugged scenery, challenging hiking, and the chance to spot rare peregrine falcons and brush-tailed rock wallabies. Yellow Pinch is the starting point for the difficult five-hour climb to either of Mount Barney's major peaks. The trail leads through eucalypt forest and, at higher elevations, cool subtropical forest and patches of heath. Along the way, watch for red-browed firetail finches feeding on grasses, colorful pale-headed rosellas flitting through forest clearings, and exquisite azure kingfishers peering into ponds and streams.

Fraser Island
Queensland

CHAPTER **20**

Bare feet sink into warm, wind-smoothed sand at the top of a towering dune. Far below, a lone swimmer lolls at the foot of the steep slope, whose sharp descent takes it beneath the sparkling, emerald-green waters of **Lake Wabby**. Thick forest cloaks the opposite bank. On the other side of the dune, the mobile sands of **Hammerstone Sandblow** stretch like sea swells to the grey-green tangle of wattles, wild hops, and coast banksias rimming the Pacific beach line. ◆ Half-submerged in the sands are leaning, wind-blasted stumps, the skeletal remains of a forest long ago buried by the drifting dune and now exhumed as winds sweep the sand westward toward the lake it will ultimately engulf. Laid bare, too, are ancient middens of shells and bones that recall the seafood feasts enjoyed a millennium or more ago by the indigenous Butchulla people. In **Roads of sand lead to fern-fringed creeks, stands of giant satinay trees, and windswept beaches where wild dingoes roam.** sheltered hollows, runner roots tenaciously embrace the drifting sands; in time, other plants will find a hold, and the sand hill will become scrub and then forest again. ◆ Continual shaping and reshaping – this is the essence of **Fraser Island**. For more than 700,000 years, fast-flowing rivers in New South Wales have cut into the sandstone of the Great Dividing Range and carried the debris to the Pacific shore, to be swept north by wind and wave. The immense sand mass of Fraser Island, 185 miles (300 km) north of Brisbane, is where most of these grains come to rest. At 75 miles (120 km) long, up to 9 miles (14 km) wide, and rising to 800 feet, Fraser is the largest sand island in the world. ◆ Yet, despite its sandy underbelly, it is far from being a barren expanse of dunes. Rather, it is covered with a variety of sand-adapted

At Cathedral Beach, ancient sand cliffs, bound together by silt and clay and colored by iron oxide, have been exposed by erosion.

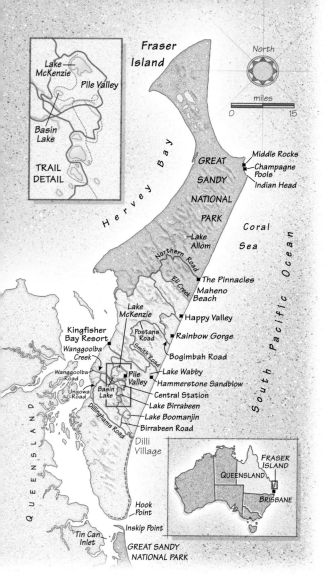

Fraser Island

TRAIL DETAIL

Lake McKenzie
Pile Valley
Basin Lake

North
miles
0   15

Hervey Bay

GREAT
SANDY
NATIONAL
PARK

Middle Rocks
Champagne Pools
Indian Head

Lake Allom

Coral Sea

Northern Road
Eli Creek

The Pinnacles
Maheno Beach

Lake McKenzie

Kingfisher Bay Resort
Wanggoolba Creek

Postans Road
Smith Road

Happy Valley
Rainbow Gorge

Bogimbah Road

Wanggoolba Road
Ungowa Road
Basin Lake
Pile Valley

Lake Wabby
Hammerstone Sandblow
Central Station
Lake Birrabeen
Lake Boomanjin
Birrabeen Road

Dillinghams Road

Dilli Village

QUEENSLAND

Hook Point

Inskip Point

Tin Can Inlet

GREAT SANDY NATIONAL PARK

FRASER ISLAND
QUEENSLAND
BRISBANE

South Pacific Ocean

honeyeaters and fairy wrens of the heathlands to the majestic white-breasted sea eagles that circle above the spray-smudged eastern beach and the migratory wading birds for whom the intertidal flats of the western shore are a favored stopover. Large mammals are fewer, but most visitors will experience the thrill of observing a dingo sauntering along the beach. There are walking trails to suit all levels of fitness, lake swimming year-round, and, during the August to October migration season, plentiful opportunities for whale watching.

The eastern beach runs almost as straight as a ruler for 60 miles (100 km) from **Dilli Village** to the jutting basalt outcrop of **Indian Head** and, at low tide, is both main thoroughfare and landing strip. If you drive onto the island from the vehicle ferry at **Hook Point**, this sea-sprayed "highway" is your first experience of beach driving. At the approach of each vehicle, flocks of terns lift from the glistening sands in a low, squawking cloud, then huffily resettle in its wake.

Life in the Lakes

From Dilli Village, one of the main inland tracks leads to the western edge of **Lake Boomanjin** and then continues north to **Lake Birrabeen**. Stop for a swim at Birrabeen – the sand is impossibly white, the water absolutely clear. Both are perched lakes, which form in the dunes high above the water table when decomposed vegetation mixes with sand and hardens into an impermeable layer. With a surface area of 500 acres, Boomanjin is the largest such lake in the world. There are 40 perched lakes on Fraser, most of which are rimmed by beaches of

Scaly-breasted lorikeets (right) inhabit the island's forests and heathlands, feeding on pollen, nectar, and fruit.

vegetation, ranging from dune grasses and creepers to flower-rich heathlands, eucalypt and banksia woodlands, and even majestic rain forest, this being one of the few places in the world where rain forest grows on sand. Inland, rain-fed, sand-bottomed lakes cradle pristine water, and springs bubble up from a vast aquifer far below the dunes, sending pristine creeks east and west to the coasts. Much of this landscape is protected by **Great Sandy National Park**, which encompasses the northern half of the island and part of the mainland near Cooloola.

Bird life is abundant on Fraser, with more than 200 species ranging from the myriad

bleached white sand that is almost pure quartz, and the water they have collected over thousands of years is remarkably clean. Some lakes, including Boomanjin, are tea-colored by tannins from fringing paperbark (melaleuca) trees; this is called "black water" and contrasts sharply with the bright white sand.

The waters are low in nutrients and support only isolated populations of tiny fish, which probably arrived as eggs on the feet of birds. The most common are the rainbow fish – no more than an inch long – that flit and dart across the sandy beds. More obvious are the numerous short-necked freshwater turtles, which range from hatchlings hardly bigger than an apricot pit to wily old females the size of dinner plates. Watch for their heads breaking the surface for air. In late spring, the females climb the banks to lay their eggs under the sand. Provided that they do not become a meal for a keen-nosed dingo or goanna, the eggs hatch underground 11 to 12 weeks later; the baby turtles then scramble to the surface and scamper to the nearest water.

At **Lake Allom**, about halfway up the island, turtles are so plentiful that you can observe them easily from the shallows or take to the water yourself and swim among them.

Central Station, five miles north of Lake Birrabeen, was once the headquarters of logging operations on the island. Today, this grassy clearing, edged with soaring hoop and kauri pines hung with staghorn ferns, is a popular camping and picnic spot; an information building has displays on the Aboriginal and European history of the island. Here, walkers have a choice of trails. A 20-minute boardwalk circuit through the filtered light of luxuriant rain forest follows the

Rising waters (above) can trap vehicles in soft sand, so avoid beach driving at high tide.

Lace monitors (right), which can grow to six feet, often scavenge around campsites.

Kings of the Sand Castle

The dingo, a subspecies of the grey wolf, evolved in Asia and arrived in Australia as a companion of seafarers about 4,000 years ago. The estimated 200 dingoes that roam wild on Fraser Island are believed to be the purest strain in eastern Australia. This is because they have had limited contact with domestic dogs, which are now banned from the island.

Each dominant male has his own territory, which he shares with his mate and their offspring. Up to 10 pups are born in early winter and raised with the assistance of older siblings. Dingoes hunt alone or in small family groups, eating anything from wallabies to insects and beached fish, although the increased presence of vehicles has discouraged them from hunting pipis (a type of shellfish) as they once did. The animals constantly patrol their beat and are seen often around campgrounds and resorts.

Dingoes may look starved but are naturally lean. Do not be tempted to feed them, do not leave food or scraps unguarded, and do not entice them closer for the sake of a photograph. To do so will blunt their hunting skills and rob them of their natural fear of humans, making them dependent on handouts and possibly aggressive in their demands for food. Far better, for both dingoes and visitors alike, is to preserve the animals' independence and natural wariness of humans, thus enabling them to hunt and roam free.

Dingoes (left) thrive on Fraser, but interaction with humans threatens to blunt their predatory instincts.

At Wanggoolba Creek (below), boardwalks make hiking easy and protect fragile rain-forest habitat.

The Eastern Beach

Cliffs of ancient colored sands, bound together by silt and clay and carved by wind and water into fantastic turrets and spires, border the eastern beach all the way from **Rainbow Gorge**, just south of Happy Valley, to the famed **Pinnacles** on **Maheno Beach**. The reds, browns, ochers, and creams of the cliffs are the result of leaching iron oxide.

At Maheno Beach, the island's largest stream, **Eli Creek**, cuts through the sands to the Pacific Ocean. A boardwalk shaded by whispering casuarinas and stilt-rooted pandanus follows the creek a short distance upstream to a small bridge, a fine spot for a dip. On a hot day, the waters are refreshingly chilly and the flow is so strong that it acts as a natural water slide, swishing you back to the beach.

Dolphins riding waves into shore are frequently spotted from the cliffs, as are migrating humpback whales. In 1770, Butchulla people standing on the island's headlands watched the earliest-known European visitor, English navigator James Cook, sail by. In his journal, Cook noted "the black bluf head or point of land on which a number of natives were assembled which occasioned my nameing it Indian Head." The waters below Indian Head are particularly rich in fish and therefore notorious for the sharks they attract. A boardwalk at **Middle**

silent, clear waters of **Wanggoolba Creek**; along its banks are rare and ancient angiopteris ferns, or king ferns, which have the largest palm fronds in the world. A 1.6-mile (2.6-km) trail leads to **Pile Valley**, where 1,000-year-old satinay trees tower up to 225 feet above the rain-forest floor. A more challenging 2½-hour (each way) walk wends from Central Station via Basin Lake and blackbutt forest to the crystal-blue waters and white sand of popular **Lake McKenzie**.

Rocks offers panoramic views of the coastline and access to the effervescent waters of **Champagne Pools** via a short, steep track. Here, a natural seawall creates deep, sandy rock pools that are filled at high tide by crashing waves. At low tide, the pools are excellent for swimming; in fact, the presence of sharks and treacherous currents elsewhere means that this is the only place on the entire eastern shore where saltwater swimming is possible. The brightly striped fish that become marooned in the pools earned them their alternative name, the Aquarium.

Eli Creek (left), with its transparent water and sandy bed, is typical of Fraser's pristine streams.

The *Maheno* (below) ran aground in 1935 as it was being towed to Japan to be scrapped.

2,000. Clan groups were concentrated on the western side of the island and used bark canoes to fish the bay and cross to the mainland.

To the Butchulla people, the island was K'Gari. That was the name of a beautiful spirit who helped create the land and, as a reward, was turned into an island paradise covered with trees, lakes, and flowers. A dawn walk on the pristine sands of the eastern beach, a stroll through a magnificent rain forest, or a dip in the crystal-clear waters of a perched lake will leave visitors to Fraser Island in no doubt that the spirit of K'Gari lives on.

Island Idyll

Human history on Fraser Island stretches back at least 5,000 and perhaps as many as 40,000 years. During periods of plentiful resources, the Aboriginal population swelled to about

TRAVEL TIPS

DETAILS

When to Go

Fraser Island has a pleasant climate year-round. In summer, the average maximum temperature is 86°F (30°C), while in winter (June–August) it is 75°F (24°C). Travelers wishing to see wildflowers in full bloom should visit between July and September, while July to October is the best time for whale watching.

How to Get There

Fraser Island is 120 miles (190 km) north of Brisbane, which has an international airport. There are regular domestic flights and bus services to Hervey Bay, the major hub for travel to Fraser Island. Vehicle barges to Fraser Island operate from Hervey Bay's Urangan Boat Harbour, from Inskip Point near Rainbow Beach, and from River Heads. Passenger launches operate daily between Urangan and Kingfisher Bay and River Heads and Wanggoolba Creek. It is also possible to fly to the island from Brisbane, Hervey Bay, Rainbow Beach, Maryborough, and Noosa.

Special Planning

A four-wheel-drive vehicle is essential for exploring Fraser Island, as most of the island's roads are sand and therefore impassable to normal vehicles. Four-wheel-drive rentals are available on the mainland or on the island at Eurong Beach, Kingfisher Bay, and Happy Valley. Drivers should ensure their vehicle is mechanically sound and equipped with essential spare parts. The speed limit is 50 mph (80km/ph) on beaches and 22 mph (35 km/ph) on tracks. Beach travel should be undertaken only during the day and around low tide, when exposed sand is firm and smooth. Creeks should not be crossed at high tide; Wathumba Creek estuary is impassable at all times. There are no medical facilities on the island, so visitors should carry a well-stocked first-aid kit.

Permits and Entry Fees

Vehicle and camping permits are required and can be obtained from the Department of Environment office at Rainbow Beach, tel: 07-5486 3160, Urangan Boat Harbour's Marina Kiosk, tel: 07-4128 9800, or the River Heads General Store, tel: 07-4125 7133.

INFORMATION

Department of Environment
P.O. Box 30, Rainbow Beach, Qld 4581; tel: 07-5486 3160; web: www.env.qld.gov.au

Fraser Coast, South Burnett Regional Tourism Board
P.O. Box 446, Maryborough, Qld 4650; tel: 07-4122 3444; web: www.frasercoast.org or e-mail: info@frasercoast.org

CAMPING

The Department of Environment has campgrounds at Dilli Village, Central Station, Lake Boomanjin, Lake McKenzie, Dundubara, Waddy Point, and Wathumpa. Basic facilities at the campsites include showers, picnic tables, barbecue grills, toilets, and tap water. Generators are not allowed. Visitors wishing to camp at Dundubara, Waddy Point, and Lake McKenzie should book and pay in advance, as these sites are very popular, particularly during school holidays. Beach camping is allowed unless signs indicate otherwise. Campers are encouraged to use portable stoves and observe fire bans, and boil or treat water before drinking.

LODGING

Eurong Beach Resort
P.O. Box 100, Maryborough, Qld 4650; tel: 07-4127 9122; web: www.fraser@is.com or e-mail: eurong@fraser~is.com

Set amid gardens just off the beach, this resort offers motel-style units, two-bedroom family apartments, luxury units, and A-frame cottages. Facilities include a swimming pool, dining room, garden restaurant, and supermarket stocked with self-catering and vehicle supplies. $$–$$$

Fraser Island Retreat
P.O. Box 224, Torquay, Qld 4655; tel: 07-4127 9144; web: www.fraserislandtours.com.au or e-mail: toptours@bigpond.com.au

Located midway along the island's surf beach at Happy Valley, this retreat offers accommodations in luxury timber cabins. Each has cooking facilities, 24-hour power, a private veranda, TV and video, and ceiling fan. Facilities include a swimming pool and barbecue area.

Kingfisher Bay Resort and Village
P.M.B. 1, Urangan, Qld 4655; tel: 07-4120 3333 or 1-800 072 555 (toll-free in Australia); web: www.kingfisherbay.com or e-mail: reservations@kingfisherbay.com

This resort has 152 hotel rooms, more than 100 self-contained villas, a 100-bed lodge for groups, four swimming pools, restaurants, bars, a shopping village, and a beauty and massage salon. Built to strict environmental guidelines, it won Australia's top architectural prize for its design. All styles of accommodation have magnificent sea or forest views that can be enjoyed from wide private verandas. $$$$

TOURS & OUTFITTERS

Air Fraser Island
Hervey Bay Airport, P.O. Box 7121, Urangan, Qld 4655; tel: 07-4125 3600; e-mail: afi@bigpond.com.au

Serving Fraser Island from a number of mainland locations, including Brisbane, Toowoomba, and Hervey Bay, this company offers a variety of air tours ranging from short scenic flights to longer expeditions that include camping packages, four-wheel-drive or bus tours, and whale-watching trips.

Stefanie Charters
7 Burrum Street, Urangan, Qld 4655; tel: 07-4125 4200; web: www.stefanie charters.com.au or e-mail: stefanie@ net-lynx.net

This company offers two- and three-day sailing tours aboard the luxury yacht MSV *Stefanie*. The two-day tour explores the waters of Hervey Bay Marine Park and the northwestern beaches of Fraser Island. The three-day tour includes two nights on the boat, a night at Hervey Bay, and a day-tour of Fraser Island. Both include whale watching during the migration seasons.

Sunrover Expeditions
1 Eversleigh Road, Scarborough, Qld 4020; tel: 07-3203 4241; web: www.powerup.com.au/ ~jgarozzo/sunrover/ or e-mail: jgarozzo@powerup.com.au

A three-day guided safari of Fraser Island from Brisbane stops on the way to the island at Teewah Beach, the wreck of the *Cherry Venture*, and Rainbow Beach. On the island, guests stay at Kingfisher Bay Resort and Village. Destinations include Lake Wabby and the Pinnacles.

Excursions

Cooloola Coast
Department of Environment, P.O Box 30, Rainbow Beach, Qld 4581; tel: 07-5486 3160; web: www.env.qld.gov.au

The Cooloola Coast covers 216 square miles of the 540-square-mile Great Sandy National Park. Like Fraser Island, the landscape is formed mainly of sand and features long golden beaches, enormous dunes, banksia woodlands, open heathlands, and towering rain forest. There is an extensive system of marked trails and excellent canoeing on the Noosa River, which leads to a series of freshwater lakes visited by pelicans and sea eagles.

Hervey Bay
Hervey Bay Tourist and Visitor Centre, 63 Old Maryborough Road, Pialba, Qld 4655; tel: 1-800 649 926.

Between August and October, several hundred humpback whales spend time in the sheltered waters of Hervey Bay on their seasonal migration south, possibly to recover from breeding or to allow calves to develop a protective layer of blubber before entering Antarctic waters. Numerous tour operators in the bay offer whale-watching trips ranging from four-hour forays to full-day outings.

Mon Repos Conservation Park
Queensland Parks and Wildlife Service, P.O. Box 1735, Bundaberg, Qld 4670; tel: 07-4159 1652; web: www.env.qld.gov.au

For thousands of years, Aboriginal groups gathered on the sands here to feast on the nesting turtles and turtle eggs. Today, the turtle rookery in this 111-acre park is the most important on the mainland. Boardwalks and viewing locations allow visitors to observe loggerhead, flatback, and green turtles; in the prime nesting season, between mid-November and mid-February, up to 20 turtles a day lumber up the beach to lay their eggs. The hatchlings emerge between mid-January and mid-March, and make a frantic dash for the safety of the water.

The Great Barrier Reef
Queensland

CHAPTER 21

t's rush hour on the outer **Barrier Reef**, and like some underwater megalopolis, the massive coral head at the Mountain dive site on **Norman Reef** is a blur of color and movement. As you fin toward the Mountain at a depth of 35 feet, the reef and its inhabitants become more distinct. Immediately in front of you, a mass of hard and soft corals seems to contain every color of the rainbow and an equally varied range of shapes, from stubby, branching staghorns through bulbous, wrinkled brain corals to extravagant gorgonian fans that spread out like intricate ferns. ◆ A mist of small fish hangs among the coral. Tiny blue gobies the size of your fingertip mingle with vivid blue-and-yellow striped angelfish, while lemon damselfish hover at the edge of the reef foraging for breakfast. Above, your air bubbles rise through schools of sweetlip emperor, with **Opportunities abound for** their exaggeratedly pursed mouths, **both divers and nondivers** and yellow-tailed fusiliers riding an ocean **to explore the marvels of this** swirl. ◆ You could easily **extraordinary underwater world.** spend your entire dive at this one spot, but you move on and begin to circum-navigate the Mountain, discovering a seemingly infinite variety of corals and marine life. Finally, just as you are about to return to the boat, your dive buddy tugs on your arm and gestures at something beneath you. There, gliding along the edge of the reef, is a small white-tipped shark. Transfixed by its sleek, smooth beauty, you start to follow it. But with one powerful flick of the tail, it accelerates rapidly and disappears into the endless blue. ◆ Just one dive on the **Great Barrier Reef** can provide you with an immediate and lasting sense of the extraordinary abundance and variety of its life-forms. Yet, in reality, what you see will be a mere snapshot of the most diverse ecosystem

A diver peers through the intricate fronds of a gorgonian fan. Corals of all kinds are constructed by, and support colonies of, living polyps.

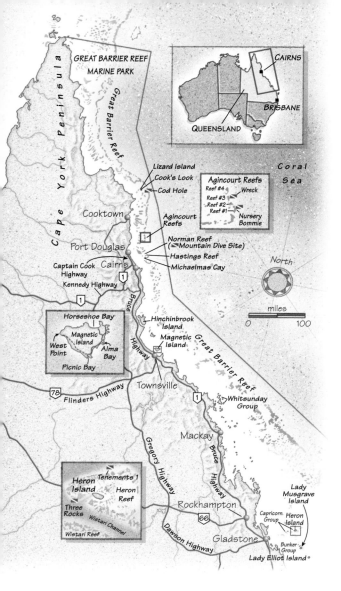

Map Labels

GREAT BARRIER REEF MARINE PARK

Great Barrier Reef

Cape York Peninsula

CAIRNS

BRISBANE

QUEENSLAND

Lizard Island
Cook's Look
Cod Hole

Agincourt Reefs
Reef #4   Wreck
Reef #3
Reef #2
Reef #1   Nursery
Agincourt   Bommie
Reefs

Coral Sea

Cooktown

Port Douglas

Norman Reef
(Mountain Dive Site)
Hastings Reef
Michaelmas Cay

Captain Cook
Highway
Kennedy Highway

Cairns

North

miles
0   100

Horseshoe Bay

Magnetic
Island
West
Point   Alma
                    Bay
Picnic Bay

Hinchinbrook
Island
Magnetic
Island

Great Barrier Reef

Flinders Highway

Townsville

Whitsunday
Group

Mackay

Gregory Highway

Bruce Highway

Heron
Island   Tenements 1
                    Heron
                    Reef
Three
Rocks
          Wistari Channel
Wistari Reef

Rockhampton

Capricorn
Group
Lady
Musgrave
Island
Heron
Island

Dawson Highway

Gladstone

Bunker
Group
Lady Elliot Island

Since 1975, the Barrier Reef has been protected by the world's largest marine reserve, the **Great Barrier Reef Marine Park**, covering 134,633 square miles and encompassed by the largest of all World Heritage areas. The reserve includes not only the 2,900 or so separate coral reefs and 300 coral cays – low islands of coral and crushed sand – that make up the Barrier Reef but also 618 continental islands.

The reefs alone harbor the greatest variety of life-forms found in any one location on Earth. Conservative estimates put the number of fish species at 1,500, and no fewer than 400 species of sponge and 500 species of seaweed adorn 400 kinds of coral. Even more astonishing is the reef's mollusk community, which includes approximately 4,000 species, ranging from tiny nudibranch sea slugs through hard-shelled scallops, oysters, and clams to cephalopods such as octopus, squid, and cuttlefish. The warm waters of the Coral Sea are also home to or visited by an extraordinary array of marine mammals, including green, hawksbill, and loggerhead turtles, dolphins, dugongs, and humpback whales. In addition, the tropical skies, islands, and cays ring with the cries of more than 215 species of birds.

Reef Builders

But perhaps the most remarkable single fact about the Great Barrier Reef is that it too is a living entity. This natural masterwork consists of billions of individual corals, each of which is made up of thousands of tiny jellyfishlike animals known as polyps. The polyps grow by dividing and multiplying, a process known as budding, and feed on nutrients produced by algae that live within the coral. As the polyps develop, they precipitate calcium carbonate from the seawater to form a hard limestone "skeleton." It is this chalky white structure that forms the basis of the reef on which the colorful living polyps continue to grow.

Sap-sucking slugs (left) are named for their feeding habits: they suck nutrients out of algae.

in the world, one tiny piece of a magnificent coral puzzle that comprises not just one reef but by far the largest collection of coral reefs on Earth.

Extending for 1,430 miles (2,300 km) along the Queensland coast, the Great Barrier Reef covers an area that exceeds that of Great Britain and Ireland combined. Indeed, so large is it that the only way to obtain a complete view is to travel into space: seen from beyond Earth's atmosphere, the reef stands out as the only visible organic structure on the surface of the planet.

Construction of the Great Barrier Reef began 18 million years ago as the Australian continent drifted northwest into coral-rich tropical seas. But it was not until the seas rose after the last ice age, around 8,000 years ago, that the pre-sent reef began to form on Australia's coastal shelf. Conditions were, and continue to be, ideal for reef development. The sea temperature remains 73°–84°F (23°–29°C) year-round, the waters are shallow and clear (levels of less than 98 feet are a prerequisite for coral growth), and levels of sunlight are high, encouraging the production of nutrients.

If any one event epitomizes the vibrancy of life on the Great Barrier Reef, it is the mass spawning of corals, which takes place each year between October and December, over several nights just after the full moon. This is a memorable sight, with the corals ejecting huge explosions of pink and orange eggs and sperm into the dark water. Fertilization then occurs in the open sea, perhaps hundreds

Coral cod (left) allow cleaner shrimps to remove parasites from their bodies.

Clown anemone fish (below) produce a slimy coating that protects them from the stings of sea anemones.

of miles from where the eggs and sperm originated, forming larvae that then lodge in the coral and begin to grow.

Outer Limits

To the first-time visitor, the scale of the Great Barrier Reef is daunting. For practical purposes, it helps to think of it as being made up of three distinct sections – north, central, and south. The suitability of each as a base for exploring the reef depends on both your travel plans and your interests.

Extending from the virtually uninhabited tip of **Cape York** to just south of **Cairns**, the northern section includes some of the most remote and pristine parts of the reef but also some of its most accessible dive sites. Indeed,

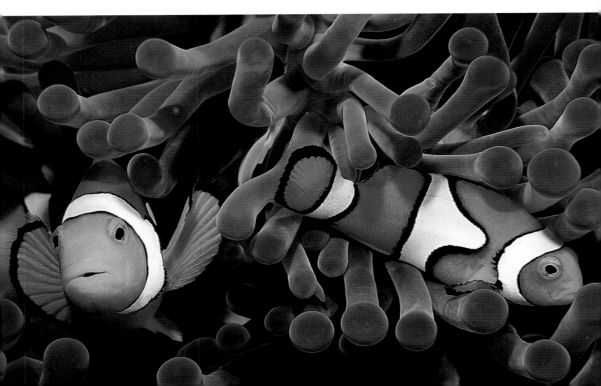

the region's coastal towns of Cairns and **Port Douglas**, with their abundance of accommodations, boat operators, and dive schools, are probably the most convenient jumping-off points on the entire mainland.

The northern Barrier Reef consists of a series of linear or "ribbon" reefs that run along the edge of the continental shelf flanked, on the mainland side, by a network of broad "platform" reefs, a few of which are topped by low-wooded islands. Just offshore lie numerous continental islands, some of which, such as Lizard Island and Green Island, have their own large "fringing" reefs.

Day trips depart from Cairns and Port Douglas to continental islands and many parts of the outer reef. At **Michaelmas Cay**, you can walk among huge colonies of migrating seabirds, including up to 20,000 sooty terns and 8,000 common noddies, and dive on the surrounding reef among forests of staghorn corals, swaying sea fans, and beautiful black coral trees. **Agincourt Reefs**, the only ribbon reefs that can be reached on a day trip, have several dive sites, including the **Wreck**, with its giant clams, soft corals, huge Maori wrasses,

Balding Bay (above), with its sweep of pristine sand and giant granite boulders, is typical of the beaches on Magnetic Island.

Scorpion fish (left) have prominent, venomous spines that can inflict a painful, occasionally fatal, sting.

The regal angelfish (opposite, top) is one of about 30 species of angelfish found in Australian waters.

and bulky parrotfish, and the **Nursery Bommie**, where schools of Pacific barracuda roam. Day tours to these reefs usually include options for nondivers including snorkeling and excursions in glass-bottomed boats and semisubmersibles. Longer multiday cruises will allow keen divers to explore outer reefs such as Norman, Saxon, and Hastings.

Another option is to stay on one of the resort islands. Although it's remote, **Lizard Island**, 150 miles (240 km) north of Cairns, offers diving just off the beach on its own fringing reef and is less than 10 miles from the outer rim of the Barrier Reef. A short boat ride from Lizard is the famous **Cod Hole** dive site, where groups of up to 10 huge, fat-lipped potato cods, each weighing up to 600 pounds, congregate. In addition, the island has 23 beaches and many excellent bush walks, including a trek to its highest point – 1,171-foot **Cook's Look** – from which Captain Cook mapped a passage through the maze of surrounding reefs in 1770.

To the Islands

Just south of Cairns, the continental shelf widens and the reef is less dense and more distant from the mainland. Nearer the shore, however, lies an abundance of fascinating continental islands, including Hinchinbrook Island and the idyllic Whitsunday Group, some of which have fringing reefs.

The principal mainland center here is **Townsville**. Less tourist-oriented than Cairns, this low-key city lies a good two and a half hours from the reef by boat. But it does have

a 650,000-gallon **Great Barrier Aquarium**, which features many of the corals and marine creatures found at sea and has even developed its own reef ecosystems.

From Townsville, it's a short hop to beautiful **Magnetic Island**, with its boulder-strewn shores and spectacular bays. Nearly two-thirds of the island is national park and includes 15 miles (24 km) of trails. Even short treks, such as the easy 0.9-mile (1.4 km) stroll to the World War II command and signal posts at **Horseshoe Bay**, provide a chance to see wild koalas propped up in the branches of gum trees. The 5-mile (8-km) trail from **Picnic Bay** leads to an area of tidal wetland at **West Point**, where wading birds patrol, yellow-clawed fiddler crabs forage, and tiny mudskippers zip

Dugongs (right) inhabit shallow coastal waters along the north coast of Australia, especially near sea-grass beds.

The Dugong

Looking like a tuskless walrus or a cross between a hippo and a dolphin, this gentle marine mammal is one of the reef's most intriguing creatures. Sailors likened dugongs to mermaids, but for a sea nymph the dugong is a touch on the Rubenesque side, weighing in at up to 880 pounds and reaching a length of 10 feet. Grey-gold, with a soft, rounded head, small eyes, and a large snout, it uses its whalelike tail fluke to propel itself slowly and gracefully and its front flippers to balance and turn.

Dugongs are the only marine mammals that feast almost exclusively on plants, and an adult consumes an average of 55 pounds of sea grass a day, a preference that earned it the alternative name of "sea cow." Indeed, the dugong is more closely related to a land mammal, the elephant, than to other marine mammals like whales and dolphins, and it can hold its breath underwater for only a few minutes at a time. Its closest living aquatic relative is the manatee.

The reef's population of 12,000 is one of the largest in the world, but even here numbers are on the decline. Causes include illegal netting, collisions with ships, and heavy discharges of silt from coastal rivers that have inhibited the growth of sea-grass beds. The dugong's extremely slow reproductive process – females calve only once every three to five years and the pregnancy lasts 13 months – also makes it vulnerable. In an attempt to address this decline, a system of 16 dugong sanctuaries has been set up along the Queensland coast.

The Crown-of-Thorns Starfish

This sinister-looking, coral-eating, spine-covered starfish is one of the most unwelcome guests on the Great Barrier Reef. With a capacity to chomp their way through up to 65 square feet of coral a year, large populations of this creature can badly damage individual reefs and pose a serious threat to the Barrier Reef as a whole. It takes most coral communities a minimum of 15 years to recover from an outbreak and, in the case of larger, slower-growing corals, up to 500 years.

COTS, as they are known for short, are usually brown or reddish grey, with red-tipped spines and between 14 and 18 arms. Growing to between 10 and 13 inches in diameter, the starfish eats by pushing its membranous stomach out of its mouth and enveloping its food. An enzyme in its stomach then breaks down the coral tissue, leaving behind a white skeleton. The faster-growing staghorn and plate corals seem to be its favorite meal, possibly because other corals are harder to grip due to their slippery surfaces or are protected by small crabs or shrimps. Unfortunately, female starfish are prolific spawners, producing up to 100 million eggs at a time.

It is not clear what causes COTS outbreaks, although prime suspects include heavy run-off from the mainland, which encourages algal blooms on which starfish larvae feed, and human overfishing of the creature's natural predators. Populations have recently increased on reefs near Cairns, and scientists fear that another serious outbreak of COTS is just around the corner. Earlier outbreaks in the 1970s and 1980s affected around 17 percent of the entire reef, with five percent suffering severe attacks.

Crown-of-thorns starfish (above) have had a devastating effect on the Great Barrier Reef in recent years.

The forms and colors (opposite, top) of reef life are so diverse that no two dives are ever the same.

centers of **Mackay** and **Rockhampton** – ensures that they are rarely visited. Fortunately, the southern region also contains some of the most accessible parts of the reef, particularly the **Capricorn–Bunker Group** off Gladstone, which includes the islands of Lady Elliot, Lady Musgrave, and Heron.

Little more than a sandy dot in the midst of the dazzling Coral Sea, **Heron Island** is a stunning 42-acre coral cay surrounded by top-class dive sites. Many are in shallow waters on the cay's own reef, **Heron Reef**, or the adjacent **Wistari Reef**. At the **Tenements 1** site on Heron Reef, you can drift dive along a horseshoe-shaped wall regularly visited by both white-tipped and grey reef sharks, as well as by large pelagic species such as tuna and mackerel. At the **Three Rocks** site on Wistari Reef, three large bommies (coral heads) rise above a steep embankment that slopes down to a depth of 59 feet. Look for white-tipped sharks at the base of the slope and brown-striped butterfly cod – also known as fire fish because of their highly venomous spines – hovering around the bommies.

Back on land, Heron resounds to the cacophonous calls of tens of thousands of

across the flats. Divers can explore several shallow fringing reefs, including those off **Alma Bay** on the eastern side of the island, where they'll find gardens of large brain, staghorn, and plate corals, and may encounter six-banded angelfish and ornately patterned boxfish.

Coral Cays

Although some of the southern reefs are among the largest in the world, their remoteness – many lie around 90 miles (150 km) from the mainland

Brown boobies (left) nest in large colonies on many of the reef's coral cays.

One-Tree Island (opposite, bottom) is a scientific research center located a short distance from Heron Island in the Capricorn-Bunker Group.

birds. It is a serenade that lasts well into the evening, when the chunky wedge-tailed shearwaters are still in full song. On the easy 1.1-mile (1.8-km) walk around the island, you may spot waders such as the golden plover, one of several migratory species that travel from Siberia, as well as – predictably – herons, of the reef variety. In the island's low-lying woodlands you may also come across diminutive land birds, including the pretty silver-eye and the buff-breasted rail, which nests in a burrow in the ground. Both green and loggerhead turtles breed on the island too, from November onward. Their hatchlings emerge eight to 12 weeks later and scramble down the beach toward the sea, desperately trying to avoid hungry seabirds. During winter, pods of humpback whales pass just offshore.

From some of the world's largest mammals to the most minuscule and delicate of sea anemones, the range of life on display on the Great Barrier Reef is truly astounding. Whether you choose to explore its gleaming coral cays on foot or discover its myriad underwater treasures by immersing yourself in the warm waters of the Coral Sea, you're sure to agree that for once the phrase "wonder of the world" is entirely justified.

TRAVEL TIPS

DETAILS

When to Go

Late April to October is the best time to visit the Great Barrier Reef. During winter, the daytime maximum temperature ranges between 77°F and 81°F (25°–27°C), with overnight minimums of between 63°F and 68°F (17°–20°C). In late spring, summer, and early fall (November to April) temperatures soar, with average daily maximums of between 86°F and 93°F (30°–34°C), and there are frequent heavy storms as well as the threat of hurricanes.

How to Get There

Cairns is the major hub for travel to the Great Barrier Reef. There are regular international and domestic flights to Cairns International Airport, which is 5 miles (8 km) north of the city. Other airports in the region include Townsville (for Magnetic Island), Hamilton Island (for the Whitsundays) and Gladstone or Bundaberg (for access to the southern reef islands such as Heron and Lady Elliot).

Special Planning

It is dangerous to swim off unprotected beaches between November and April due to the presence of deadly box jellyfish. Fully protected swimming enclosures are provided at Port Douglas, Palm Cove, and Mission Beach. Visitors should remember that the reef is home to some dangerous marine creatures and that coral can be sharp. Wear sturdy shoes for reef walks and do not touch the coral when diving.

Permits and Entry Fees

No entry fees or permits are required.

INFORMATION

Queensland Travel Centre
P.O. Box 428, Newcastle, NSW 2300; tel: 131 801; web: www.queensland-travel-centre.com.au

Great Barrier Reef Marine Park Authority
P.O. Box 1379, Townsville, Qld 4810; tel: 07-4750 0700; web: www.gbrmpa.gov.au

Queensland Parks and Wildlife Service at Reef Wonderland
Flinders Street, Townsville, Qld 4810; tel: 07-4721 2399; web: www.env.qld.gov.au

CAMPING

There are scores of campsites along the reef and on its islands. Designated Queensland Parks and Wildlife Service campsites are indicated on park maps. Where there is no ranger, visitors must self-register and pay fees using the box provided.

LODGING

PRICE GUIDE – double occupancy	
$ = up to $49	$$ = $50–$99
$$$ = $100–$149	$$$$ = $150+

Heron Island Resort
Via Gladstone, Qld 4680; tel: 07-4972 9055; web: www.poresorts.com.au or e-mail: poresorts@aol.com

Accommodations here range from premium beach houses to cabins with shared facilities. Amenities include a restaurant, bars and lounges, swimming pools, and tennis courts. Staff members conduct complimentary interpretative walks. $$$$.

Magnetic Island Holiday Units
16 Yule Street, Picnic Bay, Magnetic Island, Qld 4819; tel: 07-4778 5246; web: www.magnetic-island.com.au/mi-unit/htm

Set in tropical gardens with abun-dant bird life, butterflies, possums, and rock-wallabies, these apartments are within walking distance of the beach. All units have ceiling fans, televisions, laundry facilities, and air conditioning. $$

Novotel Palm Cove Resort
Coral Coast Drive, Palm Cove, Qld 4879; tel: 07-4059 1234; web: www.novotel/pcr.com.au or e-mail: res1@novotel/pcr.com.au

A two-minute walk from stunning Palm Cove beach, this luxurious resort has 10 swimming pools, tennis and squash courts, a gym, and a nine-hole golf course. $$$–$$$$

Oasis Resort
122 Lake Street, Cairns, Qld 4870; tel: 07-4080 1888; web: www.oasis/cairns.com.au or e-mail: oasis@internetnorth.com.au

A central location makes this pleasant hotel one of the best places to stay in the city. The 314 rooms have private baths, and facilities include a pool, gym, restaurant, and bar. $$$–$$$$

Sheraton Mirage
Davidson Street, Port Douglas, Qld 4871; tel: 07-4099 5888; web: www.sheraton-mirage.com or e-mail:smpdsales@tnq.com.au

Set on 1.2 miles (2 km) of beach frontage, this sumptuous hotel has 294 rooms and 110 villas, all with garden or lagoon views. Facilities include an 18-hole international golf course, a five-acre swimming lagoon, four restaurants, and eight tennis courts. $$$$

Whitsunday Wilderness Lodge
P.O. Box 409, Paddington, Qld 4064; tel: 07-4946 9777; web: www.whitsundaywilderness.com.au or e-mail: lodge@whitsunday.net.au

Located on South Long Island in the Whitsunday Islands, this is an enlightened and comfortable ecoresort with 10 waterfront cabins hosting a maximum of 20 guests at any one time. The cabins have private baths and private balconies, and the price includes all meals. $$$$

TOURS & OUTFITTERS

Deep Sea Divers Den

319 Draper Street, Cairns, Qld 4870; tel: 07-4031 2223; web: www.divers-den.com or e-mail: info@divers-den.com

This company's snorkeling trips, one-day dives, and dive courses cater to all levels of expertise. The most popular outing is a three-day, two-night live-aboard trip involving 11 scuba dives and including all dive equipment, meals, and accommodations.

Down Under Dive

287 Draper Street, Cairns, Qld 4870; tel: 07-4031 1288 or 1-800 079 099 (toll-free in Australia); web: www.downunderdive.com.au or e-mail: reservations@downunderdive.com.au

Down Under Dive offers a variety of dive courses, two- and three-day snorkeling trips, and reef cruises. Longer tours are conducted on the luxurious S.V. *Atlantic Clipper* and include all transfers, equipment, and meals.

Ocean Spirit Cruises

33 Lake Street, Cairns, Qld 4870; tel: 07-4031 2920 or 1-800 644 227 (toll-free in Australia); web: www.oceanspirit.com.au or e-mail: ospirit@internetnorth.com.au

Cruises set sail for a day to either Michaelmas or Upolu Cays from Cairns. Options include diving, snorkeling, and guided bird-watching tours of Michaelmas Cay.

Quicksilver

Marina Mirage, Port Douglas, Qld, 4871; tel: 07-4099 5500; web: www.quicksilver-cruises.com or e-mail: reservations@quicksilver-cruises.com

This operator takes up to 500 people daily to the Low Isles from Port Douglas on the catamaran *Wavedancer*. The company also has its own reef observatory and semisubmersible vessels that allow a close-up view of sea life.

Excursions

Haggerstone Island

Haggerstone Island Guest House, P.O. Box 1538, Cairns, Qld 4870; tel: 07-4099 4644; e-mail: visitors@greatbarrierreef.aus.net

About 370 miles (600 km) north of Cairns, near the tip of Cape York, two and a half hours away by small plane, Haggerstone is encircled by shallow fudge-colored reefs and yellow sand cays. Its exclusive tropical guesthouse, featuring a large Thai-style central hut and three wooden shacks, caters to small numbers of visitors who feast daily on freshly caught fish. The island is home to tiny sunbirds, finches, Torres Straight pigeons, and bar-shouldered doves. Just offshore, snorkelers will delight in the myriad marine life of neighboring lagoons and can view the remnants of an 1840s shipwreck. More experienced divers can make a short trip to the outer reef, where underwater escarpments plummet up to 2,000 feet to the seafloor.

Hinchinbrook Island

Department of Environment, 142 Victoria Street, Cardwell, Qld 4849; tel: 07-4066 8155; web: www.env.qld.gov.au

The largest of Australia's island national parks, Hinchinbrook is a mountainous, rain-forest-covered wilderness, just off the mainland around 120 miles (190 km) south of Cairns. Its rugged outline is dominated by 3,676-foot Mount Bowen; mangroves and fine beaches line its shores. There is superb hiking, and dugongs are regularly spotted offshore.

Whitsunday Islands

Whitsunday Information Centre, Corner Mandalay and Shute Harbour Roads, P.O. Box 332, Airlie Beach, Qld 4802; tel: 07-4946 7022.

Rising out of the ocean like verdant hillocks, this constellation of 74 islands offers a number of attractive bases from which to explore the reef. Most of the islands have fringing reefs as well as forests full of hoop pines, eucalypts, and acacias. Boat tours of the group leave from Shute Harbour and Abel Point Marina near Airlie Beach, and range from day trips to three-day adventures. Self-skippered yachts are also available.

The Wet Tropics
Queensland

CHAPTER **22**

Brooding clouds, vestiges of the wet season, curtain the sky like heavy, grey drapes. Deep within the dense tropical rain forest, still moist from an overnight shower, the Boyd's forest dragon clings like a shadowy sentinel to a slender sapling. It is perfectly still but fiercely alert, maintaining a silent command post amid the syncopated chorusing of frogs hidden in **Mossman Gorge**. ◆ In this verdant kingdom, where brilliant blooms, birds, and butterflies are the colorful exceptions, the dragon is the master of disguise. Its spiny yellow, green, and brown body, textured like a file, merges artfully with the mottled mosses cushioning the tree's stem. Its presence would go completely unnoticed but for the occasional swift turn of its prehistoric-looking head to scour the forest floor for insects, or the lightning-fast flick of its fleshy tongue to snatch a snack of ants. ◆ Today it's an unsuspecting grasshopper that's on the menu. Startled by the haunting call of a nearby wompoo pigeon, the insect has been flushed from

Nowhere in Australia do plants and animals thrive in greater abundance than in the tropical rain forests of far-north Queensland.

the safety of the tangled undergrowth and unknowingly has caught the dragon's eye. In a flash, the reptile scurries headfirst down the tree, leaps to the ground, rises up on its spindly hind legs, and waddles off in hot pursuit, as awkward as a gent in high heels. ◆ There are scores of curious creatures secreted in the shady nether world of the World Heritage-listed **Wet Tropics** of far-north Queensland: tree-climbing kangaroos, odd bats with snorkel noses, large birds wearing helmeted crowns, and giant purple pythons uncoiling to 23 feet. Indeed, this 164,372-acre rain-forest wonderland, which extends 360 miles (580 km) down the northeast coast of Queensland

The frilled lizard raises its frill to ward off predators or rival males. At other times, the folds of skin lie flat on its neck and shoulders.

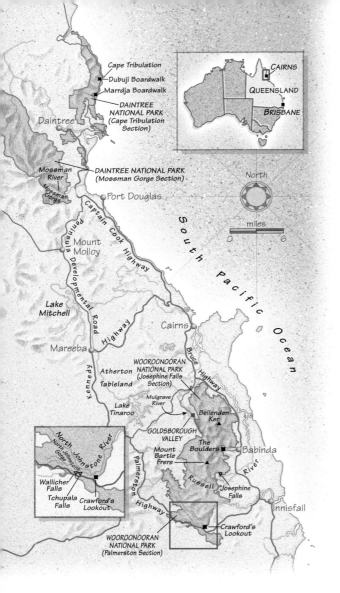

both comfortable and challenging walking tracks, scenic driving circuits, cultural tours, and nocturnal adventures, all within a few hours' drive of **Cairns**, opens a window on this most primeval of landscapes and the Aboriginal peoples it has sustained for thousands of years.

Visitors follow part of an age-old Aboriginal walking trail as they travel north from Cairns to remotely beautiful **Daintree National Park**, the jewel of the Wet Tropics. This park incorporates the country's largest tract of lowland rain forest and a mosaic of mountain forests, heaths, swamps, and coral foreshores in two distinct areas: the 161,785-acre Mossman Gorge section at its southern extremity, and the 42,237-acre sliver of **Cape Tribulation** to the north, where the rain forest greets the **Great Barrier Reef** with a broad smile of inviting white sand.

Most of the Mossman section is inaccessible, except to experienced and well-equipped bush walkers, but its defining feature, Mossman Gorge, is easily reached and the best starting point for a Daintree odyssey. Here, the pristine **Mossman River** carves a path through a steep-sided valley, tumbling over moss-cloaked granite in a series of cascading pools. The 1.7-mile (2.7-km) circuit trail, an easy amble, is the perfect introduction to its lush lowland rain forest, and especially on humid days, the forest's shade provides relief from the oppressive heat.

Running parallel to the river, the trail exposes boulders carpeted with emerald lichens, liverworts, and small lithophytes (plants that live on rocks), and trees like rose butternut, candlenut, pencil cedar, and Daintree penda adorned with rare orchids

from **Cooktown** to **Townsville**, harbors the greatest diversity of wildlife in Australia, with no less than 400 endangered species, 70 of them found nowhere else in the world. Its 19 national parks and 31 state forests are also staggeringly rich in plant life, including descendants of some of the oldest species on earth. A living museum, the Wet Tropics has unlocked many long-held evolutionary secrets.

Rain Forest Reconnaissance

While much of the Wet Tropics is rugged and remote, a plethora of

Eclectus parrots (left) live only in the rain forests of Cape York and were not discovered until 1913.

Quinkan art (opposite, top) is named for the Quinkans, or spirit-figures, that often appear in the paintings.

The Daintree River (right) snakes through a verdant tunnel of creepers, figs, ferns, and palms.

and large basket and bird's-nest ferns. The turquoise-winged Ulysses butterfly occasionally flutters by, but Australia's largest butterfly, the velvety green-and-black Cairns birdwing, prefers the heights of the rain-forest canopy.

Birdwatchers are rarely disappointed on this walk. Brush turkeys commonly scratch about the undergrowth, and the pale-yellow robin and spectacled monarch both construct their nests here, decorating them with flakes of lichen and swatches of moss. During the warmer months, keep your eyes peeled for the buff-breasted paradise kingfisher, with its distinctive royal blue, orange, and black plumage and long white tail feathers, which eschews trees to nest in termite mounds.

The traditional custodians of the north Queensland forests, the Kuku-Yalanji Aborigines, had ingenious uses for a range of trees found within Mossman Gorge. The sap of the milky pine was potent enough to stun fish, and its bark was skillfully fashioned into canoes to ply the seasonal rivers. The gummy seed of the sticky bean was an effective trap, gluing unsuspecting birds' feathers

and preventing them from flying. The Aborigines' intimate understanding of rain-forest ecology also gave them fascinating insights into food availability. When the sticky bean tree was flowering, they knew it was time to dig incubating scrub-fowl eggs from their mounds; when the wattle wore its vivid yellow dress, the mullet were plump for spearing on the coast. In a reserve within Mossman Gorge, the Kuku-Yalanji share the secrets of their traditional rain-forest lifestyle during a short cultural tour.

Time Travelers

The forebears of the ribbonwood tree, found within the Cape Tribulation forest canopy, flourished perhaps 120 million years ago – long before people first set foot on the continent. At the time, Australia was part of the supercontinent Gondwana and draped in a velourlike cape of rain forest, sewn with cycads, mosses, ferns, and conifers. The appearance of the ribbonwood's ancestors heralded a major development – the evolution of our planet's first flowering plants. Only 18 plant families of this antiquity have been identified worldwide, 10 of them in the forest refuges of Daintree National Park, and within these families at least 50 species are found exclusively in the Wet Tropics. This botanical suite represents the greatest diversity of ancient flowering plants anywhere in the world.

Until its rediscovery in 1971, the ribbonwood (*Idiospermum australiense*) was known only from a specimen collected in 1902. Today, little changed over the millennia from its ancestors, it still sports sweet-smelling cerise flowers during the dry season and can be seen along the Daintree's **Marrdja Boardwalk**, just south of Cape Tribulation. Like some botanical time-tunnel, this pathway

near Oliver Creek reveals relict cycads and zamia palms as well as more recent arrivals such as mangroves.

During drier spells, the forest rings with the calls of plump wompoo pigeons, and pairs of Victoria's riflebirds are occasionally seen engaging in a synchronized, swaying seduction. At higher altitudes, careful observers might notice the ornate bowers built on the ground by the golden bowerbird, which may be up to eight feet long and are furnished with lichens and freshly picked blooms. Lesser housekeepers like the yellow-spotted and bridled honeyeaters are more likely to be occupied feeding on insects and blossoms.

One of the Daintree's few diurnal mammals lives in thicker rain forest nearby. The smallest and most primitive member of the kangaroo family, the musky rat-kangaroo emerges from thickets of the wait-a-while palm or rustles about the forest floor collecting leaves. Its distant cousin, the Bennett's tree-kangaroo, would never be so bold. A

Boyd's forest dragons (left) have a body length of about six inches, but their tails are twice as long.

Buttress roots (right) help trees to anchor in the poor, shallow soils of the rain forest.

Rain-Forest Gardener

Saltwater, or estuarine, crocodiles (left) lie in wait for passing prey under murky water or aquatic plants.

The cassowary (right) is now an endangered species, mainly as a result of habitat loss.

One of the most significant and striking members of the Wet Tropics rain-forest community is the large flightless bird known as the cassowary. Stalking the forest for forest fruits, snails, insects, and fungi, and passing the fruit seeds in its droppings, this 6½-foot bird may be responsible for dispersing the seeds of as many as 100 plant species.

The cassowary is, however, a furtive and endangered rain-forest gardener. Although it is one of the world's largest birds, its dark plumage helps it merge with the shaded rain forest. But destruction of its lowland habitat, predation by domestic and feral animals, and road deaths have contributed to a dramatic decline in its numbers. Scientists now believe there may be as few as 1,500 birds left in their restricted Wet Tropics and Cape York range.

For most of the year, the cassowary is solitary. After a brief mating, the devoted father incubates the eggs for about two months before caring for the striped chicks for a further nine months. It takes the youngsters several years to develop their glossy dark plumage and distinctive markings – a brilliant necklace of pale blue, azure blue, and orange skin, accentuated by a pair of red wattles.

Cassowaries are often seen around Cape Tribulation, Mission Beach, Kuranda, and Wallaman Falls, so drive carefully in these areas. Avoid feeding or approaching the birds as they can be unpredictable and are potentially dangerous: the claw of the inside toe on each foot is armed with a large spike that can inflict severe injuries. If you encounter a cassowary, back away slowly, keeping it in sight.

secretive animal, it leaves tell-tale scratches or mud marks on the trees it scales, but a sudden crash of branches and a flash of brown fur as it alights from its treetop roost is usually all that is heard and seen of this creature.

While wildlife is its major attraction, Cape Tribulation also caters to those travelers simply intent on beach-combing its stunning coastline, shaded by beach almonds and beach pandanus. About a quarter of a mile from the parking lot at the cape, north of Marrdja, a platform commands glorious views of the beach and ocean. Close by, the **Dubuji Boardwalk** leads visitors through fan palms that stand 50 feet high and resemble giant lime parasols, and past swamps to shoreline mangroves – sentries at the entrance to north Myall Beach.

A spotlighting tour is a great way to maximize your chances of seeing some of the Daintree's nocturnal creatures and to experience its cloistered confines after dark. You'll undoubtedly hear the screeching of flying foxes as they drop from their daytime perches like ripe fruit to embark on a night's frenzied feeding. If you're lucky, you might come eye-to-eye with a rare or endangered possum such as the resident pygmy-possum or the striped possum, a beautifully marked species that draws attention to itself by tearing at dead wood in search of beetle larvae.

Riding the Rapids

It's a very different sound – that of rushing water – that greets more daring visitors to the heart of **Wooroonooran National Park**, between Cairns and **Innisfail**. Here, the fast-flowing **Russell River** hurries from its watershed in the **Bellenden Ker Range**, swirling cool and clear through isolated lowland forest to its meeting with the mighty South Pacific. Uncoiling like a serpent in the shadow of Queensland's highest peak, 5,320-foot **Mount Bartle Frere**, the Russell is one of the most easily accessible of the Wet Tropics' magical rivers and perfect for whitewater rafting or challenging kayaking.

Traveling the river, especially after the summer deluge, is an invigorating experience. Once the storms have abated, the Russell flows strong and high, swollen by an average annual rainfall of close to 19 feet in its mountainous catchment. Its meandering banks are fringed by overhanging crow's nest ferns and rain-forest giants including figs, tulip oaks, river cherries, and white beech. On some of their boughs, ornately patterned, nonvenomous amethystine and carpet pythons absorb the sun's energy-giving rays.

A variety of fish, including sooty grunter, native catfish, and jungle perch live in these waters, but visitors can hope for only a fleeting glimpse of another of their inhabitants – the platypus. This shy, egg-laying mammal, which emerges from its burrow at dusk to snuffle the river's shores with its duck-like beak, is most common in the river's

The Cairns birdwing (above) is Australia's biggest butterfly. Females are significantly larger than males.

Common spotted cuscuses (right) favor the rain-forest canopy and are therefore hard to spot.

Punsand Bay (below) lies near the tip of Cape York, the northernmost point on the Australian mainland.

more tranquil backwaters and unlikely to be found amid the whirlpool rapids.

Stepping out of the raft, still buzzing with energy, visitors can experience more of 196,365-acre Wooroonooran, the largest rain-forest park in Queensland, on foot. A network of graded trails entreats visitors to sample the luxuriant vegetation in the **Palmerston** section of the park, south of the Russell River, which is renowned for its generous spill of waterfalls.

From **Crawford's Lookout** on the **Palmerston Highway**, you can descend deep

Cape York Peninsula

An acute triangle of almost 50,000 square miles, the **Cape York Peninsula** is one of the wildest, least developed, and most sparsely populated regions of Australia. It's largely a four-wheel-drive frontier: roads are rough and dusty in the dry season and a quagmire in the Wet. Traveling north from Cooktown during the Dry, it takes three or four days to reach Australia's northernmost tip. It's a fascinating trip, revealing tropical rain forest corridors to the east, sparse savanna grasslands and rugged sandstone ranges in the dry inland, and crocodile-infested wetlands on the west coast.

About one-tenth of the peninsula is protected within almost 40 parks and reserves of widely varying character. Straddling the Archer River and its tributaries, **Mungkan Kandju National Park** is flush with birds, most of which live in the rain forest fringing the river banks or on its pristine lagoons. Farther north, **Iron Range National Park** protects the largest area of lowland rain forest in Australia, which is home to the stunning eclectus parrot, spotted and grey cuscus, rufous spiny bandicoot, and a dazzling array of butterflies. One of the most popular stopovers is **Jardine River National Park**, in the far north, which features delightful waterfalls, most notably Indian Head Falls.

For at least 40,000 years, Aborigines lived well off the region's abundant resources. A record of their lives and spiritual beliefs remains imprinted in the sandstone ranges between Cooktown and the Palmer River, most notably at the **Quinkan** art site in the Laura River Valley. The region's custodians, the Ang-Gnarra Aboriginal Corporation, provide tours of the rock art, which ranges from simple hand stencils to magnificent friezes of hundreds of figures and animals.

The roots of ancient strangler figs (right) form a giant curtain across the base of a host tree.

into the **North Johnstone Gorge** to visit the **Tchupala** and **Wallicher Falls**. More experienced and physically fit visitors can tackle the arduous 9-mile (15-km) trail that winds its way to the summit of Mount Bartle Frere, in the northern **Josephine Falls** section. This is a hazardous climb, hampered by slippery rocks and often poor visibility. But from progressively higher vantage points, tenacious walkers are rewarded with splendid views of the Atherton Tableland, **Bellenden Ker** (the state's second-highest peak), the **Mulgrave River Valley**, and the north Queensland coast.

A less challenging walk, to the north, takes you back in time along the historic 12-mile (19-km) **Goldfields Track**, an old prospecting route between Mount Bartle Frere and Mount Bellenden Ker. This journey of between seven and nine hours, linking **The Boulders** scenic reserve, near **Babinda**, and **Goldsborough Valley State Forest** recreation area, can be completed in either direction along a path noted for its monstrous king ferns, refreshing streams, gully crossings, and ridge-top views.

Especially beside creeks, walkers may be startled by the raucous screeches of sulfur-crested cockatoos or see smaller bush birds like the scrub-wren or thornbill flitting through the forest understory. High in the canopy, the flashes of brilliant crimson belong to king parrots dining on seeds, fruit, leaf buds, and blossoms. Whatever the perspective, from treetops to leaf-strewn forest floor the Wet Tropics is a true masterpiece, a verdant green canvas lavishly painted with some of the world's most precious and vibrant wildlife.

An amethystine python (right) consumes a rat, having first suffocated it with its powerful coils.

TRAVEL TIPS

DETAILS

When to Go

There are only two seasons in the Wet Tropics: the Wet and the Dry. The wet season extends from November to April and presents problems for travelers, with many roads rendered impassable by frequent heavy rain and average temperatures from 75°F to 91°F (24°–33°C). In the dry season, road conditions are more stable, and the average temperature is 57°–79°F (14°–26°C).

How to Get There

There are regular flights to Cairns from all major Australian cities and from some overseas airports. Rental cars are available at the airport and in town. The Mossman section of Daintree National Park lies 50 miles (80 km) north of Cairns and 3 miles (5 km) west of Mossman township. The Cape Tribulation section begins 53 miles (86 km) north of Cairns, just north of the Daintree River.

To reach the Josephine Falls section of Wooroonooran National Park, travel 28 miles (45 km) south of Cairns along the Bruce Highway and turn off 1¼ miles (2 km) south of Miriwinni. The park entrance is 5 miles (8 km) farther on. You can access the Palmerston section by continuing to Innisfail and then following the Palmerston Highway for 20 miles (33 km).

Special Planning

Travelers should check road conditions before setting out, especially during the wet season. The road beyond Cape Tribulation to Bloomfield is suitable for four-wheel-drive vehicles only.

Phytophthora cinnamoni (root rot fungus), which can decimate large tracts of forest, can be carried in contaminated soil on boots and tent pegs. Visitors who have been hiking overseas or in areas outside the Wet Tropics are asked to clean and disinfect footwear and camping gear carefully before arrival.

Crocodiles are abundant in the Wet Tropics and are protective of their territory. Pitch camps well away from deep pools and avoid swimming or bathing where crocodiles gather.

Permits and Entry Fees

Permits are required for camping at Snapper Island in Daintree National Park and are available from the Environmental Protection Agency, tel: 07-4052 3096. Campers can self-register at the campground at Noah Beach. Permits for bush camping in the Josephine Falls section of Wooroonooran National Park can be obtained from self-registration stands at the top of the Josephine Falls parking lot or at Junction Camp.

INFORMATION

Queensland Parks and Wildlife Service

10–12 McLeod Street, Cairns, Qld 4870; tel: 07-4052 3096 or 07-4052 3092; web: www.env.qld.gov.au

Wet Tropics Management Authority

P.O. Box 2050, Cairns, Qld 4870; tel: 07-4052 0533.

CAMPING

Scenic camping areas are found throughout the Wet Tropics. In the Cape Tribulation section of Daintree National Park, there are sites at Noah Beach and on Snapper Island. In Wooroonooran National Park, camping is permitted near Henrietta Creek in the Palmerston section, and bush camping is allowed in parts of the Josephine Falls section. Campgrounds are often fully booked during school holidays and the peak season (April to September), but there are many commercial campgrounds in neighboring towns. Visitors camping in national parks are asked to use portable camping stoves, bring their own firewood, and make fires only in fireplaces that are provided.

LODGING

Bartle Frere House

Josephine Falls Road, Bartle Frere, Qld 4871; tel: 07-4067 6309 or e-mail bfhouse@ fastinternet.net.au

Situated in the Josephine Falls section of Wooroonooran National Park, this establishment offers private rooms in an old Queenslander-style home and campsites surrounded by rain forest. The accommodations are conveniently located for the beaches and reefs, Cairns, and the Atherton Tableland. $

Crocodylus Youth Hostel

P.M.B. 30, Mossman, Qld 4873; tel: 07-4098 9166.

The hostel offers dorm-style accommodations and private cabins with their own baths. Facilities include a restaurant serving budget meals and a kitchen for self-catering. The staff organizes a plethora of activities including guided day and night walks, horseback riding, sunrise paddle treks, two-day sea-kayaking tours, full-day snorkeling trips, and crocodile-spotting cruises. $

Heritage Lodge

P.M.B. 14, Mossman, Qld 4873; tel: 07-4098 9138; web: www.home.aone.net.au/heritagelodge/ or e-mail heritage@c130.aone.net.au

Situated two hours north of Cairns, this resort is nestled in rain forest and offers 20 boutique-style cabins with private baths. The property is bordered by Cooper Creek and the Cape Tribulation section of Daintree National Park. Facilities include a restaurant, bar, and a freshwater swimming hole. Activities available at the lodge include four-wheel-drive safaris, horseback riding, and trips to the reefs and nearby Thornton Beach. $$–$$$

TOURS & OUTFITTERS

Daintree Rainforest River Trains
P.O. Box 448, Mossman, Qld 4873; tel: 07-4090 7676; web: www.ozemail.com.au/~dntrain/index.html or e-mail: dntrain@ozemail.com.au

The River Train departs from the ferry crossing and offers a two-and-a-half hour tour that includes an environmental cruise, guided mangrove-rain-forest boardwalk, and morning and afternoon snacks. This is the world's only floating river train operating in a World Heritage Area.

Foaming Fury
P.O. Box 460, Cairns, Qld 4870; tel: 07-4031 3460; web: www. foamingfury.com.au or e-mail: bookings@foamingfury.com.au

This one-day adventure includes a hike through the Wooroonooran National Park's rain forest to the Russell River followed by three hours of whitewater rafting. Foaming Fury is the only operator allowed to conduct tours on the Russell River.

Kuku-Yalanji Dreamtime Tours
P.O. Box 171, Mossman, Qld 4873; tel: 07-4098 1305.

A one-hour guided tour near Mossman Gorge explains the Kuku-Yalanji Aboriginal peoples' rain-forest lifestyle, traditional beliefs, and use of plants for food and medicine.

Excursions

Chillagoe–Mungana National Park

Queensland Parks and Wildlife Service, P.O. Box 38, Chillagoe, Qld 4871; tel: 07-4094 7163; web: www.env.qld.gov.au

About 124 miles (200 km) west of Cairns lies a series of colossal limestone outcrops beneath which thousands of years of weathering and erosion have sculpted chambers, passageways, and approximately 650 caves. Labyrinthine Royal Arch Cave, one of three open to the public, includes more than a mile of passageways. Donna and Trezkinn caves are both illuminated, highlighting intricate stalagmites and stalactites and iron-stained shawls.

Crater Lakes National Park

Queensland Parks and Wildlife Service, P.O. Box 21, Yungaburra, Qld 4872; tel: 07-4095 3768; web: www.env.qld.gov.au

Just a short distance inland from Wooroonooran National Park, this reserve incorporates two volcanic lakes, Eacham and Barrine, encircled by rain forest. These flooded craters and their rich red soils are reminders of the intense volcanic activity that shook the Atherton and Evelyn tablelands between three million and 20,000 years ago. Local fauna includes the saw-shelled turtle, eastern water dragon, and amethystine python. A great driving tour links the lakes with nearby Lake Euramoo, Mount Hypipamee, and Malanda Falls.

Undara Volcanic National Park

Undara Experience, P.O. Box 6268; Cairns, Qld 4870; tel: 07-4097 1411.

The world's most extensive lava tubes are 171 miles (275 km) southwest of Cairns. They formed 190,000 years ago during a series of volcanic eruptions that spread vast amounts of lava across the region. As the bubbling lava rushed along dry riverbeds, the top of the flow cooled to form a hard crust while, underneath, hot lava continued to run. Eventually the lava drained away, leaving a system of enormous natural pipes. Many tunnels, which extend for 100 miles (160 km), can be visited on tours.

SECTION THREE

Resource Directory

GETTING TO AUSTRALIA

Dozens of airlines fly to Australia from cities in North America, Europe, Asia, and Africa. Flights to Australia from North America depart from Los Angeles, San Francisco, and Vancouver. International carriers include Qantas, United Airlines, Air New Zealand, Canadian Airlines, and Northwest. From Europe and Asia, the major carriers include Qantas, Cathay Pacific, Japan Airlines, Thai Airways, Singapore Airlines, and British Airways. With Australia's increasing international popularity as a tourist destination, it is advisable to book flights well in advance, especially if traveling in the southern midsummer (around Christmas).

Australia's main international gateways are Sydney, Melbourne, Adelaide, Perth, Brisbane, Cairns, and Darwin. Sydney and Melbourne are the busiest airports, receiving flights from around the world and most of the direct flights from North America. Most flights to Perth come from Asia, Africa, or the United Kingdom. Adelaide receives flights from Europe via Sydney or Melbourne, and direct flights from Singapore. Brisbane, Cairns, and Darwin mainly serve Asia, but it is possible to make connections to Europe. Hobart takes flights from New Zealand.

VISAS

Visitors to Australia must have a passport valid for longer than their intended stay. With the exception of New Zealand citizens, all visitors must also have a visa or Electronic Travel Authority issued in their own country. Visas can be obtained from an Australian Embassy or Australian Consulate-General. Allow at least four weeks for processing. Applicants will be asked to provide proof that they have a return ticket and sufficient funds for the duration of their stay. Once in Australia, visas can be extended, although the Department of Immigration and Multicultural Affairs seldom extends tourist visas beyond 12 months.

For visitors staying in Australia for three months or less, Electronic Travel Authorities provide an efficient alternative to applying for a visa. Tourist Electronic Travel Authorities are free and allow multiple entries into Australia over 12 months, with a maximum stay of three months upon each arrival. North American travel agents and airlines can issue tourist Electronic Travel Authorities when ticketing flights to Australia.

MONEY

The Australian dollar is divided into 100 cents. Where prices are marked in single cents, they are rounded to the nearest five cents on payment.

There are no limits on importing traveler's checks, but any cash amount in excess of the equivalent of A$5,000 must be declared on arrival or departure. Major foreign currencies and traveler's checks can be exchanged at airports, money changers, major banks, and large hotels. Credit cards are widely accepted in Australia, with the most common being Visa, MasterCard, American Express, and Diners Club. Automatic Teller Machines are ubiquitous; credit cards linked to foreign bank accounts can be used at most machines to withdraw cash.

Bank trading hours in Australia are generally from 9:30 A.M. to 4 P.M. Monday to Thursday and 9:30 A.M. to 5 P.M. on Friday, though major city branches may remain open until 5 P.M. on weekdays and some banks are open until noon on Saturdays.

Note that tipping is not as widespread as in the U.S. or Europe, and it is not essential to tip waiters, taxi drivers, or hotel staff. However, if the service is particularly good and you wish to show your appreciation, a gratuity of up to 10 percent will be much appreciated.

HEALTH & INSURANCE

Australia's medical services are as good as any in the western world. Through reciprocal arrangements, residents of the United Kingdom, New Zealand, Finland, the Netherlands, Malta, and Italy are entitled to free or subsidized medical treatment through Medicare, Australia's national healthcare service. Residents of other countries are advised to take out medical insurance. Travelers who plan to visit remote regions should buy high-coverage policies to protect against the costs of emergency air transportation. Visitors who intend to engage in adventurous activities should check their policies thoroughly, as many exclude "dangerous activities" such as scuba diving.

Vaccinations are not required unless visitors have come from or visited a yellow-fever-infected country within six days prior to arrival, and health certificates are not needed to enter Australia. Despite its proximity to Southeast Asia, Australia is free of diseases such as malaria, yellow fever, cholera, typhoid, and rabies. Those journeying to remote regions should carry a well-stocked first-aid kit at all times and know what to do in an emergency.

GETTING AROUND

By Plane

Many international packages include domestic air travel discounts. Both of Australia's main domestic carriers, Qantas and Ansett, offer discounts of 25 to 40 percent to international

visitors and sell a range of air passes that permit a number of single flights for a set price. Advance Purchase Excursion round-trip tickets offer savings of up to 55 percent on normal economy fares. These fares must be booked and paid for in advance (21 days in advance generally gives the best discount), and the trip must include a Saturday night. Advance Purchase Excursion tickets are non-refundable, although departure dates can be changed.

Ansett Australia; tel: 131 300; web: www.ansett.com.au

Qantas Airways; tel: 131 313; web: www.qantas.com.au

By Rental Vehicle

North American visitors renting vehicles must be over 21 years of age and have a valid driver's license. Premiums are often charged for drivers under 25.

The four major car rental companies are Budget, Thrifty, Hertz, and Avis. There are also numerous small operators offering a wide variety of vehicles, from prestige cars to old cars known as "rent-a-wrecks." Basic insurance, which covers injury to other people and collision damage, is normally included in the price of vehicle rental. Insurance to cover personal injury can be arranged for an additional charge. Many companies offer one-way rental, usually at an additional cost.

Avis, Budget, and Hertz have four-wheel-drive rentals, with Avis and Hertz offering one-way rentals between the eastern states and the Northern Territory. Visitors renting four-wheel-drive vehicles should take out the highest level of insurance available as excess charges typically run into the thousands of dollars. They should also closely inspect the insurance contract, as damage incurred during off-road touring is often not covered. Some operators require previous off-road experience for those renting four-wheel-drive vehicles.

Avis Australia; tel: 1-800 225 533.

Budget; tel: 132 727; web: www.budget.com.au

Hertz; tel: 133 039; web: www.hertz.com.au

Thrifty; tel: 1-800 652 008; web: www.thrifty.com.au

By Bus

Australia's two main bus operators – Greyhound Pioneer and McCafferty's – have a variety of passes that give travelers substantial discounts. McCafferty's offers a single pass that covers travel from Cairns down along the east coast and then up through Central Australia to Uluru and Alice Springs. Greyhound Pioneer's unlimited travel pass gives passengers seven days of travel over a 30-day period. Numerous bus companies operate at the local level and serve smaller towns.

Greyhound Pioneer; tel: 132 030; web: www.greyhound.com.au

McCafferty's; tel: 131 499; web: www.mccaffertys.com.au

By Train
The major interstate services are the *Indian-Pacific* (Sydney to Perth), *The Ghan* (Adelaide to Alice Springs), *The Queenslander* (Brisbane to Cairns), the *Great Southern Pacific Express* (Sydney to Cairns), the *Overland* (Melbourne to Adelaide), and the *Spirit of the Outback* (Brisbane to Longreach). Although rail services are state operated, it is possible to buy passes that cover the whole network. (Rail Australia coordinates bookings between state rail agencies.) The Austrail Pass and Austrail Flexipass are available only to international visitors and must be purchased before arrival in Australia. The Austrail Pass offers economy-class travel anywhere for 14-, 21- and 30-day periods, with seven-day extensions also available. The Austrail Flexipass offers eight, 15, 22 or 29 days of economy-class travel within a six-month period.

Rail Australia; tel: 132 232; web: www.countrylink.nsw.gov.au

ADVICE FOR DISABLED TRAVELERS
Facilities for visitors with disabilities are constantly improving. Most airlines serving Australia offer special assistance prior to departure, in flight, and upon arrival. On rail services, assistance and special equipment are available. Bus travel is more problematic, but some operators have facilities for travelers in wheelchairs. Vehicles with hand controls can be hired from major car rental companies. Many hotels, restaurants, entertainment venues, and tourist attractions cater to those with disabilities. In general, the best way for disabled travelers to ensure assistance is to call ahead and inform business operators of their special requirements. The following organizations provide information for travelers with disabilities:

National Information Communication and Recreation Network
P.O Box 407, Curtin, ACT 2605; tel: 02-6285 3713 or toll free in Australia: 1-800 806 769; web: www.nican.com.au or e-mail: nican@spirit.com.au
This network maintains a database of nearly 4,500 entries on organizations, activities, and services for people with disabilities.

Australian Tourist Commission
Level 4, 80 William Street,
Woolloomooloo, NSW 2011; tel: 02-9360 1111; web: www.australia.com
The "Special Interests" section of the commission's website has comprehensive travel advice for travelers with disabilities.

TOURIST OFFICES
The Australian Tourism Commission can provide a wealth of information, including the free "Australian Vacation Planner," which is written specifically for travelers from North America. State tourism authorities will supply travelers with free brochures and maps.

In the United States
Australian Tourism Commission
2049 Century Park East, Suite 1920, Los Angeles, CA 90067; tel: 310-229-4870; web: www.atc.net.au or www.australia.com

In Australia
Australian Tourist Commission, Level 4, 80 William Street, Woolloomooloo, NSW 2011; tel: 02-9360 1111; web: www.australia.com

Canberra Tourism, Canberra Visitors Centre, Northbourne Avenue, Dickson, ACT 2601; tel: 02-6205 066 or 1-800 026 166; web: www.canberratourism.com.au

Canberra Tourist Bureau, Jolimont Centre, Northbourne Avenue, Canberra City, ACT 2601; tel: 1-800 026 166; web: www.canberratourism.com.au

Darwin Region Tourism Association, Corner Mitchell and Knuckley Streets, Darwin, NT 0800; tel: 08-8981 4300.

New South Wales Government Travel Centre, 19 Castlereagh Street, Sydney, NSW 2000; tel: 132 077; web: www.tourism.nsw.gov.au

Northern Territory Tourism Commission, Tourism House, G.P.O. Box 1155, Darwin, NT 0801; tel: 1-800 621 336; web: www.nttc.com.au

Queensland Government Travel Centre, Corner Adelaide and Brisbane Streets, Brisbane, Qld 4000; tel: 131 801; web: www.qttc.com.au

RACV Travel Centre, 230 Collins Street, Melbourne, Vic 3000; tel: 1-800 337 743; web: www.tourism.vic.gov.au

South Australian Tourism Commission, P.O. Box 1972, Adelaide, SA 5000; tel: 08-8303 2033; web: www.tourism.sa.gov.au

South Australian Travel Centre, 1 King William Street, Adelaide, SA 5000; tel: 1-300 366 770; web: www.tourism.sa.gov.au

Tasmanian Travel and Information Centre, Corner Davey and Elizabeth Streets, Hobart, Tas 7000; tel: 03-6230 8233; web: www.tourism.tas.gov.au

Tourism Tasmania, G.P.O. Box 399l, Hobart, Tas 7000; tel: 03-6230 8233; web: www.tourism.tas.gov.au

Victorian Tourism Information Service, Melbourne Town Hall, Corner Little Collins and Swanston Streets, Melbourne, Vic 3000; tel: 132 842; web: www.tourism.vic.gov.au

Western Australian Tourism Commission, 16 St. Georges Terrace, Perth, WA 6000; tel: 08-9220 1700; web: wa.gov.au/gov/watc

Western Australian Tourist Centre, Forrest Place, Perth, WA 6000; tel: 1-800 812 818; web: wa.gov.au/gov/watc

NATIONAL PARKS ORGANIZATIONS
Environment Australia can supply general information on Australia's national parks and wildlife. National parks are managed by state authorities, and the head office of each can supply more specific information on individual parks, including advice on camping and environmental care.

National
Environment Australia, John Gorton Building, King Edward Terrace, Parkes, ACT 2600 or G.P.O. Box 787, Canberra, ACT 2600; tel: 02-6274 1111; web: www.environment.gov.au

Biodiversity Group of Environment Australia, 153 Emu Bank, Belconnen, ACT 2617 or G.P.O. Box 636, Canberrra, ACT 2601; tel: 02-6250 0200; web: www.biodiversity.environment.gov.au

New South Wales
National Parks and Wildlife Service, 41 Bridge Street, Hurstville, NSW 2220; tel: 02-9585 6333; web: www.npws.gov.au

Northern Territory
Parks Australia North (a division of Environment Australia), 81 Smith Street, Darwin, NT 0800; tel: 08-8946 4300; web: www.environment.gov.au

Parks and Wildlife Commission of the Northern Territory, Gaymark Building, Mansfield Lane, Palmerston, NT 0830; tel: 08-8999 4401; web: www.nt.gov.au/paw

Queensland
Department of Environment and Heritage, 160 Ann Street, Brisbane, Qld 4000; tel: 07-3227 8166; web: www.env.qld.gov.au

South Australia
Department of Environment and Natural Resources, 77 Grenfell Street, Adelaide, SA 5000; tel: 08-8204 1910.

Tasmania

Department of Parks, Wildlife and Heritage, 134 Macquarie Street, Hobart, Tas 7000; tel: 03-6233 6191; web: www.parks.tas.gov.au

Victoria

Parks Victoria, 378 Cotham Road, Private Bag 8, Kew, Vic 3101; tel: 03-9816 7066; web: www.parks.vic.gov.au

Western Australia

Department of Conservation and Land Management, 50 Hayman Road, Como, Perth, WA 6152; tel: 08-9334 0333; web: www.calm.wa.gov.au

TOUR OPERATORS

Australia has hundreds of tour operators, ranging from large companies offering package deals that cover many major attractions to small family-operated concerns that cover only small areas. Below is a sample of the wide range of operators based in North America and Australia. The Ecotourism Association of Australia can supply a list of more than 200 accredited ecotour companies.

U.S.-Based Operators

Ansett Australia, tel: 888-426-7388; web: www.ansett.com

Cartan, 1334 Parkview Avenue, Suite 210, Manhattan Beach, CA 90266; tel: 800-841-1994; web: www.cartan.com

Go Downunder, 5865 South Kyrene Road, Suite 2, Tempe, AZ 85283; tel: 800-387-8850; web: www.goway.com

Newmans South Pacific Vacations, 6033 West Century Boulevard, Suite 1270, Los Angeles, CA 90045; tel: 800-862-5494.

Qantas Vacations; tel: 800-523-5312 (U.S.) or 800-268-7525 (Canada); web: http//qantas.power.net

South Pacific Travel Shops, Offices are located throughout the United States. In Los Angeles, tel: 310-568-2059; New York, tel: 212-972-2775; Chicago, tel: 312-214-4044; web: www.south-pacific-travel.com

Swain Australia Tours, 6 West Lancaster Avenue, Ardmore, PA 19003; tel: 800-227-9246; web: www.swainaustralia.com or e-mail: info@swaintours.com

Australia-Based Operators

Amesz Tours, P.O. Box 1060, Midland, WA 6056; tel: 08-9250 2577; web: www.amesz.com.au

Australian Ecotours/Peregrine Bird Tours, 2 Drysdale Place, Mooroolbark, Vic 3138; tel: 03-9726 8471.

Denise Goodfellow, P.O. Box 39373, Winnellie, NT 0821; tel: 08-8981 8492; e-mail: goodfellow@bigpond.com

Discovery Ecotours, G.P.O. Box 381, Darwin, NT 0801; tel: 08-8981 1100; web: www.discoveryecotours.com.au

Ecotourism Association of Australia, G.P.O. Box 268, Brisbane, Qld 4001; tel: 07-3229 5550; web: www.ecotourism.org.au or e-mail: meaghan@eastwind.com.au.

Ecotour Travel Agency, 447 Kent Street, Sydney, NSW 2000; tel: 02-9261 8984.

Go Bush Safaris, P.O. Box 71, Gladesville, NSW 2111; tel: 02-9817 4660; e-mail: john@sinclair.org.au

Peregrine, 258 Lonsdale Street, Melbourne, Vic 3000; tel: 03-9662 2700. Peregrine's North American representative office is Himalayan Travel, 110 Prospect Street, Stamford, CT 06901; tel: 203-359 3711; web: www.gorp.com.himtravel.htm or e-mail: worldadv@netaxis.com

World Expeditions, Third Floor, 441 Kent Street, Sydney, NSW 2000; tel: 02-9264 3366; web: www.world-expeditions.com.au or e-mail: enquiries@worldexpeditions.com.au

ENVIRONMENTAL ORGANIZATIONS

Australia has warmly embraced the environmental movement, and a number of well-established organizations can provide information on issues such as the greenhouse effect, rain-forest preservation, and endangered species. For visitors who want to take a more hands-on approach, the Australian Trust for Conservation Volunteers, a non-profit organization, runs practical conservation projects such as track preservation and tree planting.

Australian Conservation Foundation, Head Office, 340 Gore Street, Fitzroy, Vic 3065; tel: 03-9416 1166; web: www.acfonline.org.au

Australian Trust for Conservation Volunteers, Head Office, P.O. Box 423, Ballarat, Vic 3353; tel: 03-5333 1483; web: www.atcv.com.au

Birds Australia, Head Office, 415 Riversdale Road, Hawthorn East, Vic 3123; tel: 03-9882 2622; web: www.raou.com.au

Friends of the Earth, 312 Smith Street, Collingwood, Vic 3066; tel: 03-9419 8700; web: www.foe.org.au

The Nature Conservation Council of New South Wales, Level 5, 362 Kent Street, Sydney, NSW 2000; tel: 02-9279 2466; web: www.nccnsw.org.au

Tread Lightly! Australia, P.O. Box 220, Crows Nest, Qld 4355; tel: 07-4698 4963; web: www.tread-lightlyaustralia.com.au

Wilderness Society, Head Office, 130 Davey Street, Hobart, Tas 7000; tel: 03-6234 9799; web: www.wilderness.org.au

WEBSITES

There are thousands of sites that can provide the international visitor with useful information. Here is a list of the some the best places to start "surfing" Australia.

www.anzwers.com.au
A fast, reliable Australian search engine that will provide quick access to Australian sites.

www.aussie.com.au/aussie.htm and **www.about-australia.com/about.htm** These sites, called "Aussie Index" and "About Australia" respectively, provide good general information for the tourist.

www.australia.com or **www.aussie.net.au**
The Australian Tourist Commission's website has a wide range of useful information on traveling to Australia.

www.csu.edu.au/education/ australia.html
Charles Sturt University's Guide to Australia provides detailed background information on Australia as well as hundreds of links to government departments, national parks organizations, and tour operators.

www.nttc.com.au
This Northern Territory Tourist Commission website includes listings of a wide range of Aboriginal tour companies.

www.travelaus.com.au/
A guide to Australian holidays, travel agents, and tour operators.

www.walkabout.fairfax.com.au
This two-million-word, regularly updated guide to traveling in Australia is run by the Fairfax newspaper company, publisher of *The Age* and *The Sydney Morning Herald*. It includes good general information and entries on hundreds of Australian destinations.

www.yha.com.au
YHA Australia's site provides general information on hosteling and membership and provides a searchable database of Australian youth hostels.

FURTHER READING

Touring Guides

There are hundreds of guidebooks that provide visitors with ideas about where to go, how to get there, where to stay, and what to see. Below is a sample of some of the better guides that travelers may want to keep in their vehicle or backpack.

The Australia Bed & Breakfast Book: Homes, Farms, B&B Inns, by J. Thomas (Pelican Publishing Co., 1999).

Discover Australia: 4WD, by Ron and Viv Moon (Random House, 1997).

Discover Australia: Motoring Guide, by Ron and Viv Moon (Random House, 1997).